LANGUAGE IN CULTURE AND CLASS

The Sociology of Language and Education

A. D. Edwards

Senior Lecturer in Education
University of Manchester

HEINEMANN EDUCATIONAL BOOKS LTD
LONDON

Heinemann Educational Books Ltd

LONDON EDINBURGH MELBOURNE AUCKLAND TORONTO
HONG KONG SINGAPORE KUALA LUMPUR NEW DELHI
NAIROBI JOHANNESBURG LUSAKA IBADAN
KINGSTON

ISBN 0 435 82269 1
Paperback edition 0 435 82270 5
© A. D. Edwards 1976
First published 1976

Published by Heinemann Educational Books Ltd
48 Charles Street, London W1X 8AH
Printed and bound in Great Britain by
Morrison & Gibb Ltd, London and Edinburgh

LANGUAGE IN CULTURE AND CLASS

Preface

This book originated in an investigation of social class differences in children's speech and the extent to which these could be fitted into the framework of Bernstein's theory of sociolinguistic codes. There are residues of this research in Chapters 3 and 4, but the book is not a rewriting of that academic exercise. Theses rarely make good reading because of their conventional aridity of style and caution in argument. They are prepared initially for an 'audience' of two or three, presumed to be expert and paid to be sceptical. Books are hopefully expected to have a readership more sympathetic, open to learning, and numerous. The opportunity to lay aside the strait-jacket of doctoral exposition in writing about matters which were still a consuming interest was part of the reason for beginning this book. There was also the hope of providing some sociological guidelines through an increasingly complex field of inter-disciplinary enquiry.

When I was planning my research in 1967-8, the Sociology of Language was an academic territory still waiting to be defined, let alone explored. What there was of *directly* sociological study was dominated by the work of Bernstein. Its range and depth justifies the detailed discussion of it in Chapter 3. But with that formidable exception, the territory looked empty enough to be fairly quickly surveyed. This was the optimism of ignorance. I had little idea at that time of the growing convergence of interest in 'social' linguistics from the linguistic and social scientific sides. There has since been a remarkably rapid growth of theory and research, under various 'social' labels and from many perspectives. It is now a major task to keep in touch even with those aspects of it most obviously related to other sociological concerns. I have tried to provide some guidance to the varieties of perspective, evidence and explanation. There are other guides available, but most of them have a predominantly linguistic orientation. I am writing not as a *socio*linguist, but as 'a mere sociologist looking at language'. Though the sharpness of the distinction is rejected during the course of the book, my primary interest is not in language but in what their use of language can tell us about people—about their social background, aspirations and loyalties, their perceptions of each other and of the situations in which they interact. I have in mind the three partly overlapping groups I encounter in my teaching—language specialists interested in a sociological view of matters they are used to seeing in other ways; students whose main concerns are social scientific, and who have come to regard language as more profoundly important in social life than as merely the unproblematic medium through which ideas are expressed and interaction proceeds; and teachers interested in what the sociology of language might have to say to them about the large-scale causes of educational failure and the small-scale analysis of classroom communication. Their interests are not incompatible. Any meaningful examination of 'language in education' requires a solid background of more general analysis. And as will be argued in the last chapter, the study of classroom language can reasonably be regarded as basic sociolinguistic research.

When I began my research, I was fortunate to work with several colleagues at Exeter University whose interests in language were strong but different. They stimulated my interest, and widened my awareness of possible areas of study. I am grateful to Patrick Creber, Geoffrey Fox, and Patrick McGeeney. Dr David Evans combined energetic encouragement with a vigorous scepticism about sociology, and his own research into the language of mongol children forced me to think hard about the relationship between knowledge and performance. The completion of the research at Manchester University was greatly helped by Dr Patricia McEldowney and Dr Alex Cook, and by the encouragement of Dr Eric Batten. I am especially grateful to David Hargreaves for the stimulus of working with him on an interdisciplinary course which has provoked many arguments about the potential contribution of sociolinguistics to the study of social interaction (and about his insistence on the much greater potential contribution of symbolic interactionist theory to the study of sociolinguistics). I also appreciate his direct help with parts of this book. My three children have given me more peace than I had any right to expect, while remaining healthily unimpressed by the labours of academic writing or the mysteries of sociology. My greatest debt is to my wife Ann, not for the dutiful labour of checking and correcting (which I took for granted) but for many months of unfailingly cheerful and lively support.

A.D.E. *May 1976*

Contents

I.

Sociology and Language

1. SOCIALLY REALISTIC LINGUISTICS

> In linguistics, abstracted speech sounds, words, and the arrangement of
> words have come to have so authentic a vitality that one can speak of
> 'regular sound change' . . . without knowing or caring who opened their
> mouths, at what time, to communicate what to whom.
>
> (Sapir 1949, pp. 578–9.)

> . . . if our concern is social relevance and social realism, we must recognise
> that there is more to the relationship between sound and meaning than is
> dreamt of in normal linguistic theory.   (Hymes 1972b, p. 317.)

Everyday life would be insupportable if we did not perceive objects and
events in highly selective ways. To be immersed even briefly in 'total
reality' would mean being lost in a buzzing confusion. But in selecting
and organizing what we see, we lose much of what *could* be seen. The
words with which we abstract from and make sense of our experience
serve also to restrict it. The scientist's abstractions are part of this
general process of achieving coherence through exclusion. And they are
also imposed by the nature of his discipline. In acquiring its particular
language, he 'puts on a set of coloured spectacles . . . a veritable *a priori*
form of perception and cognition through which he views the world'
(Wright Mills 1963, p. 459). Contained in it are critical decisions about
what to observe, how to classify the observations, what kinds of
relationship and explanation to look for. Some of these decisions
represent a deliberate narrowing of the gaze, an open declaration that
'*this*, and not *that*, is *our* business'. Others are the more compelling
because they are taken for granted, part of the 'normal' world in
which he works. The more he immerses himself in 'the austerities of a
well-defined science', the more he risks becoming 'estranged from man
himself' (Sapir 1949, p. 580).

The main achievements of modern linguistics, especially that pre-cision often envied by practitioners of woollier disciplines, have come from a rigorous concentration on structure abstracted from use. Bloomfield's (1926) definition of language as 'the totality of utterances that *can be made* in a speech community' clearly identifies the *system* as the primary concern. Beneath the bewildering variety of actual speech lay homogeneous and invariant rules which careful study would uncover. Hoping to make linguistics 'scientific', he was prepared to exclude some traditional areas of investigation as not (or not yet) open to precise 'objective' description. For the time being, it was to be an autonomous, self-contained field of knowledge, its phenomena ex-plicable only by other linguistic phenomena. By comparison, the assumptions underlying the now predominant generative-transforma-tional model are even more austere. In Chomsky's (1965, p. 3) famous statement:

> Linguistic theory is concerned primarily with an ideal speaker-listener, in a homogeneous speech community, who knows its language perfectly and is unaffected by such grammatically irrelevant conditions as memory limita-tions, distractions, shifts of attention and interest, and errors (random or characteristic) in applying his knowledge of the language in actual performance.

The special domain of linguistics is defined here at a level far removed from 'actual speech'. While extra-linguistic facts about speaker and situation undoubtedly influence how speech is produced and under-stood, they are seen as the concern of the social sciences, from which linguistics is detached. In the academic division of labour, the *linguist's* 'working hypothesis' is the need to study knowledge of language apart from the uses to which that knowledge is put (Chomsky 1972, pp. 111–13). He must do so because no body of speech is more than a partial and distorted representation of the rules underlying it. The assumption of a homogeneous speech community unrealizable in the 'real world' is a necessary idealization for this approach. It has been outlined here because it contrasts so sharply with what the *sociologist's* interest in language is likely to be. Where the linguist (or, more accurately, this kind of linguist) reveals homogeneity, the sociologist will look for socially patterned diversity. Where the linguist accounts *jor* differences within a speech community as 'free variation', the sociologist will see some of them as systematically related to the social identities of the speakers, or to the social setting in which they spoke. From one perspective, these differences will seem superficial; from the other, a matter of great social significance, to the participants as well as to the 'expert'.

The contrast is sharp partly because it omits inconvenient differences within linguistics itself. It ignores the long tradition of dialect studies, explicitly concerned with socially patterned variation and often 'professedly sociological' in orientation (Pickford 1956, p. 211: also McDavid 1946; 1966). It also ignores the close inter-relationship of linguistics and anthropology, especially in America, with a language and its 'surrounding' culture seen as so inseparable that neither was comprehensible without close knowledge of the other (Greenberg 1948; 1971: Whiteley 1966). Some generative linguists too have seen the restriction of attention to 'pure' data as only a transitional stage, necessary to establish the model's formal and empirical credentials before widening its scope (De Camp 1969).

Whether temporarily or not, the 'pure' linguists have not neglected 'language in use' out of wilfulness, idleness or incompetence. Their emphasis on the structure of language has been deliberate. An equally deliberate rejection of such abstraction is apparent in what Hymes (1964a; 1971) calls 'the ethnography of speaking', a widening of view to take in the context in which speech is used and the rules of appropriateness which may govern particular linguistic choices. Like Chomsky's reference to the ideal speaker and listener, this kind of description too rests on a theory—'a theory of speech as a system of cultural behaviour' and of linguistics as a *social* science (Hymes 1971, p. 51). Structural linguists assumed reference (or naming) to be the main function of language, words 'standing for' objects and actions and conveying information about them in a direct and explicit way. Such referential language can be self-sufficient. In its written form, we may understand it even though it was recorded in a distant time and place by someone of whom we know nothing. But where language is part of a whole process of interaction, its meanings are inseparable from its context, and it tells us far more than is carried on the surface of the words. It may be patterned in ways which reveal or define who the speakers are, what their relationship is, and how they perceive the situation in which they speak. A 'socially realistic linguistics' tries to account for these patterns. It is not concerned with idealized speakers, but with 'persons in a social world' who must know 'when to speak, when not, what to talk about, with whom, when, where, and in what manner' (Hymes 1972a, p. 277).

The different perspectives can be illustrated in the use of the term 'competence' by Chomsky and Hymes. Chomsky argues that most accounts of language acquisition fail to explain the gulf between what is heard and what is 'known'. From the partial selection of language data that they encounter, children derive rules that enable them to distinguish the 'correct' from the ill-formed and the fragmentary in an infinite number of sentences. Despite all the differences in this data, members of the same speech community 'acquire grammars that are remarkably similar' (Chomsky 1972, p. 112). Whatever explanatory weight should be given to an innate human disposition to acquire language, or to possible common characteristics ('universals') in the deep structure of *all* languages, the competence which underlies performance 'is to a large extent independent of intelligence and of wide variations in individual experience'. From 'degenerate and restricted data' comes infinite ability (Chomsky 1972, p. 64). This approach is seen by Hymes (1972a) as a valuable weapon against explanations of linguistic differences between groups of children as being inherent or even racially determined. But it also seems irrelevant to many of the problems facing those labelled as 'deprived'. The gap between the possible and the actual, between what they 'know' and what they say, is too often poignantly wide. His own concept of *'communicative* competence' moves beyond the ground rules of the language to attitudes and habits regarding its use. The speech community is characterized not only by a common grammar, but by shared ways of speaking, and of understanding and evaluating speech. As a child learns his language, so he learns what language can do, what uses are most rewarding for him, what it can tell him about others and others about him. If he moves out of his 'home world', he may find that some of the communicative rules have changed. More ominously, he may not realize that they have changed, and so face misunderstanding or hostility.

Contained in this wider concept of competence is a different view of what constitutes 'correctness' in speech. Generative linguists seek to discover 'a system of formal principles capable of determining the grammatical sentences in a language, and capable of associating with each of these sentences those structural properties on the basis of which it can be correctly interpreted' (Fillmore 1972, p. 273). From this perspective, correctness is a matter of grammar alone. But from the social (or socio-linguistic) rules that he has learned alongside the rules of grammar, a competent member of the speech community will know that what is formally correct will often be socially impractical or even socially dangerous. What is *appropriate* as well as correct 'is not a property of sentences, but of a relationship between sentences and contexts . . . We must not assume that grammar is the form in which speech is organised in use' (Hymes 1972b, pp. 321, 329). Certainly it is not the *only* form in which speech is organized. Consider these two examples of 'rules of address', rules which would have no place at all in a formal grammar.

(a) *Sheriff:*   'Vergil. That's a funny name for a Philadelphia boy.
                What do they call you in Philadelphia, Vergil?'
    Vergil Tibbs: 'They call me *Mr.* Tibbs.'
       (From the film, *In the Heat of the Night.*)
(b) 'What's your name, boy?', the policeman asked.
   'Dr. Poussaint. I'm a physician.'
   'What's your first name, boy?'
   'Alvin.'
       (A. F. Poussaint, 'A Negro Psychiatrist Explains the Negro
       Psyche', *New York Times Magazine*, 20 August 1967.)

In both examples, the relevant rules are clearly recognized by the participants. Deviations from them might reflect the application of different rules, or be deliberate departures from normal usage which would carry unmistakable social messages. They are most unlikely to be 'errors'. In his home town near Memphis, the black policeman Vergil Tibbs will be 'boy' to any white man in authority. The first words addressed to him in the film are—'On your feet, boy'. His professional identity is then unknown, and they are addressed to the racial category rather than to the man himself. In nominally egalitarian Philadelphia, he is accustomed to a respectful formality. Dr Poussaint tries to bring his encounter under the control of these same Northern rules, reinforcing the attempt with an occupational reference that would then have elicited the same title in reply. 'I beg your pardon, Doctor' would have been a victory for him. Instead, the policeman's deliberate repetition of 'boy' reflects the asymmetrical status of a Southern situation, and both are aware of the social meaning it carries. 'For the moment, my manhood had been ripped from me . . . No amount of self-love could have salvaged my pride or preserved my integrity.'

These are straightforward examples. But as will be seen in detail in the next chapter, judgments of correctness will often include or be dominated by some sense of what is appropriate. They will depend on context as well as text, on the ways in which 'settings authorise linguistic choices' among alternatives *all* of which are *grammatically* correct (Fillmore 1972, p. 277). And all languages provide means of expressing superiority or deference, intimacy or formality. Any competent speaker will have some of them in his verbal repertoire.

The contrast in perspectives can also be illustrated in the approach to variations in form. If the language of a speech community is assumed to be homogeneous, 'its diversity trips one up round the edges'. If the analysis begins with diversity, it can 'isolate the homogeneity that is truly there' (Hymes 1971, p. 276). Chomsky's linguistic theory is directed towards the invariant rules from which an infinite number of correct sentences can be generated and understood. Variability is seen as either the result of switching from one set of rules (or system) to another, or as a matter of performance only, of those 'grammatically irrelevant conditions' which are outside the linguist's domain. The second approach removes inconvenient differences from serious attention by labelling them as random or 'free' variation. But a 'socially realistic' description will often show them to be highly systematic, predictable in terms of certain characteristics of the speaker or the situation. And it may concentrate on features which would not appear at all in an austere grammatical analysis. Take the following example:

> Shorty would take me to groovy, frantic scenes in different chicks' and cats' pads, where with the lights and the juke down mellow, everybody blew gage and juiced back and jumped. There I met chicks as fine as May wine, and cats who were hip to all happenings.
> (*The Autobiography of Malcolm X*, Penguin Books, 1968.)

In terms of the syntactic structure of American English, this display of hipster slang is standard. Its strangeness is wholly lexical. And it is a deliberate strangeness, a demonstration of separation from the 'square' world and of a knowledge shared with 'everyone I respected as hip in those days'. Elsewhere in the book, as will be seen later, Malcolm X records his ability to switch styles according to circumstance. This double source of variance appears, massively documented, in Labov's description of New York City speech. This study will be outlined later in the chapter, but it exemplifies the 'realistic' approach. The speech of individual New Yorkers (their idiolects) was found to be 'studded with oscillations and contradictions' inexplicable by any data within the linguistic system. The 'homogeneity that is truly there' was apparent only in relation to the social stratification of the community, and to the level of formality in the situation in which speech was recorded. The frequency of occurrence of some feature like the final and preconsonantal /r/ in e.g. *bare, beer* and *guard* could be related to the speakers' origins, education, occupation, perception of its social significance, and monitoring of their speech so as to conform to the prestige (or some other) pattern. The previously unaccountable variation had been described as 'free'. But when the individual speech pattern 'is studied in the larger context of the speech community, it is seen as an element in a highly systematic structure of social and stylistic stratification'. Such study had to include areas previously considered 'inaccessible to formal linguistic analysis', such as the informants' subjective reactions to the variables concerned (Labov 1966a, p. v).

The relevance of *this* kind of linguistics to the interests and concerns of sociology is apparent.

2. SOCIOLOGICAL LINGUISTICS, SOCIOLINGUISTICS, AND THE SOCIOLOGY OF LANGUAGE

Hymes' account of communicative competence rests on a basic assumption, that to cope with the reality of communication through speech 'requires a theory in which sociocultural factors have an explicit and constitutive role' (Hymes 1972a, p. 271). Many years earlier, Malinowski had described as the dilemma facing linguists whether they could justifiably restrict their attention to 'words alone'. Structural linguists had regarded such study as not only possible but essential. But if the main function of speech was to 'direct, control and correlate human activities', then how could it be detached from its context of situation? Its description led inevitably to 'sociological investigation, to the treatment of linguistics as a branch of the general science of culture' (Malinowski 1937, p. 172). It was already a branch of cultural anthropology, announced as such in composite labels like ethnological philology and anthropological linguistics, and reaping and conferring huge benefits from its importance in the work of Boas and Sapir. Malinowski himself was drawn into linguistics by his realization that to reach below the surface of a people's life demanded a full knowledge of its language. It was not enough to rap out a few words of Swahili. The other great figure of the 'London School' of linguistics, J. R. Firth, was a linguist drawn towards ethnography by his emphasis on how much the meaning of words depended on the settings in which they were used. But though he wrote a paper on 'sociological linguistics' as early as 1935, the term remained at his death a coin with little currency. Disregarding the example of anthropology, sociologists largely ignored language as an object of specialized enquiry. It was so obviously basic to social life that its infinite diversity was taken for granted. It was simply the unproblematic medium through which ideas were expressed, attitudes recorded, and interaction proceeded. Even when investigating their own academic territory, they rarely made use of linguistic data. In J. B. Carroll's *The Study of Language* (1953), the token two pages allotted to 'linguistics and sociology' stand alongside the forty-two on 'linguistics and psychology'. The allocation may also reflect Carroll's own professional identity, but it was largely justified by the tradition of neglect. Writing in the same year, Hertzler traced the paths that a sociology of language *might* take: the functions of language as a means of cultural transmission and of symbolizing and maintaining group consciousness; language as a reflection and determinant of social differentiation and stratification; the 'special languages' of castes, social classes, and occupational and other groups; the uses made of linguistic 'evidence' in placing people socially; the special forms of language used for such purposes as conveying respect or maintaining social distance; and the 'channelling' of thought and action through the ready-made categories which a language provided. This was a challenging territory for investigation. Yet twelve years later, introducing a long survey of 'language structure, function and process in relation to societal structure, function and process', Hertzler was still bemoaning the paucity of sociological research, and the consequent need to re-interpret material from other disciplines in the light of concepts from his own (Hertzler 1965, pp. 6–8). 'Language and Society' remained a mainly anthropological preserve (e.g. Hymes 1964b: Landar 1966). A 'sociologist of language' could quickly gain the appearance of an expert in an almost empty field.

The field has filled up since with a remarkably rapid growth of theory and research under various 'social' labels (e.g. Bright 1966: Lieberson 1966: Fishman 1968; 1971; 1972: Burling 1970: Gumperz 1971: Pride 1971: Giglioli 1972: Gumperz and Hymes 1972: Robinson 1972: Bernstein 1971; 1973: Trudgill 1974b). The proliferation represents a sudden convergence of interests. Linguists increasingly pay attention to the social patterning of language in use. Social scientists revive or develop an intense interest in the significance of symbolism in social life (e.g. Moscovici 1972: Dreitzel 1970). And the result of their work is often impossible to categorize. Is it linguistics or social science? Is it socially realistic linguistics, or linguistically sensitive sociology?

The questions are raised most obviously by the main labels— sociolinguistics and sociology of language. Fishman, for example, uses both as titles of successive books, sometimes insists on their distinctiveness, and sometimes slides to and fro between them in an example of apparently 'free' variation. Can the terms be used interchangeably, or do they express a significant difference?

In its still short but very active life, sociolinguistics has raised enough uncertainty and roused enough suspicion to be described as— 'at worst a poorly-defined inter-disciplinary activity, at best an empirical discipline without a theoretical basis' (De Camp 1969, p. 158). It suggests a general application of social scientific methods and findings, and especially those of anthropology and sociology, to serve a more effective study of language. For, like the earlier composite terms, it implies a *primary* concern with language. Indeed, De Camp makes a curt distinction between the sheep and the goats, between proper sociolinguists whose work is rooted in linguistic theory, and 'mere sociologists looking at language' and manipulating its data for their own purposes. The term also has a satisfyingly 'hard' and scientific ring to it, carrying at least the promise of rigorous precision to stiffen the social realism. Some linguists, of course, could claim with Halliday (1975, p. 26) that they had been 'doing sociolinguistics' all their professional lives while simply calling it linguistics. Others have announced their conversion to a wider view, redefining their task as the study of 'how far, and for what purposes, and in what settings, people "use" their grammars' (Fillmore 1972), or seeking to replace the 'somewhat antiseptic ideal speaker/hearer' with 'sociolinguistic man' and his many-sided competence (Troike 1969). Generative linguists have turned to the study of dialect (e.g. Bailey 1966), and argued for the construction of 'polylectal' grammars capable of accounting for varieties within a speech community in ways more sensitive than simply adding a few additional rules to a unitary core (Bickerton 1971; 1972). By accommodating the extent and patterned character of linguistic variation, such grammars might at last bring 'a stampede of sociologists into the linguistic corral, looking to see what was in it for them' (Bickerton 1972, p. 17). They would *hope* to see systematic patterns of choice which could be related to social roles, activities and situations. And if such socially realistic linguistics became standard, rather than a hyphenated addition to the 'pure' science, then sociolinguistics could wither away except as a description for research with an especially heavy social emphasis. If its very existence 'reflects a gap in the disposition of established disciplines with respect to reality', then its goal should be to preside over its own liquidation (Hymes 1972b, p. 324). There would then be neither the need nor the excuse for sociolinguistic research detached from the mainstream of linguistic theory (De Camp 1969, p. 158).

The sociology of language is a looser, vaguer term, falling easily into the growing company of sociologies of this and that. In its concern with the uses and users of language as 'aspects of more encompassing social patterns or processes', it also seems less vulnerable to redundancy (Fishman 1971, p. 9). The emphasis is less on the social organization of language than on the uses of language in the whole organization of social behaviour, and on the use of linguistic data in identifying and interpreting other social phenomena. It is concerned with who speaks (or writes) what language (or variety) to whom, and to what end, in the main spheres of interaction. And it includes matters not normally considered in linguistics—e.g. language loyalty, and language as source and symbol of group solidarity or segregation. At the micro-level, in Ervin-Tripp's definition (1971a, p. 15), it examines 'components of face-to-face interaction as these bear on, or are affected by, the formal structure of speech'. But this implies a linguistic priority, and the sociologist will probably be less interested in the formal structure as such than in *what* it can tell him about the identity and relationship of the speakers, and *how* it is used to define them. Fishman also blurs the admittedly crude distinction I have been making by throwing the main weight of his definition on to the variations in forms of language. 'The task of descriptive sociology of language is to describe the general or normative patterns of language use within a speech network or speech community so as to show the systematic nature of the alternations between one variety and another among individuals who share a repertoire of varieties' (Fishman 1972a, p. 48). This seems to me an exercise in 'descriptive *sociolinguistics*', the heading actually used by Fishman earlier in the article. Trying to find the 'right' label for a scholar, or even a single piece of research, is an often pointless and misleading task. But it is *roughly* correct to see a predominantly social emphasis in the sociology of language, a tendency to proceed *from* language *to* social structure and see it as one aspect of 'more encompassing social patterns'.

The roughness of the contrast, and the raggedness of the 'boundary', may be seen more clearly by considering some of the relationships between language and other forms of social behaviour that inter-disciplinary research has indicated or relied on.

1. It was the '*systematic covariance of linguistic structure and social structure*' which Bright (1966, p. 11) saw as the concern of sociolinguistics. Establishing such concomitant variation need not imply any causal relationship. People like this, or in this kind of situation, happen to use that language or way of speaking. Mapping speech against various social facts may produce fascinating results and be justified for its own sake. But it also lends itself to a 'mindless empiricism', the accumulation of information without much sense of its purpose or meaning. A sense of purpose may come from either the linguistic or the 'social' side of the investigation.

2. *Linguists may make use of sociological methods and concepts so as to pursue their own enquiries more effectively*. While early dialect studies owed most

to geography, some recent investigations of urban speech have relied heavily on sampling and other techniques long familiar in sociology (Labov 1966a: Wolfram 1969: Trudgill 1974a). Its neglect of these techniques was a main sociological criticism of the *Linguistic Atlas of the United States and Canada*, an encyclopaedic mapping exercise which consumed decades of academic labour (Pickford 1956). His use of them entitles Trudgill to raise his book to the level of *sociological*, rather than merely *social*, dialectology (1974a, pp. 1–2). The much longer relationship of linguistics with anthropology is apparent in the preparation of 'sociolinguistic profiles' as an aid to language planning in many African countries (Ferguson 1966a; 1966b: Greenberg and Berry 1966: Whiteley 1971; 1972). These portrayals of the whole 'language situation' of a society demand deep and detailed cultural knowledge. They include information about who speaks and when, and also about attitudes to a language, to its 'appropriate' communicative functions, and to its symbolic value as an expression of ethnic and other loyalties.

3. *Linguistic data may be used by sociologists looking for those 'reflections of social structure that are revealed in language'* (Grimshaw 1966, p. 191). It has long been used in anthropology in the study of migration and settlement patterns, culture-contact and cultural assimilation, and also (in Sapir's phrase) as a 'complex inventory' of the interests, occupations and preoccupations of a society. The more important was an area of experience, the more extensive and differentiated was the vocabulary which ordered it. We will see this fact reflected in criminal argot, where finely detailed discriminations are made in those activities critical to the group (see p. 22). Knowledge of the argot can then be used as an index of involvement (Lerman 1967). Sociologists were slow to make use of such indices, and McDavid (1946) took them to task for neglecting the facts so copiously contained in the *Linguistic Atlas*. If they *had* then taken an interest in language studies, they might have argued that the dialectologists' preoccupation with rural communities and their simple notions of social class made their work largely irrelevant to sociology's preoccupation with social stratification in industrial society. More recent linguistic research has offered a rich vein of data on e.g. the discreteness of stratification, the integration of ethnic groups into the dominant culture, and the transmission of (and resistance to) prestige patterns of behaviour. Its results are reported elsewhere in this book, and only the briefest examples will be given here. Labov's investigation of New York speech was deliberately presented in non-technical form because of the significance of its results for sociologists. Since it seemed possible to establish the dis-

tribution of features of speech, identify class norms, and measure situational variations around them, all this evidence could be used in the study of social structure and social process, as indications of status, mobility, aspiration and insecurity (Labov 1964; 1966c; 1968). In bilingual and bidialectal contexts, speech and reactions to speech have been used as evidence of group loyalty and group stereotypes (e.g. Herman 1961: Lambert 1967: Giles 1970), while in face-to-face interaction, subtle shifts of style or mode of address provide sensitive indices of self-identification and role-allocation, deference and intimacy (e.g. Gumperz 1964: Lennard and Bernstein 1968: Slobin *et al.* 1968).

4. Some of the research already referred to goes beyond correlation to causation. *Social structure may be seen as determining language use,* an approach which clearly rejects the self-contained nature of its phenomena assumed in some linguistic theory. Labov (1966a, p. 15) quotes from a lecture given in 1905 in which the French linguist Antoine Meillet recognizes both the 'proper autonomy' of language and the nature of linguistics as a *social* science:

> . . . it is probable, a priori, that every modification of social structure is expressed by a change in the conditions from which language develops . . . the only variable to which we can turn to account for linguistic change is social change, of which linguistic variations are only consequences.

Over fifty years later, another French linguist, André Martinet, also recognized the impact on language of 'outside influences', but admitted no obligation to study them. In his strictly professional capacity, the linguist had to be excused if he 'declines the invitation to investigate sociological conditioning' (cit. Labov 1966a, p. 13). But without such investigation, many 'purely' linguistic facts would be impossible to explain. The kind of research foreshadowed though not practised by Meillet is exemplified in Friedrich's studies of kinship terminology in Tsarist and post-Revolutionary Russia, and of pronoun forms in nineteenth-century Russian literature. In the first, the social consequences of industrialization, and the greater independence of women and the growth of their legal rights were seen as greatly reducing the degrees of kinship regularly recognized and labelled. Terminology followed behaviour. 'It is change in social systems that primarily precedes and predetermines change in the corresponding semantic systems.' So direct an approach to the problem of 'causal relationships between society and language' was defended as the main 'thrust and responsibility of the new science of sociolinguistics' (Friedrich 1966, pp. 31–2). In the second, choice of *ty* or *vy* (the intimate/superior or the distant/deferential 'you') was seen as determined by ten 'components of social culture' (age, kin relation, topic of conversation, etc.), and predictable from them if due allowance was made for the cross-cutting influences of contradictory constraints. A more evolutionary attempt at social explanation is Joos' (1952) account of 'phonetic drift', in which changes in the sound of speech are related to the accentuation of prestigious forms by 'top people' anxious to preserve the prestige-marking gap between themselves and their eager pursuers. The result was an ever-moving target for emulation, and a continual process of phonetic change. Citing the analysis with approval, Fischer (1958) places it 'in the field of sociology of language rather than linguistics proper'. His own account of young children's use of -in or -ing (e.g. goin'/going) in recorded interviews related their choice to the sex, class, personality of the speaker, the formality of the conversation, and the specific verb chosen. From a purely grammatical perspective, these would appear as free variants. But a wider view which included their meaning to the conversants showed them to be 'socially-conditioned' or 'socio-symbolic'. Fischer's perceptive argument is only thinly supported by the evidence he presents. But essentially the same approach is followed by Labov (1966a), with most detailed documentation. Whatever the usefulness of his results to sociologists (and of their findings to him), his main concern was the solution of *linguistic* problems, especially of understanding the mechanisms of linguistic differentiation and change. Using 'determined' as an abbreviation for 'is closely correlated with and appears to measure social influences which are logically and temporarily prior' to it, he sees language as perhaps the most highly determined form of human behaviour (Labov 1966a, pp. 314 and 509).

5. *Language may also determine social structure.* The most famous example of this reversed relationship is the 'Whorfian hypothesis' of linguistic relativity, in which language is seen as 'inter-penetrating' experience, influencing *what* we see by the particular categories and modes of perception which it makes available, or most readily available. Words *and* thoughts run mainly along the 'grooves of habitual expression'. In referring to our world, we partly create it (Whorf 1956, pp. 212–13 and 252: Sapir 1949, p. 162). This is too complex an area to be more than touched on here. Instead, a more limited and sociological example will be given because it illustrates a point of great importance to this and the next chapter.

Wright Mills (1939; 1940) saw in language a whole system of social control, a means of describing *and evoking* common patterns of social behaviour. Morally, men perceive situations and anticipate the consequences of conduct in terms of 'vocabularies of motive', moral categories through which interaction is defined, controlled and accounted for. The observer of a particular society or group must discover what motives are regularly ascribed to actions within it, what actions are labelled in what ways, and therefore what motives carry conviction when describing others or oneself. For we are normally restricted to the common motivational currency of the culture, the standardized 'real' motives of that time and place. Mills' argument moves brilliantly between the wider context and the immediate situation. By labelling motives, we place the relevant actions in a recognizable category within which they 'make sense'. The labels provide both justifications and *cues* for action. Arising out of a particular context and acting back upon it, they are both determined and determinant.

This dual relationship will be apparent in much of what follows. And we shall see, an individual's speech may 'betray' his social origins against his will or without his knowledge. It may also be *intended* to proclaim his social identity or affiliation, and as such is used to *work on* his world. Similarly, all speech communities have rules of appropriate usage which are normally disregarded at some cost. But recognized ways of expressing respect or friendship may also be used to define a situation or relationship, or to challenge a previous definition.

6. The kinds of relationship between language and social structure outlined in the last two sections move beyond correlations to causes. They also indicate how the co-variation approach, the matching of essentially independent data, loses vital inter-relationships between them. When Hymes (1967b) argued that linguistics 'needed' the sociologist, he was continuing his attack on its isolation of 'pure form' as the proper object of study. But the collaboration he hoped for did not mean adding 'a speech-less sociology' to a 'sociology-free linguistics'. What he wanted was the integration of social and linguistic variables from the outset of the research. The context had to be an inseparable part of linguistic description, not merely an 'environment' within which linguistic choices were made. Speech may *reflect* social structure, or be *determined by* the stylistic level demanded of speakers of a certain rank or in situations of a certain type. But the social constraints are themselves announced and reinforced by that choice of style, and might be modified or challenged if the choice were different. The detailed examples which end this chapter will, it is hoped, clarify the argument.

What is left, then, of the earlier distinction between sociolinguistics and sociology of language in terms of the priority of their concerns? I think there is still an essential difference in emphasis, and in what it is that the two perspectives seek to reveal. Where one gets to in inter-disciplinary research is better evidence of primary interest than where one starts from. For example, research might find that some linguistic feature was more often used by speakers of high social status, by women, and by incomers to the community (e.g. Levine and Crockett 1966). This would be a sociolinguistic enterprise if establishing and accounting for such variation was the end of the task. But if the data was used to define social categories, or to indicate social ambition or insecurity, the 'flow' of the analysis from language to social structure is sociological. Asymmetrical borrowing between the 'partners' is common in inter-disciplinary research. There is also the mundane but formidable matter of relative expertise. Any 'mere' sociologist (like myself) must be at least temporarily shaken by De Camp's (1969) plea for competent linguists to dominate the 'search for truth about the social nature of language', and so exclude the charlatan. He is probably more per-manently aware of the danger of narrowly utilitarian and possibly haphazard use of whatever linguistic techniques and concepts seem immediately useful to him. I felt the problem acutely in my own research (Edwards 1976b). On one side of the fence lies the danger of what Firth (1935) called 'loose linguistic sociology without formal accuracy'; on the other is the possibility that a preoccupation with 'formal accuracy' will produce data impossible to interpret in any sociological way.

Dangers are not removed simply by being recognized, nor does a vague boundary become much clearer from having its vagueness described. But having done both, I still feel entitled to 'get on with things', emphasizing again that the relationships between speech and other forms of social behaviour have become an exciting area of enquiry which may be entered from several directions and explored in a variety of ways. In the detailed examples which follow, the 'covariance of linguistic structure and social structure' is assumed to be relatively easy to identify and account for, the often extreme difficulty of doing so being considered later in the book. Some of these examples are of investigations which were sociologically oriented from the start. Others were done under a different label, but lend themselves to sociological interpretation. They are all intended to give some 'reality' to the rather abstract exposition so far, and to introduce some of the main concepts and findings of a sociology of language.

3. LANGUAGE DIFFERENCE AND SOCIAL DIFFERENCE: SOME EXAMPLES OF THE SOCIOLOGY OF LANGUAGE

The material reported in this section ranges from large-scale analysis resembling the sociolinguistic profiles mentioned earlier to intensive study of particular communicative events. As such, it illustrates the two contexts, of 'culture' and of 'situation', which are examined in the next chapter. It is a representative selection less in factual content than in the variety of approaches displayed. Some of the examples are given in detail, others in outline because they serve mainly as 'trailers' for fuller treatment elsewhere.

(i) *Language and social function: stable and unstable bilingualism in Canada and the United States*

The starting point of sociolinguistics is described by Hymes (1972b) as the identifying of social functions and the discovery of ways in which linguistic features are selected and grouped together to serve them. Where these features are delicate matters of style, they may be hard to identify, let alone interpret. But in plurilingual societies, the structure that 'serves' the function may be a whole language.

A common language is a powerful symbol of group identity. It can be the focus of fierce loyalties, as language riots in Belgium, India and elsewhere have shown. These loyalties express a simple sense of property, and also a realization that when language 'barriers' disappear, other forms of cultural separateness often disappear with them (as we will see, these barriers may be largely in the mind, the symbolic value of one's 'own' language bearing little relation to its purely linguistic distinctiveness). In societies which have been conquered, or colonized, or are plurilingual by accretion, use of the 'standard language' is often a means and a measure of acculturation to the 'mainstream'. And plurilingualism may be a passing phase as one language succumbs to the greater prestige and usefulness of another. But it may also be an integral part of the society, reflecting and symbolizing persistent social divisions. Where several languages co-exist in this way, the active continuance of each will depend on its retaining some function. Fishman (1972b) uses the term 'domain' to describe the cluster of situations, or spheres of interaction, in which one language (or variety) is normally used.

In Canada, two European languages have co-existed for centuries. In the United States, a phase of extensive plurilingualism soon lapsed into relative homogeneity. These two 'language situations' can be briefly described. When Lord Durham arrived in Canada in 1838 to report on the recent political upheavals there, open war between British and French was still in living memory. He found in the predominantly French province of Lower Canada 'a struggle not of principles but of races . . . two nations warring in the bosom of a single state'. A 'deadly animosity' separated the inhabitants into two 'hostile divisions'. In his famous Report, Durham recommended the subjection of the French to 'the vigorous rule of an English majority', and envisaged the end of their distinct cultural identity, including their language, in not much more than a generation. But his intentions were negated, not fulfilled, in that time. The British North America Act (1867) which made Canada a federation declared that—'either the English or the French language may be used by any person in the debates of the House of Parliament of Canada and of the Houses of Legislature of Quebec . . . and any person pleading in any Court of Canada'. More than a century later, two 'nations' continue to live side by side, the French having preserved their language from the absorption which Durham foresaw. In his Report, he had drawn a lengthy parallel with the French of Louisiana, who had been successfully absorbed into the mainstream of American society. But they had presented a relatively easy and local problem. By the end of the century, the United States was the most heterogeneous nation on earth. One in seven of its inhabitants had been born beyond its shores. The 'huddled masses' and 'teeming refuse' of Europe had poured in by the million, often settling in distinct ethnic enclaves. Yet the 'melting pot' dissolved linguistic like other differences, and the dissolution was intended. In 1919, Theodore Roosevelt could present as policy, and largely as fact, that—'We have room for but one language, and that is the English language, for we intend to see that the crucible turns out our people as Americans . . . not as dwellers in a polyglot boarding-house' (cit. Kochman 1972b, p. 212). If the first-generation immigrant learned to speak English with difficulty, his son was likely to speak the 'native' language with no less difficulty, and his grandson not to speak it at all.

This difference in outcome could be explained solely by legal recognition or neglect. In Canada, French was given formal equality. But in American courts and legislatures, and in schools from the first day in kindergarten, a single common language was used. Fishman extends the explanation in an explicitly sociological direction, arguing the dependence of form on function (1972a, pp. 51–4). In a mono-lingual society, one language serves all communicative purposes (there may, of course, be sharp differences between its varieties). In a bilingual society, a language survives as long as it meets communicative needs that cannot be met as readily, or appropriately, in the other. In both Canada and the United States, educational and economic success have normally required fluency in English. Yet in Montreal, each new generation of French-Canadians has continued to learn French as their first language because the early world of home, neighbourhood and church has been a French-speaking world. Even if they became bilingual in secondary school and the 'higher' occupations, this remained the 'home world' to which they returned each day, the world of primary-group relationships. As a result, the domains of French and English were kept functionally separate. In the United States, English was clearly essential for 'getting on' in an officially open society. But the immigrants were from such diverse backgrounds that it was usually the lingua franca for almost all purposes. Except in some of the ethnic enclaves (e.g. Frey, 1945), there was soon no separate domain in which the old tongue was essential, no network of valued relationships only supportable through its use. There was nothing to be *done* with it. Until recently, the only areas where this pattern of linguistic extinction did not apply were where the prospect of 'success' was so remote as to be meaningless as a motive for using English, or the segregated worlds of e.g. the Amish and some Indian and Spanish-speaking communities. It is now challenged by the strong sense of ethnic identity apparent in the use of 'Black', or 'Negro Non-standard' English (see pp. 49–50).

The main example here may seem too easy. After all, the French in Canada were a large minority, strongly entrenched and concentrated in a particular region, and their language was given a formal equality of status. But formal recognition does not guarantee survival, nor is the lack of it a mark of doom. Though Spanish is its official language, there is stable bilingualism in Paraguay because Guarani both symbolizes a sense of separation from the colonial past and is the language of familial and familiar relationships (Rubin 1962). For all the formal uses and prestige of the standard Bokmal in northern Norway, the dialect retains its place as the language of friendship and of local life. Even the Breton language survives as long as the 2% of the French population who speak it continue to find some spheres of interaction in which to safeguard it through *use* (Gumperz 1964: Ferguson 1962). Stable bilingualism often rests on two complementary sets of values, the intimate/informal and the impersonal/formal. And as we will see, the co-existence of standard language and dialect, of formal and colloquial speech, is open to the same kind of analysis.

(ii) *The social stratification of English in New York and Norwich*

A professor of sociology, born and raised in New York City, began a lecture with an (r) index of 50 to 60; as he proceeded and warmed to his subject, the index dropped precipitously as low as (r) −05; then as he began to make his final points, the (r) index began to rise again, though it never quite reached its initial value. A Negro woman, living on welfare in a bare tenement apartment, used a carefully articulated speech with (r) −19; now and then she interrupted herself to scold her children, using a radically different style of speech with (r) −00.

. . . Behind cases like these, and many others, one can see the outlines of a pattern.   (Labov 1966a, pp. 56–7.)

Labov's research in Lower East Side revealed a speech community, not simply a collection of people living side by side and randomly influencing each other's speech. A pattern could be identified in performance and even more in its evaluation, a pattern generally disliked by New Yorkers themselves for the way it seemed to 'place' them unfavourably in the eyes of other Americans. A considerable diversity between and within the speech of individuals was a consistent one— i.e. it was predictable in relation to certain characteristics of the speaker, the addressee and the setting. Where previous research had dismissed it as unaccountable free variation, Labov's investigation showed that individual speech patterns were 'part of a highly systematic structure of social and stylistic stratification'. The evidence came from the careful recording of five sounds—e.g. as in the example above, the frequency with which the final or preconsonantal (r) was sounded in words like *guard, bare,* and *beer.* Such phonological variables have considerable research advantages. They can be precisely measured, their high frequency makes it possible to collect a quantity of data quickly, and they have some immunity to conscious suppression by the speaker. They also tend to co-occur, 'so that a single social process may be accompanied by correlated shifts of many phonological indexes' (Labov 1968, p. 241). They are *socio*linguistic variables because of their correlation with aspects of the social context.

The approach is vividly apparent in one self-contained part of the research which deserves a paragraph to itself for the ingenuity of the method. The speech of salesgirls was recorded in three Manhattan stores, drawn from the top, middle and bottom of the price and fashion scale (the equivalent, let us say, of Harrods, Marks and Spencer's, and Woolworth's). Each unwitting informant was approached with a factual enquiry designed to elicit the answer—'Fourth floor'—which contained the significant pre-consonantal (r). A pretence not to have heard it obtained a repeat performance in careful, emphatic style.

Data was thereby collected from 264 speakers with a minimum of effort, and the results showed 'a clear and consistent stratification of (r) in the three stores'. Those from the top used it most, those from the bottom used it least, and those in the middle showed the greatest upward shift in repetition, suggesting an evaluative consensus with their social 'superiors' but a greater insecurity in performance (Labov 1966a, pp. 63–89).

These results highlight the main themes of the research. Over the whole sample, frequencies of phonological occurrence were correlated with e.g. occupation and ethnic group, and most closely with a combined index of socio-economic status (education + occupation + family income). In general, 'a variant that is used by most New Yorkers in formal styles is also the variant that is used most often in all styles by speakers who are ranked higher on an objective socio-economic scale' (Labov 1966a, p. 405). The reference to 'formal styles' is to the contextual manipulations used in the recording of speech—from the 'formal' reading of word lists through 'casual' conversation to 'excited' accounts of near escapes from death. Formality was defined according to the amount of attention that could be given to the sound of the words. In 'formal' speech, individuals often 'monitored' their performance in the interests of self-presentation, so revealing social loyalties, anxieties and aspirations. And far more effectively than was possible with direct questioning, this stylistic variation indicated shared awareness of prestige features and stigmatized ones. Indeed, there were many inaccuracies in the self-reporting of speech, sharp contrasts between usage and evaluation reflecting not the sounds produced but the norms imposed. And unless overtly stigmatized in such stereotypes as the 'dem guys' and 'toity toid street' of 'Brooklynese', these norms were outside conscious awareness. There was close agreement across the whole sample in rating tape-recordings for 'the best job this man could hold given the way he speaks', but few informants could specify what the 'relevant' features were. To reveal these 'internal evaluative processes', Labov constructed 'a chain of inference . . . (leading) to a quantitative measure of overt behaviour' (1966a, p. 406). The main links in the chain came from the stylistic shifts mentioned earlier, and these are illustrated in the table opposite (Labov 1966c, pp. 61–2). Despite marked differences in casual usage, shared norms of 'correctness' produced parallel changes when speech was more carefully monitored, with the significant exception that lower middle-class speakers 'take the lead' in the most formal contexts of all.

As a linguist, Labov was mainly concerned with the explanation of phonetic change. But the relevance of his evidence to sociologists was strongly emphasized. Thus the lower middle-class informants were especially hostile to stigmatized features, showed the greatest stylistic fluctuations, and tended to 'over-correct' in their pursuit of respectability (e.g. 'Between you and I'). This linguistic insecurity was seen as evidence of social insecurity and ambition in a mobile society. It was also important evidence of reference group behaviour, of norms related to those the informants admired rather than those with whom they had that direct and regular contact which makes possible the internalization of those norms, and the consequent consistency of the behaviour governed by them (Labov 1966a, pp. 475–6; 1966b). Women also used fewer stigmatized forms than men, and were more sensitive to prestige patterns. 'Lower class' speech has certain connotations of toughness and virility which led some men to *accentuate* its characteristics in careful speech, so showing the importance in a heterogeneous society of cross-cutting influences within the 'overall hierarchy of values' (1966a, pp. 440 and 495).

Occurrence of final and pre-consonantal (r)

	Lower Class %	Working Class %	Lower Middle Class %	Upper Middle Class %
Casual Speech	2.5	4.0	4.0	19.0
Careful Speech	10.5	12.5	20.5	32.0
Reading (a passage)	14.5	21.0	27.0	37.0
,, (word lists)	23.5	35.0	61.0	47.0
,, (minimal pairs)	49.5	55.0	77.5	60.0

Trudgill's 'study in sociological dialectology' in Norwich is closely modelled on Labov's work, shows a similar application of sociological techniques to the facts of linguistic diversity, and produces similar results from a wider range of sociolinguistic variables. He too stresses the fluidity of class boundaries in industrial society, and the need to investigate norms as well as usage by controlling the contexts in which speech is recorded. The main 'sociological' approach was to look for clusters of linguistic scores, or breaks in the continuum, 'which may reflect breaks in the social class continuum itself' (Trudgill 1974a, p. 59). The results of doing so offered some support for a broad middle-class/working-class (or non-manual/manual) cleavage. It can be illustrated in one of the non-phonological variables, the occurrence of -s in third-person singular, present tense verb forms. Lower working-class speakers used almost 100% s-less forms in casual speech ('It go well', 'He don't like it, do he?') and 87% even in formal contexts. For them, the form was so little stigmatized as to have no real social significance. The middle-middle class (his 'top' group) used almost none at all in *any* context, suggesting a gulf in normative influences and a minimum of direct contact between groups. The greatest adjustments *to* s-forms in 'formal' speech were made by the lower middle class (71% to 95%), and by the upper working class (20% to 62%). These were the groups closest to the 'line', anxious either to dissociate themselves from the working class or to acquire some middle-class attributes (Trudgill 1974a, p. 62). As in Wolfram's (1969) research in Detroit, and to some extent in Labov's, especially large gaps appeared in the scores of these socially 'adjacent' groups. And Trudgill too found that women were often in the van of 'correct' usage and evaluation, a fact which he attributes to their greater concern with status and appearances in a sexually unequal society. Even in this relatively genteel city, some features of working-class speech seemed to be associated with masculinity, and so to be emphasized in some contexts by some speakers (e.g. by male adolescents).

There is a danger that the apparent polarization of social class differences in usage may suggest the existence of two distinct 'social dialects', one predominantly local and the other leavened by national (or 'standard') features, with speakers switching on occasion from one to the other. But like Labov (1969a), Trudgill describes the situation as a case of 'inherent variability'—i.e. the variation is seen not as the result of a mixture of varieties, but as an integral part of the linguistic system and the linguistic counterpart of social heterogeneity. There is a continuum, a matter of relative *frequencies* of occurrence of some feature or another. (We shall see the importance of the approach later in this book.) What he describes as the 'Norwich diasystem' is something which members of the speech community can 'draw upon in their variable speech production, and use . . . in the comprehension and social interpretation' of the speech of others. It is part of their communicative competence, knowledge which can be used to identify themselves and others, and to define relationships and situations.

(iii)   *Argot, jargon and slang*

These thieves and caterpillars in the commonwealth . . . have devised a language among themselves which they name 'canting' but others 'peddlars' French, a speech compact . . . of English and a great number of odd words of their own devising, without all order or reason, and yet is such that none but themselves are able to understand.

(From a warning against 'rogues and vagabonds' published by Thomas Harman in 1567; quoted in J. Dover Wilson, *Life in Shakespeare's England*, Penguin Books, 1944.)

Regional and social class dialects are the most widely investigated forms of intra-societal differentiation. But at all levels of analysis, from the nation to the small group, common ways of speaking serve to unite and to demonstrate unity, and Sapir deplored linguists' neglect of those 'sub-forms of a language' current among occupational and other groups held together by ties of common interest. 'The complete absence of linguistic indices . . . is obscurely felt as a defect or sign of emotional poverty. The extraordinary importance of minute linguistic differences for the symbolisation of psychologically real as contrasted to politically or sociologically official groups is intuitively felt by most people. "He talks like (one of) us" is equivalent to saying, "He is one of us" ' (Sapir 1949, p. 16). The language of special 'interest groups' serves both to conduct its particular business and to symbolize its separate identity; it is 'partly the instrument of effective common action, and partly the means and symbol of group loyalty . . . it is zealously fostered as the outward expression of the unity of thought, feeling and action' (Lewis 1949, p. 49).

Slang is distinguished from *argot* by being less secret, more public, more generally available and, of course, more 'respectable'. As the language of deviant groups, argot is itself a mode of deviance, a gesture of defiance against the straight world. Its contents are highly specific to the group and its activities, and no generalized knowledge of 'deviant sub-cultures' will be sufficient to reveal them. The Elizabethan Thomas Harman felt it his duty to uncover the variety of villainies among the idle vagabonds, and so identified 'three and twenty sorts of wicked people'. They included *priggers of prancers* (horse-thieves), *freshwater mariners* (beggars posing as ship-wrecked seamen), *demanders for glimmers* (females pretending to have lost all their goods through fire), *doxies* (the later gangsters' molls), and the enticingly named *bawdy baskets* (female pedlars). Though his industry is commendable, Harman's list of categories could only have been the tip of the lexical iceberg without prolonged participant observation in these sub-cultures of roguery. The apparent lack of 'order and reason' in their speech was an intended opaqueness, reinforcing solidarity within and separation without. More than three centuries later, Arthur Morrison's novel of East London low life describes the Sunday morning parade of the 'High Mobsmen'. Swaggering along in their check suits, gold chains, lumpy rings and billycocks, they were pointed out by name or exploit:

Him as done the sparks [diamonds] in from Regent Street for nine centuries of quids. Him as done five-stretch for a snide [forged] bank bill, and they never found the 'oof [takings]. Him as maced [swindled] the bookies in France, and shot the nark in the boat.

(*A Child of the Jago*, repr. MacGibbon & Kee, 1969, pp. 100–1: first pub. 1896.)

The modern edition of the novel provides a glossary of nefarious activities as finely discriminating as that of 1567—e.g. busters are burglars, magsmen are confidence tricksters, and fags, hookers and dippers are subtle varieties of pick-pocket.

It is mainly lexical items like these that characterize argot, and all rackets develop their own. From them flows a rich supply of innovations into more general slang, prostitutes especially being said by Maurer (1939) to act as linguistic entrepreneurs because of their double contacts with the under- and upper-world. This is a field of enquiry rich in the exotic and the bizarre, and it was studied with enthusiastic intensity by David Maurer. Though he was a professor of English, his purpose was often explicitly sociological. He saw in argot a powerful reinforcement of group rapport, and a defensive reaction to the hostility of the 'outside' world. Rarely used merely to conceal critical meanings, it was nevertheless a sort of union card (Maurer 1950). And among the various rackets, prostitution alone seemed to lack verbal inventiveness. This was attributed mainly to a lack of group solidarity and professional pride, and a certain striving for conventional respectability which made its practitioners ambivalent towards their trade compared with the 'braggadocio' apparent in others. Nor did they need the shrewd psychological approach of those 'grifters' who lived on the quickness of their wits and their facility with words (Maurer 1939). The con-men, who lived by words, might be expected to display especial verbal skills. And this is what Maurer found. They seemed to derive a creative pleasure from toying with language:

> They love to talk . . . and their proclivity for coining and using argot words extends much beyond the necessary technical vocabulary. They like to express all life-situations in argot, to give their sense of humour free play, to revolt against conventional usage. Thus they have a large stock of words and idioms for expressing ideas connected with travel, love-making, the creature comforts, recreation, money, the law . . . And one may rest assured that they will use good, rich, roistering, ribald words which will radiate connotations for the initiate. (Maurer 1940, pp. 272-3.)

This is a description of language use in which denotation (simple reference, or naming) is far less important than connotation, the associations a word has for the initiated. Argot was seen as reflecting a way of life, as the key to attitudes, evaluations and modes of thinking. Its use could therefore be used as an indicator of participation in the particular sub-culture. Using it this way, Lerman (1967) emphasized that the most detailed preliminary study was necessary to find the 'correct' words for *that* group at *that* time, the instability of argot being strong evidence of its mainly symbolic function. Once a word is taken over by outsiders, its in-group value is lost and a replacement will probably be found. In less 'deviant' form, the jazz musicians described by Becker (1963) used many esoteric words, like 'riff', because they were technically indispensable. But they also used many others, like 'bread' for money, for which conventional synonyms were readily available, but which expressed their sense of separation from the world of the 'squares'.

More 'respectable' occupations use language in similar ways, though perhaps without that 'sinister vivacity' which Maurer attributed to deviant groups. It can then be called *jargon*. Modern students might well sympathize with Samuel Butler's complaint of 'a Babylonish dialect that learned pedants much affect', and academic jargons mixture of intellectual necessity, mere convention and trade solidarity will be discussed in Chapter 5. All 'learned professions' have terms for which Standard English provides no equivalents or only vague ones, and which therefore make possible condensed and unambiguous communication between fellow-professionals. Such terms also keep laymen at a respectful, or at least uncomprehending, distance and so enhance the majesty and the mystery. This double function is also apparent in the jargon of less time-honoured occupations, e.g.:

'Wow. More downtime on the lay barge—roughnecks in the dog-house.' A telex to that effect from the North Sea might conjure up visions of riotous offshore high-jinks. Like some other aspects of the oil business, however, the message is more prosaic than it sounds. It simply means—'Waiting on weather. Work on the barge laying submarine pipelines has been held up again, and the drilling crews are taking shelter.' The translation . . . is provided by courtesy of the Bank of Scotland, who publish today a glossary of oil jargon that is increasingly sweeping into business conversation.
(*The Guardian*, 28 April 1975.)

That glossary is intended so to remove the mystification of the jargon that 'ordinary' businessmen could start 'talking the same language as the oilmen'. And in so far as the jargon is only a matter of technical terms, it may achieve its purpose. But in so far as it expresses a strong sense of identity in a self-consciously pioneering branch of technology, then no glossary could guide the outsider through all the meanings it conveys.

The last example is again of language largely unintended for outside ears. Until the Opies' book was published in 1959, the 'language of school-children' was one of the least recorded of all varieties of speech in Britain. Linguistically, it 'offers a constant welcome to innovation' and reflects a delight in the sheer sound of words. But the strength of

L.C.C.—2

tradition is striking too. As nowhere else in the language, words and rhymes, repartee and ritual, survive substantially unchanged from earlier centuries. Though the Opies give many examples of the speed of oral transmission, a topical jingle being recorded hundreds of miles apart within weeks of the event it commemorates, it is this continuity which they emphasize most. A rhyme known to be 130 years old will have passed through the keeping of not less than twenty successive school generations. Though sharp regional and even local variations remind us of the intensely local life of the past, much of the traditional lore and its formulation can be found all over the country.

This continuity may make us lose sight of an essential function of the jokes, rhymes, songs and formulas. They are intended to protect many activities from adult understanding and control. 'Grown-ups have outgrown the schoolchild's lore. If made aware of it they tend to deride it, and they actively seek to suppress its livelier manifestations . . . And the folklorist and anthropologist can, without travelling a mile from his door, examine a thriving unselfconscious culture' (I. and P. Opie 1959, pp. 3–4). It is the culture of 'the greatest of the savage tribes', and its language is for intra-tribal communication. A child has to learn the right forms. When he has done so, they provide ready-made phrases for fun, for licensed obscenity, for defusing hostile situations, and for mocking the adult world. And if the 'correct' word for a 'good thing' is 'super' or (as in my children's school) 'ace', then nothing else will do. A referential equivalent will merely betray ignorance or non-affiliation. The ritual declarations too have to be exact—'promissory notes, affidavits, deeds of conveyance, receipts and notices of resignation, are verbal, and are sealed by the utterance of ancient words which are recognised and considered binding by the whole community' (I. and P. Opie 1959, p. 121).

To remake the point in more sociological form, the child achieves his purposes through his use of communal and habitual words and sequences. There are forms for every time and purpose in peer-group life. Their use makes transactions possible, and also proclaims and maintains the group. Through his successful use of these verbal resources, the child shows his knowledge of his sub-culture, and his adherence to its norms. He demonstrates his similarity to others, not his difference from them.

(iv) *Speech and social identity: indicators, stereotypes and markers*

I remember being beaten up by the inevitable bully for talking posh in Hunslet. Interesting, because I must have had a broad Leeds voice: but

there was just that edge to it which the Hunslet ear picked up and thought
was upstaging them.

> (Richard Hoggart, *Speaking to Each Other*, Vol. 1, Chatto &
> Windus, 1970.)

. . . the freckled girl tried at his own suggestion to give him clear ideas upon
the subject of 'as' and 'has'. A certain confusion between these two words
was becoming evident . . . Hitherto he had discarded that dangerous letter
altogether, but now he would pull up at words beginning with 'H', and draw
a sawing breath—rather like a startled kitten—and then aspirate with
vigour.

Said Kipps one day, "As 'e—I should say, ah, Has 'e . . . Ye know, I got
a lot of difficulty with them two words, which is which.'

'Well, 'as' is a conjunction and 'has' is a verb.'

'I know,' said Kipps, 'but when is 'has' a conjunction, and when is 'as' a
verb?'   (H. G.Wells, *Kipps*.)

The previous section emphasized the functions of a 'special language'
in *group* life. But all linguistic varieties have important implications for
the way individuals are regarded and regard themselves. Since speech
differences often *reflect* other forms of social differentiation, they can
be used to 'locate' a speaker socially. His knowledge of the judgments
likely to be made may lead him to bring his speech under control so
as to present himself in some desired way. The young Richard Hoggart
could not help the taint of poshness which brought him trouble. Kipps'
speech too is patterned by his origins, and to be fit to enjoy his new-
found fortune he must change the pattern. He is no less aware than his
mentor of the social connotations of the elusive 'h', but traditional
grammar could offer no help to his efforts at 'new-self' presentation.
Brief as the two examples are, they illustrate the distinction which
Labov (1971) makes between indicators, stereotypes and markers.
'Indicators' are features of speech regularly distributed throughout a
social class, ethnic or other group, and used by each individual in
roughly the same way in any context. They may be below the level of
consciousness, and are certainly outside the speaker's control. 'Stereotypes' refer to features which have 'risen to overt social consciousness'
and which, like the dropped 'h' in Kipps' speech, elicit from the
hearer some standardized response. As Estella says of the young Pip in
Great Expectations—'He calls Knaves "Jacks", this boy. And what
coarse hands he has! And what thick boots!' The word and the
coarseness go together. 'Markers' show both social and stylistic
differentiation. They are to some extent under the control of the
speaker, and he is probably aware of their significance. The 'hyper-
correction' found in lower middle-class speech provides an extensive

example. Clearly, the same feature—e.g. the length of a vowel or the use of a dialect word—may be an indicator of one speaker's origins and a marker of another's presentation of a particular identity.

My concern first is with the use made by others of the evidence contained in speech, even when the speaker is an unwitting source of the information. This evidence is often sought for almost as an end in itself, though there are generally good practical reasons for it too. It 'helps to define the situation, enabling others to know in advance what he will expect of them, and what they may expect of him' (Goffman 1971, p. 13). Though Goffman does not include it among his carriers of information (or 'sign vehicles'), speech is an important source of data from which at least initial assessments are made. They often begin with paralinguistic features, qualities of voice suggesting e.g. toughness, sexiness or diffidence (Crystal 1971). There has been a formidable research problem here in identifying *what* features are responded to, and in providing standardized labels for them (e.g. Laver 1968). Shaw's expert phonetician, Professor Higgins, identifies Eliza Doolittle as Lisson Grove (Paddington) on the evidence of a few words; Miss Eynsford Hill is betrayed as Earl's Court by her pronounciation of 'pneumo*w*nia'; and Colonel Pickering has his entire breeding (Cheltenham), education (Harrow and Cambridge) and occupation (Indian Army) summarized from his speech. Such party tricks are merely fictional. Yet Labov's New York informants agreed closely on the occupational suitability of recorded speakers without being able to explicate the evidence. And they could recognize stigmatized forms and their social correlates while being unaware of the presence of those forms in their own speech. These correlates are, of course, matters of belief, and often loosely or falsely related to the 'facts'. If 'no-one who speaks like that' could possibly be respectable, or well-educated, or in a position of authority, then anyone who *does* speak like that will find difficulty in being taken seriously.

Ways in which speech elicits *categorical* assessments of the speaker have been investigated in detail by Wallace Lambert and his associates. They used the 'matched-guise' technique in which, unknown to the subjects, the voices of the same speakers are heard using different languages (or dialects, or accents). Subjects are then asked to rate the apparently different speakers on various traits. Since all other bases for evaluation are controlled, their resulting judgments 'must be' derived from the stereotyped images evoked by the language (Lambert 1967, p. 91). The method assumes too easily that a speaker will sound 'the same' in two languages or dialects, a weakness that is especially apparent in research dependent on impersonations of accent not in the speaker's normal repertoire (see e.g. Strongman and Woosley 1967). It is also possible that the listeners may reveal not their 'more private feelings', as Lambert claims, but their *knowledge* of stereotypes that might not influence them at all in their *direct* contacts with 'representatives' of the category. In a first Canadian investigation, English-Canadian subjects rated speakers in their English 'guises' more favourably for good looks, intelligence, dependability and 'character' than in their French. This may seem a caricature of the social scientist's capacity to discover the obvious. But the *unexpected* result was that the English guises were rated more favourably by *French-Canadian* subjects on all those qualities, and *also* on leadership, self-confidence, likeability and sociability. Indeed, the French guises were generally rated more favourably by the English than the French judges. The results suggested uniform norms of evaluation arising from 'community-wide stereotypes', and a typical minority-group reaction by the French-Canadians, who saw themselves as kinder and more religious but as essentially second-class citizens (Lambert *et al.* 1960). A follow-up study with French-Canadian children found no down-grading of the French guises (Anisfeld and Lambert 1964). This may have reflected a greater absorption in the ethnic culture at the earlier age, and a slighter awareness of the facts of political and economic power in the wider society. It is possible, too, that a different result might have been obtained, even from adults, if the tests had been done at a time when separatist feeling was especially strong (e.g. at the time of de Gaulle's 'Vivre Quebec Libre' speech). Using the same technique on varieties of American English, white *and* black judges were found to favour Standard 'Network' English on all traits. But where white reactions were least favourable to the most strongly negro-sounding speech, black reactions were least favourable to 'educated White *Southern* speech' (Tucker and Lambert 1969). The 'common' evaluative pattern has to be significantly qualified here. And compared with standard-English guises, Jewish-accented speech was rated erratically by Jewish judges, suggesting ambivalent feelings about their ethnic identity and an inconsistent stereotype in American society (Anisfeld *et al.* 1962). Another investigation was carried out in Israel, where language use carries especially critical information about both origins and current affiliations. The speakers used Arabic and two varieties of Hebrew—Ashkenazic, with its European and 'sophisticated' associations, and Yemenite. The responses of Jewish and Arab subjects showed predictably reversed stereotypes, each group seeing in itself a similar bundle of good qualities. The Jewish subjects, almost all of European parentage, regarded the Yemenite guises as kind and friendly, but also as less intelligent, ambitious and wealthy—responses which suggest the familiar image of the 'country cousin' (Lambert *et al.* 1965).

The clustering of responses in these various studies illustrates an obvious aspect of stereotypes, and one commented on in an early study of personality assessments based on qualities of voice. There is a 'totalising effect . . . prejudicial to accurate and detailed judgement' in which several qualities are subsumed under a common label (Allport and Cantril 1934, p. 57). The groupings identifiable in Lambert's research are competence, social attractiveness and personal integrity. Speakers of the 'dominant' language or dialect may not be 'nicer', or more 'honest', but they are definitely more 'successful'. The same effect is apparent in reactions to British regional accents (Giles 1970; 1971).

Facts of the kind outlined here are an aspect of everyday knowledge that communicatively competent speakers can often use to 'give off' controlled impressions. In plurilingual societies, choice of one language rather than another may be a salient index of affiliation, especially if the speaker's position is 'marginal' or if the situation makes of his choice a public affirmation of group loyalty (Herman 1961). The local dialect may also be used quite deliberately to announce, maintain, or perhaps revive, identity with the local culture (Blom and Gumperz 1972). And as we saw earlier, awareness that a word or phonetic feature is stigmatized as 'low class' may lead to its relative suppression in careful speech, or to its accentuation as a demonstration of toughness or proletarian sympathies. It is then a linguistic 'marker', expressing something of the speaker's perception of himself, or of himself in a particular context. The use of speech to 'place' others implies a complementary fact, the use of speech to present oneself. 'Trial by language' is a trial which the 'defendant' may be unaware is taking place, or in which he may be unable to offer any 'defence'. It may also be a trial in which he tries to conceal his 'true' identity, or rejects the jurisdiction of the court in favour of another set of standards. By offering such a rich variety of social correlates, 'each of which has attitudinal correlates in our own and our listeners' behaviours', speech is a powerful means of 'reminding ourselves and others of social and ethnic boundaries, and is thus a part of the process of social maintenance or change' (Williams 1971a, p. 381).

(v) *Language and situation*

Mr. Shalford always wrote 'By Order', though it conveyed no earthly meaning to him . . . When he wanted to say he had a six-ha'penny longcloth to sell, he put it thus to startled customers: 'Can do you one six half, if y' like'. He always omitted pronouns and articles and so forth; it always seemed to him the very essence of the efficiently business-like. His only preposition was 'as', or the compound 'as per'. He abbreviated every word he could; he would have considered himself the laughing-stock of Wood Street if he had chanced to spell socks any way but 'sox'. But, on the other hand, if he saved words here, he wasted them there; he never acknowledged an order that was not an esteemed favour, nor sent a pattern without begging to submit it. (H. G. Wells, *Kipps*.)

If language provides individuals with means of 'locating' themselves and others, it also locates situations. Halliday's (1964) distinction between dialect, which he defines by *user*, and register, which is defined by *use*, exemplifies the two kinds of placing. As we will see, the contrast is too simple because a dialect may itself be reserved for certain kinds of situation. But it is still primarily related to *who* speaks in that way. Register refers to *situationally* specific language, to the 'correlation of a particular set of linguistic features with a particular set of situational features' (Hasan 1968, p. 11). 'Apologies for absence were received' characterizes a *type* of situation which is recognizable from the words alone. 'If my Right Honourable Friend will pardon the allusion, his recent pronouncements have deviated from the strict paths of veracity' —identifies a particular situation. Parliamentary debate is contained within the limits of 'parliamentary language', limits which are firm but wide. There is no need for the speaker to be as ponderous as in that example, but he *must not* call his opponent a 'liar'.

Register is not equivalent to e.g. argot because of this situational emphasis. A person may so 'live in' his argot as to become almost incapable of speaking in other ways. Register refers to forms of speech appropriate to certain circumstances or activities, often extremely difficult to identify even when we 'feel' they are there. There are, of course, rules of style which limit what can go with what. 'Ain't' calls for 'gonna' if the two are in close proximity, and a monologue or con-versation begun on one level of formality does not normally move too sharply from it. If it does suddenly break the 'rules of co-occurrence', it is likely to be for emphasis or comic effect. But any register will itself contain a variety of styles, and I am not concerned here with how speech 'hangs together' stylistically except in so far as this can be interpreted by referring to the situation in which it is used. These situational constraints are rarely so unambiguous as to make inter-pretation easy, and too vigorous a description of them may mis-leadingly imply a one-way relationship, the determination *of* speech *by* its social context. As was argued earlier, the situation may itself be defined by the choice of words. Mr Shalford saw his style as entirely appropriate to the serious business of selling drapery, and indeed demanded by it. But he also used it to symbolize business efficiency, and to establish a 'proper' shop-keeper–customer relationship. The complex inter-relationships between language and situation are so much the main concern of the next chapter that they are only touched on here, and the examples that follow were chosen for their relative clarity.

In their research in a small Norwegian town, Blom and Gumperz (1972) showed how the choice of standard language or local dialect was often 'patterned and predictable on the basis of certain features of the local social system'. In some contexts, the dialect carried negative connotations of parochialism and lack of sophistication. In others, failure to use it was seen as an expression of aloofness. In general, only dialect was used in the home and with close friends, and only the standard in more formal and less local contexts. But a shift from one to the other often carried important social meanings. A lecturer might switch *to* dialect to indicate that questions and discussion were now appropriate. Two officials switching *from* it at the end of a coffee break might be announcing their intention of getting back to business. The effectiveness of the switching depended on the participants recognizing and using the 'normal' relationship between linguistic and situational features.

The other examples are of verbal 'duelling' and display, highly 'focused' speech events such as are found in any culture. Such events represent defineable units of verbal interaction to which the participants can usually give a specific name and which are governed by clearly recognized rules (see p. 70). There are often tight limits on who can participate, stereotyped opening and closing routines, and definite rules of sequence. Successful performance in them depends on a high level of *socio*linguistic skill. In their study of duelling rhymes among Turkish adolescents, Dundes *et al.* (1972) are describing events in which *linguistic* creativity in its usual sense is apparently absent. The 'aggressor' makes his selection from a store of ready-made insults, the surface meaning of which is sexual. The aim is to place the opponent in a 'female', passive role and to keep him there, so symbolizing a general interactional superiority. Retorts are no less ready-made, and must end-rhyme with the original insult. Play continues until an insult is not, or not appropriately, 'capped'. Among Black American adolescents, 'playing the dozens' is a similarly standardized activity. Insults are exchanged in the form of rhymed couplets, and the limited scope for improvization makes heavy demands on the players' knowledge of the repertoire (Labov 1972: Foster 1974, pp. 179–237). But this is only one of many formalized examples of verbal display. 'Sounding' also involves conventional exchanges, but leaves more room for innovation. There are basic formulas to be filled in with either traditional items or original creations—e.g. 'Your mother is/is like/got/..........'

'Your mother is so......she............'

'Your mother is so....that when she . . . she . . .'

Labov records some vivid examples of the 'art' (e.g. 'Your mother play dice with the midnight mice'), a term justified by the skills often shown by the participants and their appreciation of stylistic complexities and subtleties. 'Signifying' describes a form of indirect boasting, taunting or threatening, one which relies on metaphor (e.g. 'Nigger, I'm gonn be like white on rice on you ass' i.e. 'I'm going to be all over you'). Used to describe blacks speaking in the presence of whites, 'shucking' or 'jiving' refers to a 'deliberate orchestration' of words, gestures and intonation to express false humility or respect. It was a skill heavily developed as a form of verbal self-defence (Kochman 1972a). A more aggressive version of 'putting whitey on' is apparent in the verbal pyrotechnics of Muhammad Ali. 'Talking broad' is a form of licensed unconventionality—obscenity, scandal-mongering, and other deviations from respectable conduct. Jesters, poets and comedians have long been similarly licensed, enjoying a 'traditionally honoured privilege of living both inside and outside the confines of normal usage' (Nash 1972, pp. 92–3). 'Talking broad', however, refers not to a characteristic of persons, but to *occasions* in which *all* the participants share the situationally specific freedom (Abrahams 1972a).

These examples are of great sociological significance. They show a value being placed on 'art for art's sake' which is not normally associated with the groups being described. In all of them, the main function of speech is not referential, but expressive or directive. The meaning is *not* carried on the surface of the words. All are in-group activities, dependent on detailed sub-cultural knowledge and largely inaccessible to outsiders. They are examples of interaction that might seem spontaneous to the uninitiated, but which in fact are highly structured. And they show a gulf between surface and 'real' meaning which can only be crossed by recognizing *what kind of speech* is occurring. Recognizing a particular utterance as e.g. 'sounding' depends on placing it situationally. A 'ritual insult' must not be taken as a statement of fact, or violence may result. An appropriate insult, or retort, can be used to depersonalize a potentially explosive confrontation, so ritualizing it on to a safer, rule-governed level. 'Because verbal duelling treads a fine line between play and real aggression, it is a kind of linguistic activity which requires strict adherence to socio-linguistic rules' (Mitchell-Kernan 1972a, p. 176).

These examples have shown the varieties of relationship and inter-relationship between language and social life which were earlier outlined in more abstract form. Which determines which is a false question because of the ways in which language both reflects and regulates social relationships, is shaped by the environment and itself shapes 'reality'. Some of the work described was highly technical linguistically, though showing an acute awareness of social influences on its data. Some of it depended on detailed description of social settings, roles and events, the analysis and interpretation borrowing heavily from social science or representing an 'outgrowth' from what were primarily social scientific concerns. Either way, some measure of integration rather than mere 'addition' is apparent.

Because of my own sociological interests, and intention in writing this book, I must return finally to the distinction argued earlier between sociolinguistics and sociology of language. It was a difference partly of relative expertise, largely of emphasis and primary concern. Socio-linguistics is defined by Trudgill (1974b, pp. 32–3) as 'that part of linguistics which is concerned with language as a social and cultural phenomenon'. It makes use of social scientific methods and findings, and when it does so in pursuit of questions which interest linguists, it can be termed 'sociolinguistics proper'. His own study of the 'Norwich diasystem', Labov's account of phonetic stratification, variability and change in New York, and Friedrich's investigation of pronominal usage, could all be described in this way. Trudgill sees the sociology of language as 'more specifically concerned with how, when, and why people in different communities use language varieties, and with social, political and educational aspects of the relationship between language and society'. The main interest here is in what their use of language can tell us about people—about their social background, aspirations and loyalties, and about their perceptions of each other and of the situations in which they interact. Lambert's research on stereotyping, Labov's on marking, and Mitchell-Kernan's on ritual insults, can all be used in this way. 'The greatest challenge for sociolinguistic research is to develop the methods, concepts and findings that will enable one ultimately to approach language, from the linguistic side, not only as grammar, but also as language organised in use: from the social side, to approach social structure, cultural pattern, values and the like, in terms of their realisations in verbal and symbolic action' (Hymes 1972c, p. 9). This present book is concerned primarily with that social side, with sociological perspectives on 'the means of speech in human communities, and their meanings to those who use them'.

2.

Context of Culture and Context of Situation

The traditional distinction between 'language' and 'speech' is between the system and its use, the potential and the actual. In Malinowski's terms, *context of culture* describes the environment for the total set of linguistic options available, the sum of all that is feasible and formally correct. *Context of situation* describes the environment for a particular selection made from them, a choice which may be heavily constrained by norms of appropriateness. Simply, a speaker's repertoire is determined by who he is; his choice from it can be related to the circumstances of the moment—to setting, participants and communicative purposes. 'Language is the set of rules to which all speech codes must comply, but which speech codes are generated is a function of the system of social relations' (Bernstein 1965, p. 151).

Like the whole arrangement of this chapter, the contrast in terms may imply too sharp a distinction between the two broad sources of difference. It is usually impossible to anwer the question—'Who uses language, or dialect, or way of speaking?'—without at once having to ask—'And when does he do so, and to convey what meanings?'. Even 'simple' societies differentiate between colloquial speech and the 'higher' styles reserved for ceremonial and other occasions. Most societies will have several varieties which distinguish their users geographically or socially, *and* others which are reserved for (or conventionally associated with) particular activities. Descriptive convenience should not lose sight of this interaction between user and use. It can be illustrated from Geertz' (1960) account of stylistic levels in Java. He describes three social divisions, and three main linguistic styles. It would be convenient simply to match the pairs. And it is true that peasants speak mainly on the 'lowest' level, townsmen on the second when not talking to close friends, and aristocrats on the 'highest' when talking to non-intimate equals. But the quali-

fications are already apparent. Everybody uses the lowest level sometimes—e.g. in talking to children. Peasants who have the second level
in their repertoire use it to their social superiors. Aristocrats use the
lowest level to their inferiors. Matters are further complicated linguistically, and socially, by the use of low and high 'honorifics'—items
that can raise or lower the style without involving a whole change of
level. They make it possible, for example, to offer respect without
simultaneously conveying the speaker's sense of inferiority. Townsmen
may use low honorifics when speaking with unfamiliar equals, so
maintaining distance without deference. The addition of high honorifics
to the high style pays respect to an aristocratic equal. The linguistic
result is a slow delivery, long words and elaborate phrases—'a kind
of stately pomp which can make the simplest conversation seem like a
great ceremony' (Geertz 1960, p. 254). Further complications arise
from situational influences—where the speakers are, what they are
talking about, what one hopes to get from the other—which cut across
the constraints 'normally' imposed by the respective rank of the
participants. These complications are especially acute in 'modern'
contexts like political meetings, where there is no clear guidance from
traditional rules. Yet *some* decision must be made, because it is almost
impossible to say anything without indicating either respect or
familiarity. The means of expression reflect the background of the
speaker; the choice he makes from those available to him reflects his
assessment of the addressee's status relative to his own, and perhaps
some appropriate adjustment to the facts of the situation in which they
meet.

The convenient over-simplicity of the distinction being duly recognized, the first part of this chapter is concerned mainly with
'context of culture', and of sub-culture. Discussion of speech repertoire,
diglossia and domain provides both a convenient bridge to the detailed
examination of 'context of situation', and an extended reminder of the
unreality of their separation.

1. THE SPEECH COMMUNITY

Comparisons of linguistic and other forms of social behaviour have
often been difficult because of the existence of two largely 'autonomous'
sets of data. Those social scientists interested in language have tended
to start with the group, large or small, and then discover the nature and
variety of its linguistic resources. This is the approach adopted in the
sociolinguistic 'profiles' mentioned earlier (p. 11). But the target of

linguistic analysis has tended to be 'a body of verbal signs abstracted from the totality of communicative behaviour on the basis of certain structural or genetic similarities' (Gumperz 1962, p. 28). These could then be formally described as 'a' language. From this perspective, a language consists of all the varieties which share a single superposed variety (e.g. a standardized, literary, form), and which are 'either mutually intelligible or connected by a series of mutually intelligible varieties' (Ferguson and Gumperz 1960, p. 2). The speech community is then the body of those who share the language, a kind of 'X-speaking union'. At a suitably high level of abstraction, even the varieties will disappear. As was argued earlier, the 'homogeneous speech community' postulated by Chomsky is a deliberate idealization, necessary to the discovery of deep-level uniformities to which the surface forms of speech can be related, and from which they are derived. Whatever its advantages to linguistic theory, this approach is sociologically irrelevant. It may occasionally be possible to mark out the geographical or social boundaries of a language found nowhere else, and find speakers who can use no other. This would then be a speech community presenting no problems of definition whatsoever. But the facts of language rarely coincide with those of nature or social life. In reality, the speech community may be defined politically in ways that bear little relation to purely linguistic similarity. Most languages are used in more than one *social* community, and most societies are plurilingual. 'One nation —one language', and even 'one speaker—one language', are the exceptions rather than the rule. While the 'mere fact of a common speech' is undoubtedly a potent symbol of group solidarity, what Sapir (1949, p. 15) called its 'condensation symbolism' depends only loosely on linguistic facts. Dialects of the 'same' language are sometimes less mutually intelligible than politically discrete 'languages' like Swedish and Norwegian, Serbian and Croatian, Hindi and Urdu, when an informant's statement of which language he claims as his own may be linguistically meaningless but socially significant. Even where the community is formally homogeneous, analysis above the level of deep structure is likely to show *sets* of differences in phonology, vocabulary and even grammar sufficient to justify the identification of dialects. But at least one 'standard' variety will be recognized by all as *their* language, even if not a part of their regular usage. Neighbours on either side of the Dutch–German border will have little difficulty in understanding each other. They will still regard themselves as using different languages, and will probably do so on formal occasions and in their contact with the standardized forms used in newspapers and radio. Sociolinguistic definition of a speech community is therefore likely to start with the socio-cultural unit, and establish its repertoire of ways of speaking.

This social emphasis is apparent in Gumperz' view of it as—'a social group which may be monolingual or multilingual, held together by the frequency of social interaction patterns, and set off from the surrounding area by weaknesses in the lines of communication' (1962, p. 31); and as 'any human aggregate characterized by regular and frequent interaction over a significant span of time, and set off from other such aggregates by differences in the frequency of inter-action' (1964, p. 137).

Reference here is to the quantity rather than the mode of com-munication, to who speaks to whom and how often, and not to how they speak. Frequent social interaction could take place between the same speakers in several languages and many varieties. In principle, a ghetto might contain within its borders almost all the social contacts of its members even though they spoke the 'same' language as the wider community. In practice, such isolation would almost certainly create and maintain divergences from a once common tongue, but Gumperz' definition gives no indication of interest in the correlation of linguistic and social facts. Indeed, it seems *too* removed from language, and a later version restores the balance. A speech community is now described as—'. . . any human aggregate characterised by regular and frequent social interaction by means of a shared body of verbal signs, and set off from similar aggregates by significant differences in language usage' (1968, p. 381). Reference here is to common ways of speaking and, by implication, of interpreting speech. There is shared knowledge of the formal system, and of norms of appropriate usage; the textbook-trained expert in the language may still be communicatively at a loss for all his formal competence. This sharing does not imply a single 'body of verbal signs' and of rules for their use. Any speech community will have spatially and functionally differentiated varieties in regular use within it, and any competent member will have some of them in his repertoire. What the definition leaves open is how sharp the differences should be to justify setting off one speech community from another, or sub-dividing an initially homogeneous unit. Clearly, this will not be a hard-and-fast judgment, but will depend on the vantage point adopted, and the type and detail of the differences described. As will be seen, differences in Black American speech have been described as 'free' or superficial variation around a common core of rules, as in some respects a different *linguistic* system, and as governed by signi-ficantly different *sociolinguistic* rules which lead to deep communicative misunderstandings in contexts like classrooms. Depending then on the observer's perspective, any group with a continuing existence can be treated as a speech community if its language code, *or* its use of language, displays features which regularly mark it off from others in some way. All Gumperz' definitions outline a 'field of action where the distribution of linguistic variants is a reflection of social facts' (1968, p. 384). Its description will not start from a language and the question—'Who speaks it?', but from the group and the question—'What language(s) or varieties of language do they use?'.

2. LANGUAGE AND DIALECT

A dialect is defined by McDavid (1968) as—'an habitual variety of a language, set off from other such varieties by a complex of features of pronunciation, grammar or vocabulary'. This makes a superordinate-subordinate distinction; one is 'part of', or 'a version of', the other. But the level of abstraction is again critical, as is the need to separate linguistic from 'political' definitions. The great achievement of nineteenth-century linguistics was the revelation of a common Indo-European base for many of the world's languages. A similarly global view led Whorf to group together English, French, Italian, etc. as 'Standard Average European', cut to the same basic plan and transmitted from what was in some sense a single speech community. A less encyclopaedic linguist than Whorf might still call French a dialect of Romance. That it is often the facts of history rather than linguistic distinctiveness which bring recognition of 'a' language is illustrated in the position of Dutch and Flemish within a 'German' continuum stretching from the Channel to the Oder and the Bohemian Mountains, and in the officially constructed breaks in the even longer continuum from Bombay to Assam.

Use of the terms 'language' and 'dialect' in apparent opposition to each other gives an appearance of neatness to what are extremely ragged and uncertain linguistic edges. It is for this reason that Haugen attempts a *functional* distinction between them. 'As a social norm . . . a dialect is a language that is excluded from polite society . . . an un-developed (or underdeveloped) language. It is a language that none has taken the trouble to develop into what is often referred to as a "standard language". It has not been employed in all the functions that a language can perform in a society larger than that of the local tribe or peasant village' (1966, pp. 925 and 928). This neatly summarizes what has commonly happened. Many 'languages' are former 'dialects' that have gone up in the world. In Tudor England, the 'King's English' was the dialect of the politically and economically dominant south-east, assisted by the standardizing effects of the printing-press. It was the Piedmontese Mazzini, Cavour and Garibaldi who were the 'makers' of a united Italy, and the Piedmontese Victor Emmanuel was its first king. But Piedmont was geographically peripheral. It also lacked associations with the glories of the Renaissance past. The dialect of the geographically and culturally central Tuscany became the national language, and 'Piedmontese' was soon faced with extinction. These are examples of a standard language emerging as the result of its 'natural weight'. Others have been imposed by conquest or colonization, either to facilitate administration in the rulers' interest or as a symbol of cultural superiority. Not surprisingly, then, a new standard has been imposed in many post-colonial countries to assert the separation from subservience, and the rebirth of an indigenous culture. The promotion of Gaelic in Eire is an obvious example, though it has a tough struggle against the international currency of English. In Tanzania, the choice of Swahili as the national language is seen by Whiteley (1972) as both a gesture of cultural independence, and a deliberate decision to open up the political life of the country to that large part of the population denied access to English. Where there are several *internal* candidates for the status of becoming the 'standard', the choice between them will have large political implications. Whichever is chosen will seem to open up the spoils of office to its native speakers. It may be safer then to choose an 'outside' language despite its colonial associations, or (as in Indonesia) to avoid the language of the dominant ethnic group, or even to avoid a choice altogether. Belgium, Switzerland and Canada are all examples of officially sanctioned diversity, though such legal equality may not extinguish 'sociological inequality' (Kloss 1967). The problems more commonly faced by linguistic minorities are sometimes removed by their dramatic conversion into a linguistic majority in their own autonomous state. This was the achievement of the Czechs, and is the hope of the more extreme Welsh nationalists. The possibility of its occurrence often brings punitive measures—e.g. the exclusion of the language from schools, or from all public places—from a central government which realistically sees minority-language loyalty as politically subversive. Linguistic intolerance was an important aspect of the standardizing policies of post-revolutionary Russia, and of the successor states to the Austro-Hungarian Empire. Their aim may be the outright extinction of the 'offending' language (Lord Durham's hope for French in Canada), or its relegation to 'second-class', dialect status (the persistent Spanish policy towards Catalan).

The nature of standard languages is a topic beyond the scope of this book (for an interesting and lucid account, see Trudgill 1974b, pp. 129–56). Emphasis here will be on some obvious social facts associated with them. The rise and fall of dialects is no reflection of their 'purely' linguistic qualities. There are no inherently 'primitive' languages. But the *functional range* of a language, what it can be used to do, may well be limited by the nature of the society. That a language is 'standard' does not mean that it is the language of all the people some of the time. It need not even be the language of some of the people all the time. The essential reference is to a codified language, distinct from colloquial, 'popular' speech, which provides a means of communicating across (or 'above') other varieties and which is normally the language of public affairs. It may act as a unifying force politically, and be expected on public occasions, even by those who can hardly understand it, from an almost ritualistic sense of propriety. It is certainly the language—or, more correctly, is in the repertoire—of those whose political, business or professional activities are most widely spread. Its 'ideal goals' are described by Haugen (1966) as 'minimal variation in form . . . maximal variation in function'. In fact, it may be as explicitly excluded from the intimate world of family and friends as the dialect is from school-room and court-room.

The argument has emphasized the distinction between a linguistic and a social inferiority. The word 'dialect' is rejected by McDavid in favour of 'variety' because of its irredeemably pejorative associations, its implication of a lack of sophistication. Its use 'reflects a lack of appreciation of the dignity of every naturally acquired language as an intimate part of the speaker's cultural experience' (1969b, p. 57). But this declaration of the rights of languages cannot remove the 'facts'. Dialects are not equal in 'fact' *because of* these pejorative associations, and the frequent monopoly of positions of power by those who can speak the standard language. Who has access to that language is therefore an important question. The classic administrative and liturgical languages—Sanscrit, Arabic and Latin—were kept quite distinct from popular speech. They were the prized accompaniment of an élite who carefully guarded their skill. Ability to communicate with fellow experts in distant places was achieved at the cost of a gulf between the language of the rulers and the ruled. The majority were effectively excluded from major areas of activity and information, and forced to rely on mediating groups who marketed their special knowledge without diffusing it. In India, Gandhi's efforts to build a common language on popular rather than scholarly usage were largely intended to mobilize popular opinion behind the national movement, and avoid this separation of élite communication from popular comprehension (Gumperz 1971, pp. 137–42). In modern Kenya, the choice of English as the main language of government is seen by Whiteley (1972) as reflecting a relatively élitist ideology, and as a means of *separating* the work of professional administrators from the instabilities of tribal politics. The unifying effect of a standard language will therefore depend on the context. Its use may unite the successful and aspiring, and at the same time accentuate the polarization of the *whole* society. Learning it may be part of the package labelled 'success', at the cost of cultural uprooting.

The ragged edges of any language-dialect distinction are especially obvious when describing *creole* languages. A *pidgin* language is a lingua franca, hurriedly put together for purposes of trade or colonization. It is a limited selection from one or more languages, and its linguistic simplicity is obvious. A creole is a pidgin which has become the native language of a speech community, and so developed to meet a full range of communicative purposes (Hall 1972). Its lexical, grammatical and functional scopes expand together. But it will probably continue to *seem* inferior, a 'debased version' of the predominant 'parent' language. Its 'mongrel' character is likely to be compared with the 'purity' falsely ascribed to the original, and it retains connotations of political subservience. Jamaican Creole will be taken as an example which also illustrates some of the social facts already discussed. According to Cassidy (1969), it is 'definitely a language', and the native speech of four-fifths of the island's population. Its origins lie in the simplified English of the slave days, with strong African residues. That plain statement needs immediate qualification. Creole *was* simplified in some respects, because those features of English phonology and syntax most unlike African usage were harder to acquire and maintain. There was therefore some loss of vowel contrasts and consonant distinctions, and a general loss of the inflections which mark plurals, possession and tense in Standard English (e.g. *the two book*, *John book*, *him fetch the book*). As in the last example, only number is marked in using pronouns, case and gender being distinguished by the context. In features like these, the Creole was 'simpler' than the parent languages (Cassidy 1961, p. 405). It is not any less systematic because of it. The 'same' meanings are conveyed in other ways, and new complexities emerge. While linguistic description is beyond the scope of this book, several aspects of 'Jamaica Talk' are of great sociolinguistic significance. First, it represents a long continuum. Cassidy places 'deep' Creole at one end and 'London English' at the other, with 'every sort of variation' in between. Only the extremes are mutually unintelligible. The range is illustrated in these brief extracts—from a Creole story cited by Bailey (1966), a humorous 'labrish' (gossip) column which emphasizes 'folk talk', and an example of sports reporting which is almost hyper-correct in its standardness. Interestingly, the last two are from successive pages of the 'Jamaica Weekly Gleaner' (U.K.), 13 November 1974.

Wantaim, wan man en ha wan gyal-pikni nomo. Im ena wan priti gyal fi-truu. Im neba laik fi taak tu eni an eni man. Im laik a nais buosi man fi taak tu . . .
(Once upon a time there was a gentleman who had an only daughter. She was a gay and dandy girl. She didn't like to talk to just any man. She wanted a fine gay man to talk to.)

You mean you don't done talk bout Tuesday night, and Muhammad Ali? From I was born, I never see nutten so. Dere is tump and tump, but the tump that Ali gave Foreman set off some reactions the likes of which I wonder if we will ever see again . . . Talk about egalitarianism, is dere . . . to see leaders and followers, friends and foe, jump like leggo beast.

The match was almost totally devoid of worthwhile play. The purple and white team over-passed, very often in needless lateral movements, while their central strikers were ahead and advantageously placed to try reasonable shots at goal.

Because of his own insistence on a continuum, Cassidy's reference to 'bilinguals who can use the speech of either end' is misleading. It suggests speakers who can switch into and out of discrete speech systems. An individual speaker may understand a large part of the scale, and use a considerable range. He will represent a 'span', not a point, along it. Of course, his choice may normally incline towards the 'London-end', or towards 'the inherited talk of peasant and labourer'. But he may also shift to and from along it in a single conversation, even a single sentence, without being conscious of the change. This will be more likely on public occasions, or when he feels in some way 'on trial', because such variability has a 'simple' social explanation. It is the co-existence of a prestigious and a socially stigmatized vernacular which brings extensive cross-interference (Bailey 1966, p. 2). Standard English is associated with education, prosperity and authority. The deeper forms of Creole are no less indelibly associated with poverty and ignorance. Those with the necessary facility are likely to monitor their speech in the prestige direction on formal occasions (Bailey found that the mere presence of a tape-recorder had this effect). And in a pre-echo of Labov's work on lower middle-class hyper-correction, Cassidy writes of the determined rejection of folk speech by the parvenu: 'the nervous conformity, the hard-won correctness, are inevitably flat and flavourless' (1961, pp. 3–4). Creole may have force and warmth, and be used at most social levels to convey intimacy, but the 'prizes' go to those with a command of Standard English. Children therefore confront it on a sudden and overwhelming scale when they enter school, and 'success' depends on its acquisition. Suggestions in the 1950s that the cultural shock might be reduced if the first years of schooling were conducted in Creole brought outraged reactions. Its spheres of activity were too far 'below' the serious business of education (Le Page 1968: Cassidy 1969).

Cassidy feared the gradual extinction of Creole beneath the weight of socio-political inferiority. Elsewhere too, the tangible advantages of knowing a standard language may engulf other varieties altogether. But the social diversity of modern industrial societies is too great, and the separation of public and private spheres of action too sharp, for there to be any clear trend towards linguistic homogeneity. Nor would it be functional if there were. 'A complete language has its formal and informal styles, its regional accents and its class or occupational jargons, which do not destroy its unity so long as they are clearly diversified in function, and show a reasonable degree of solidarity with one another' (Haugen 1966, p. 933). Diversity of function will be considered under the heading of 'repertoire'. This next section is concerned with sources of group difference within a formally homogeneous speech community—i.e. with 'dialects' in the everyday meaning of the word.

3. ETHNIC, GEOGRAPHICAL AND SOCIAL CLASS DIALECTS

Good English, Well-Bred English, Upper Class English . . . sometimes too vaguely referred to as Standard English—this form of speech differs from the various Regional Dialects in many ways, but most remarkably in this, that it is not confined to any locality, nor associated in anyone's mind with any special geographical area; it is in origin . . . the product of social conditions, and is spoken as essentially a Class Dialect.   (Wyld 1920, pp. 2–3.)

I don't think the Lancashire accent is very attractive . . . I think the ideal accent is absolute English, spoken without any accent at all. Affected it's even worse than a regional accent. It would be nice to have pure English. I think this would be the ideal of everybody.
('Mrs Grayson', quoted in J. Seabrook, *City Close-Up*, Allen Lane, 1971, p. 84.)

It was the false association of dialects with linguistic inferiority which led McDavid to prefer the more general and neutral term 'variety'. They were not formally underdeveloped parts of a whole, but varieties of some common system. Nearly fifty years earlier, Bloomfield (1927) had firmly rejected any equation of standard and non-standard with knowledge and ignorance. Supposedly 'incorrect' dialect forms were no more haphazard or unstable, and no easier to learn. Someone who habitually says 'I seen' has learned no less than if he said 'I saw'. 'He has simply learned something different.' *Why* he has done so may tell us a great deal about the internal divisions of the society, both natural and social. Dialect differences reflect, and reinforce, different frequencies of interaction. They also have a symbolic value in identifying the group. Their extent and sharpness can be described in terms of what Bloomfield (1933) called 'density of communication', the amount of verbal interaction within and between groups. Where there are barriers to inter-group communication, whether of geography or of caste, class or race, innovations will not be diffused and divergences will be maintained. The greater the distance between speakers, spatial or social, the more unlike their speech will be. That we talk like those with whom we talk most, or talked most in our formative years, may seem blindingly obvious. But as was seen earlier, the situation is complicated by a frequent tendency to talk like those we wish to emulate, or with whom we feel some special affinity.

While differences between geographical and social extremes in a society may be sharp, dialects represent those stretches of a continuum which have been marked off and labelled. The reasons for doing so may be linguistically obvious, as when natural breaks or weaknesses in lines of communication set some area apart from the wider community (e.g. Sauris, a physically isolated linguistic 'island' in the Carnian Alps —see p. 56), or when a social group contains most of the social contacts of its members (e.g. the Amish of Pennsylvania). But the divisions may also be made on other than linguistic grounds. A Suffolk dialect was the dialect of those who lived in a particular administrative area, and clear differences between those on either side of the county 'line' would obviously not be expected. Ethnic or other social groups may be studied, for wider reasons, in ways which include a search for distinctive forms of speech. Which 'social dialects' are identified can then be seen as a *product* of some more general research perspective. An example of this has been the detailed description of black 'ghetto speech', and the continued neglect of middle-class non-standard varieties which might also be linguistically distinctive (Wright 1975). The reference to *social* dialects is to dialects lacking the obvious geographical base of the term as conventionally understood. And it makes some of the complexities of dialect-mapping immediately apparent. Regional dialects will 'contain' social dialects, because ethnic and other social influences cut across those of mere proximity. From a different perspective, regional variations can be identified within social class or ethnic dialects. It is the supposed freedom of the 'standard' dialect from such variations that contributes largely to its prestige. As identified in the quotations which began this section, it is the neutral, 'pure', form of the language.

(i) *Standard dialect*

The *standard dialect* is that variety normally used in print, and on those occasions when speech most closely resembles the written form. Its standardized nature is most apparent in writing, and it is easy to exaggerate both its uniformity and consistency in speech. It contains its own varieties of formal and colloquial style, and some regional and perhaps social class differences. Nevertheless, it is the variety 'which draws least attention to itself over the widest area, and through the widest range of usage' (Quirk 1968, p. 100). It is 'superposed' on other varieties in a double sense—because it obscures other differences, providing a common currency of communication, and because its use is normally expected *on* public occasions and *of* those in authority. It can be analysed socially in the same way as a standard language in a multilingual society. Quirk comments on the 'temptation' to define it circularly as 'the speech of educated people'. In fact this is a good sociological definition. Standard English does not achieve its pre-eminence through its aesthetic qualities, sincerely though these may be believed in. It does so because of the prestige of its 'representative' speakers, and of the activities in which its use is normally 'required'. Such people's speech legitimates their right to do the things they do; what they do enhances the prestige of their speech. It is an excellent example of socially constructed reality. Those who do not have it in their repertoire suffer many of the disadvantages of those who lack the standard language in more obviously heterogeneous societies. 'To choose any one vernacular as a norm means to favour the group of people speaking that variety. It gives them prestige as norm-bearers, and a headstart in the race for power and position . . . The language of the upper classes is automatically established as the correct form of expression. They cannot only say, "L'état, c'est moi", but also "Le langage, c'est le mien" ' (Haugen 1966, pp. 933 and 926).

Traditionally, dialect has referred to differences in accent, vocabulary and grammar. Where geographical or other barriers are marked, this will still be a realistic description. Elsewhere, relatively high levels of geographical and social mobility, together with the standardizing influence of mass media, have reduced the most obvious differences in speech to a matter of accent, with some survivals in vocabulary and idiom reflecting the more local life of the past. There *may* have developed an 'endless middle' in speech, as in other aspects of behaviour. This seems unlikely, both because of the symbolic value of speech differences, and of the continued social segregation of interaction networks in industrial societies along both ethnic and social class lines. There are also those profound differences in the uses to which language is put which are said to have identifiable formal consequences (see Chapter 3). What is certain is that items of grammar, vocabulary and especially accent continue to provide easily recognized linguistic clues to social origins, and means of linguistic self-presentation. It is not the extent or 'depth' of the differences which concerns us here, but their social recognition and evaluation. On the day I write this, *The Guardian* has a reminiscence of Harold Nicolson's inability to take seriously anyone who spoke with a 'common voice', and its education correspondent describes a group of London sixth-formers who 'rate themselves middle-class although their accents do not always suggest this'. Both references are to *Received Pronounciation*, or to 'decent' approximations of it, which dilutes the notion of 'standardness'. It is perfectly possible to speak Standard English with a regional accent, and most industrial countries have regionally distinct RPs, with no single national pattern. This is obviously true of the United States. Even in England, it is only roughly true to describe accents as socio-regional, with the widest differences among agricultural and unskilled manual workers, and a regionally neutral pattern at the 'top' of the social pyramid (Halliday 1964). To the extent that it is regionally neutral, it is anything but socially so. It is, as Wyld described it, a 'class dialect'. It is what Lord Reith demanded of his staff at the B.B.C.—'a common denominator of educated speech'. While he emphasized its function of being comprehensible to all conditions of men, it is difficult not to see some wish to align the B.B.C. alongside the political, administrative and cultural Establishment.

(ii) *Ethnic dialects*

You, Razovitch, you shocker . . . Mamzer, I'm sorry for your father. Some heir he's got. Some Kaddish. Ham and pork you'll be eating before his body is in the grave. And you, Herzog, with those behemoth eyes . . . Your mother thinks you'll be a great lamden, a rabbi. But I know you, how lazy you are. Mothers' hearts are broken by mamzerein like you. Eh, do I know you, Herzog? Through and through.

(Saul Bellow, *Herzog*, Penguin, 1965, pp. 137–8.)

It is not only the foreign words that identify this outburst as non-standard American. Some of the word-orders are not standard either. Together, they exemplify a form of Jewish speech commonly found in the big cities, but with an ethnic location. Such dialects cut across other linguistic differences. They often contain reminders of the 'native' language, the intrusion of 'foreign' sounds, words and structures, and they often reflect the residential and perhaps occupational segregation of the group. Labov's New York research found evidence of e.g. Jewish, Italian and Polish enclaves. An initially different language is partly preserved by such relatively closed spheres of social interaction. The continuing divergences can strengthen group feeling, and they can also create a linguistic self-hatred or insecurity, an internalization of others' hostility and contempt (see p. 50). They may be deliberately maintained to confuse outsiders, and to conceal information from them. In a more profound way, it has been suggested that otherwise powerless minority groups may place a high value on verbal skills in their battle for survival, and show an unusual sensitivity to language. They have to learn to talk themselves out of trouble, and to present themselves verbally so as not to cause offence (Abrahams 1970: 1972b).

A white ethnic dialect was deliberately chosen as the opening example because of the still lingering absurdities of gross *physical* 'explanations' for some characteristics of Black English. But it is this American 'dialect' which will be used to focus the discussion because of the important sociolinguistic issues it raises. The first of these is whether it is a dialect at all. To describe it as a distinct 'language' reduces the risk of confusing a socio-political with a linguistic inferiority (Stewart 1971). To *deny* its distinctiveness has obvious assimilationist implications. Such 'political' questions have always been inherent in its study. Because of the persistent legend of a 'debased' version of Standard English, linguists were long unwilling to look too hard in case they *did* find too many differences. It was difficult to study it on its own terms, and not as a 'stigmatised poor relation' (Bailey 1965: see also McDavid and McDavid 1951). Revealing extensive differences threatened the 'melting-pot' myth of American society. The more recent revival of ethnic self-consciousness has emphasized both present differences and a distinctive history of cultural transmission (Dillard 1972: Stewart 1969; 1970). It has led to detailed formal description, and to the ethnographic study of black speech events like 'signifying' and 'playing the dozens' (for a highly readable account, see Burling 1973). This research has demonstrated the extent of variation within a 'common' language, and especially the fully developed, systematic nature of speech too often characterized from ignorance as being *sub*-standard.

Are the differences sufficient, and sufficiently consistent, to identify a distinct 'Black English'? Relating the question to everyday knowledge, the answer is yes. Except where black people have lived mainly in the company of whites, or vice versa, the ethnic identity of a speaker can usually be guessed accurately from brief extracts of recorded speech (Shuy 1969). Whether the judges are black or white, middle-class or working-class, makes little difference to their judgment. The most frequent clues are provided by accent, but there are also differences in morphology (e.g. as in Jamaican Creole, the absence of inflections) and in grammar. A native of Detroit, or New York, would have no difficulty in identifying these sentences as Black English—

John, he live in New York
He be here
I don't get none
I aks Tom did he wanna go the pictures

But such lists of equivalents can give a misleading impression of both uniformity and consistency. Black English is not 'a' dialect, and there are varieties within it to which the terms Black English Vernacular (BEV) and Negro Non-Standard English (NNE) draw attention. Again, the emphasis is on a continuum, from what Stewart calls the basilect (the furthest extreme from Standard American, largely used and then outgrown by young Negro children) to the acrolect (the closest approximation to it). Most black speakers will command a considerable span of this continuum, and be skilled in adapting their speech to particular circumstances (see p. 43). It is a matter of argument whether this shifting should be described as bi-dialectal, or as a change of style within a single entity (Houston 1969). The full range of standard forms is likely to appear some time in the speech of most blacks, and there is a danger of mistaking infrequency for absence, and of over-generalizing those features which seem obviously different. For example, the omission of the copula (the verb 'to be' in e.g. *he here*, *Jim coming*) is a well documented aspect of NNE, yet it is absent only in certain *linguistic* environments—e.g. in present-tense forms, and where contraction is possible in Standard English, as in 'He's coming' (Labov 1969a). Its more general appearance might also be expected in certain *social* environments.

As will be apparent already, the 'technical' disagreements among linguists are marked, both about the consistency and the 'level' of the

differences (for an excellent summary, see Trudgill 1974b, pp. 65–76).
Have the African residues, the Creole simplifications, and the long
history of social segregation resulted in features comprehensible only
by looking 'deep' into the speech system? (Bailey 1965: Dillard 1972).
Are the differences mainly in surface structure, and in frequencies and
contexts of occurrence? (Labov 1969a: Fasold 1969; 1970). Are
largely phonological differences often mistaken for differences in
syntax so that e.g. the loss of a final (s) is 'heard' as an absence of
tense (Houston 1969)? A compromise position seems not only sensibly
cautious but also realistic. Mainstream Black English has most features
in common with Standard English, some in common with other non-
standard varieties, and some exclusive to itself. In BEV, these exclusive
characteristics are accentuated. They have been so stigmatized, so
associated with poverty and ignorance, as to be a social handicap
which some of its users recognize and deplore (Mitchell-Kernan
1972b). For contrasting motives, urban black adolescents are increasingly likely to 'monitor black', emphasizing divergences in their
speech for manifestly separatist reasons. Even a single item may
provide the means of marking ethnic identity:

> The first time I heard the expression 'baby' used by one cat to address
> another was up at Warwick in 1951 . . . The term had a hip ring to it, a real
> colored ring . . . I knew right away I had to start using it . . . The real hip
> thing about the term was that it was something that only colored cats could
> say the way it was supposed to be said. I'd heard gray boys trying it, but
> they couldn't really do it. Only colored cats could give it the meaning we all
> knew it had without ever mentioning it—the meaning of black masculinity.
>
> (Claude Brown, *Man-Child in the Promised Land*, MacMillan, 1965.)

(iii) *Geographical dialects*

> Well, ivery day the flax and the vittles, they was brought, an' ivery day that
> there little black impet used to come mornins and evenins. An' all the day
> the mawther she set a tryin' fur to think o' names to say to it when te come
> at night. But she niver hit on the right one. An' as that got to-warts the ind o'
> the month, the impet that began to look soo maliceful, an' that twirled
> that's tail faster an' faster each time she gave a guess . . .
>
> (Ronald Blythe, *Akenfield*, Penguin Press, 1969.)

Linguistic analysis identifies those formal features which justify drawing
an obviously blurred boundary around 'a' dialect. Social analysis
establishes *who* its speakers are, and in traditional dialectology this has
meant—where are they from. The extract from a Suffolk version of the
Rumpelstiltskin story illustrates the dialect of a region by-passed by
the main lines of communication from London, and so separated from

the mainstream of economic activity. It also reflects the more local, geographically segregated life of the past. Economic backwaters are linguistic backwaters too, retaining old patterns and less affected by innovations. They therefore had an obvious attraction for dialectologists in search of survivals. Urban dialectology was mainly a development of the 1960s, making extensive use of social scientific research methods and, as was seen in Chapter 1, contributing valuable evidence to the study of social stratification. It also emphasized the unreality of the single residential criterion that the term 'regional dialect' suggests. No rural area is without its social divisions either, and it is normally easier to identify regional origins from speech as social status declines. This fact has an obvious corollary. Regional dialects come to be associated with 'low' levels of occupation and education, and so to elicit stereotypes of their users. Of course, responses to them are more discriminating than that. In Britain, rural accents are often regarded as 'charming', their speakers as 'slow' but amiable. Those of the conurbations are more likely to be regarded as 'coarse' (Wilkinson 1965). That this response seems less common in America might suggest a less intense nostalgia for the joys of rural life. Using Lambert's matched-guise technique (see p. 28), some British research has suggested a hierarchical ranking of regional differences which may be an important source of social handicap. Though there is some evidence of accent-loyalty on such social qualities as honesty and reliability, RP speakers are regarded as more 'competent' (Cheyne 1970: Giles 1971). This was the dimension derived by Lambert from those traits (e.g. intelligence, self-confidence) associated with occupational success. Giles (1970) examined more closely the bases of evaluation. Tape-recorded speech was rated for 'aesthetic quality', how pleasant it sounded; for 'communicative efficiency', which might suggest a measure of its comprehensibility but was in fact a rating of how 'comfortable' listeners felt with it; and for 'social status', the prestige associated with it. RP scored highest on all three dimensions. But there were some interesting differences within the overall judgments. 'Affected RP' rated highly on prestige, but was properly downgraded in other respects: 'Irish' was considerably more 'aesthetic' than 'prestigious'; and 'Birmingham' fared consistently badly. Speakers' awareness of such different evaluative criteria is evident in Labov's research. While New Yorkers were likely to feel that other Americans regarded their speech as coarse and ugly, it seemed to have some favourable connotations of toughness and urban sophistication.

Even at the level of accent, then, response to regional differences is complex. Where a dialect is considerably more than accent, it may be retained at *all* social levels as a symbol of local pride or, as is more likely, be used in intimate relationships and for distinctively local activities (Gumperz 1964: Blom and Gumperz 1972). And whatever the extent of the differences, they may be emphasized in a deliberate rejection of wider affiliations. In general, the separation of regional from social class correlates of speech differences is unrealistic. But the relationship between them is poorly mapped. We know that regional dialects are least marked among those in the 'higher' occupations. But how far down the social scale does the standard variety extend? How does this differ from one region to another, since some dialects make their users less vulnerable to unfavourable stereotypes than others? And as a matter of importance in considering classrooms, from what spheres of activity are they excluded?

(iv) *Social class dialects*

> Mrs. Yule's speech was seldom ungrammatical, and her intonation was not flagrantly vulgar, but the accent of the London poor, which brands as with hereditary baseness, still clung to her words, rendering futile such propriety of phrase as she owed to years of association with educated people.
>
> (George Gissing, *New Grub Street*; first published 1891.)

The 'hereditary baseness' which Mrs Yule could not escape was not transmitted in the genes. It was acquired from the company she had once kept. Before Mr Yule so 'unwisely' married her, the 'accent of the poor' would have been almost her entire linguistic environment. Most communication across social class lines was then between superiors and subordinates, a formalized interchange in which only the 'higher' servants and other employees presumed to imitate the speech of their 'betters'. Sharp differences in speech reflected and reinforced social distance. In a more open society, social and linguistic divisions become blurred. People move around more, their acquaintances are quite likely to come from diverse backgrounds, and a wider range of linguistic models are available both directly and through the media. Especially in large cities, an 'inherent variability' in language use results from this relative fluidity and heterogeneity in social life. Even so, Labov's research showed marked social class differences in phonological usage despite common norms of 'correctness', and seemed to offer sociologists unusually precise measures of social origins and aspirations (see pp. 19–20). His work stimulated other urban studies which provided further evidence of 'social and stylistic stratification'. In Detroit, for example, a count of actual to potential multiple negatives (e.g. 'he didn't hit nobody') in Negro speech ranged from an upper middle-class minimum of 2% to a lower working-class maximum of 70%. The striking generalization was the frequent presence of stigmatized features in lower-class speech, and their virtual absence in that of the higher status groups (Shuy 1969; 1971). Trudgill (1974a) replicated one aspect of the Detroit survey in his own research in Norwich—the frequency with which the final 's' was missing in some verb forms (e.g. 'he run fast', 'he don't know, do he'). The results were strikingly close, showing the same gulf between lower middle-class and the upper working-class groups. He found a similar social and stylistic hierarchy in other variables—for example, in that most familiar attribute of lower-class speech, the dropping of the 'h'. Like Labov, he comments on their usefulness as indicators of social structure, especially of a broad middle-class/working-class division. They tell us something about the frequency of verbal interaction within and between those social aggregates so easily called 'classes'. But in tabulated form, they can give a misleading impression of discreteness. What is summarized are frequencies of occurrence. Because these features form part of that knowledge used to assign social status, however provisionally, to those we meet, the members of the speech community are often aware of their social significance. The frequencies are therefore strongly influenced by the contexts in which they are elicited.

More profound differences in language forms and functions are examined in detail in Chapters 3 and 4. These cannot be reduced to surface features of accent, vocabulary, or even grammar. But in reaction to the more sweepingly generalized accounts of communicative deficiencies, some critics have turned to the concept of 'social class *dialects*' because of the theme of 'different but (linguistically) equal' which has run through this chapter. That equality in principle leaves unaffected the social reality constructed by the ways we respond to speech. Bernard Shaw was well aware of it. Professor Higgins' powers extended beyond the precise location of individuals from the way they spoke—

> You see this creature with her kerbstone English, the English that will keep her in the gutter to the end of her days? Well sir, in three months I could pass that girl off as a duchess at an ambassador's garden party. I could even get her a place as a lady's maid or shop assistant, which requires better English. (*Pygmalion*, Act 1.)

The existence of speech 'indicators' reflects relationships between what the speaker is, and how he speaks. The existence of speech 'markers' shows the speaker's ability to recognize those relationships, and to control his speech accordingly. It also emphasizes the unreality of assuming one speaker—one language (or dialect). I hope the section that follows will make that unreality even more apparent. For the concept of 'speech repertoire' refers to the range of linguistic resources available. It may include a standard language, a regional dialect, and a local dialect; or it may be described as a formal style, a colloquial style, and an occupational jargon. Sociologically, the linguistic distance between the ends of the repertoire may not be very important. What matters are the activities and opportunities to which the varieties are related. Societies of very different linguistic diversity show 'the general phenomena of variety in code repertoire, and switching among codes' (Hymes 1967a, p. 9).

4. SPEECH REPERTOIRE

'The totality of dialectal and superposed variants regularly employed within a community make up the verbal repertoire of that community' (Gumperz 1968, p. 385). What languages or varieties are used, what distinguishes their speakers, and to what distinctive uses are they put? What does the fully competent member of the community need to know to participate fully in its life? That last question draws attention immediately to inequalities in repertoire. Control over communicative resources varies with the individual's position in the community, both ascribed and achieved. The more narrowly confined his sphere or activities, and the more socially homogeneous the groups with whom he normally interacts, the narrower his repertoire is likely to be. Reciprocally, the narrower it is, the more confined his life—and his 'life chances'. Earlier reference to the linguistic continuum in Jamaica emphasized the occupational advantages of a 'span' oriented towards its Standard end. It is worth recalling that problems also arise from the uprooting effects of such facility. If non-standard forms express ethnic identity, or have powerful connotations of warmth and intimacy, their submergence may alienate the 'assimilated' and 'upward-mobile' from their community of origin. The danger explains why *bi*-dialectal policies are so passionately advocated in some American inner-city schools; Negro children are not to lose their distinctive speech, but to extend their repertoire (see Chapter 4). The problem of excessive 'standardization' may be acute for political leaders needing a base of popular support. It is explicitly recognized as such in the following extract:

> After a Harlem street rally, one of these downtown 'leaders' and I were talking when we were approached by a Harlem hustler . . .; he said to me, approximately: 'Hey, baby. I dig you holding this all-originals scene at the track . . . I'm going to lay a vine under the Jew's balls for a dime—got to

give you a play . . . Got the shorts out here trying to scuffle up on some bread . . . Well, my man, I'll get on, got to go peck a little and cop me some z's.' And the hustler went on up Seventh Avenue.

I would never have given it a second thought, except that this downtown 'leader' was standing, staring after that hustler, looking as if he'd just heard Sanskrit. He asked what had been said, and I told him . . . The point I am making is that, as a 'leader', I could talk over the ABC, CBS, or NBC microphones, at Harvard or Tuskegee; I could talk with the so-called 'middle-class' Negro and with the ghetto blacks (whom all the other leaders just talked *about*).

(*The Autobiography of Malcolm X*, Penguin Press, pp. 421–2.)

The examples that follow are concerned with the repertoire of the *community*, not of the individual, and especially with the functional differentiation between the available variants. The term 'linguistic range' refers to the *linguistic* distance between them. 'Compartmentalization' refers to 'the sharpness with which the varieties are set off from each other, either along the superposed or the dialectal dimension . . . when several languages are spoken without their mixing . . . or when special parlances are sharply distinct from other forms of speech' (Gumperz 1968, p. 386). Both descriptions will reflect the density of inter-group communication, the extent of the barriers to social interaction, and the clarity with which roles are differentiated in terms of when, where, and with whom they are appropriate. In highly urbanized societies, a 'shallow linguistic contrast in styles is a direct correlate of the fluidity of roles' (Gumperz 1962). The 'shallow' contrasts may retain considerable social significance, but they are less easily identified, at least by the outside observer. Two of the three examples here are of *plurilingual* communities, because the linguistic expression of functional differences is more 'visible' there.

(a) *Language diversity in northern India*
The complex inter-relationships of linguistic and social difference are especially apparent in India. In the area he studied, Gumperz (1971, pp. 1–76, 129–50) distinguished three main varieties of speech in ascending order of generality, each with its own functions and network of communication. The local village dialects were often unintelligible outside a narrow area, and those limited to its use led lives severely restricted in space and scope. The regional dialects were the native speech of the small-town dwellers, and a necessary 'second-language' for those coming into the towns to trade. The regional language was the medium of a written literature, and the spoken language of big business and administration. Around Delhi, it closely resembled the

regional dialect, and so was the main language of the well-educated. Elsewhere, the differences between it and colloquial speech were large enough to make it a formally acquired second language for almost all its users, a variety reserved for official and cultural occasions. Viewed from above, such diversity brings acute administrative problems because of the gulf between the everyday language of most of the population, and the written language used to convey official orders and information. From below, there are obvious problems for the villager wishing to move beyond his 'home world'. 'If he wants to be able to read the sort of literature that reaches him in the village and thus remain in direct touch with the outside community, it is not enough that he know the Devanagari alphabet. In order to read Hindi, he has to learn a great deal of new terminology and new syntactic constructions. In order to transact business, he has to master the Urdu script and Urdu literary style, and it would be useful if he knew at least some English' (1971, pp. 21–2). If he is deficient in any of these respects, his participation in some spheres of activity will be either limited or blocked, or else he will be forced to rely on middle-men. In a very direct sense, linguistic knowledge is power. The highest proportion of native speakers of the standard regional language were migrant workers, professionals, and government employees. As cause *and* effect, these were the politically active and reformist groups. Perhaps unable to understand a villager living only a hundred miles away, they could understand each other over a much greater distance. It was therefore possible to identify a regional speech community 'connected by a network of communication which extends from one urban centre to another without touching the intervening rural areas' (1971, p. 56). This compartmentalization of varieties, and of the activities associated with them, tended to polarize town and country, and to separate the mass of the population from much of the practice of politics.

(b) *Plurilingualism in Sauris*

Sauris is a linguistic enclave in north-east Italy, physically isolated by its position in the Carnian Alps. Most of its adult population speak three languages: standard Italian, a dialect of Friulian (the regional language), and a local German dialect largely unintelligible to other German speakers. There is little linguistic overlap within this repertoire; despite some intrusion of individual words and phrases, a speaker normally chooses one or another as he thinks appropriate. Functional appropriateness is so clearly defined that the languages can almost be seen as 'diatypes'—i.e. they are reserved for quite different uses. Indeed, they long represented three *spatially* distinctive worlds—the village, the region, and the nation. 'Now that the region and the outside world are so unmistakably represented *inside* the village and its daily activities, the diatypic spaces which now co-exist there have become psychologically rather than physically distinct' (Denison 1971, p. 176). Italian is the language of church, officialdom, school, conversation with children, and interaction with (or in the presence of) strangers. Friulian is the everyday language of some incomers, but it is also in general use in talking to (or in the company of) acquaintances from the surrounding area, and in some bars and other places of communal meeting. German is, or was, the language of spontaneous, intimate conversation, especially among women. That change of tense indicates a state of unstable plurilingualism. Parents' recognition of the importance of fluent Italian to 'getting on in the world' has made some homes an entirely Italian domain. More commonly, parents speak German to each other and Italian to their children, even in the same conversation. A quite sudden local linguistic change reflects the opening up of contact with, and opportunities in, the wider society. Yet most children continue to learn German in adolescence as a means of entry to village life, and the dialect persists, despite the obvious 'objective' disadvantages, because of the warmth associated with it and its role as 'the most intimate and unequivocal marker of village identity' (Denison 1968, p. 586).

(c) *Dialectal varieties in Swabia*

A sociolinguistic profile of the Schwaben area near Stuttgart showed six varieties in regular but clearly differentiated use: (1) rural dialect (2) provincial vernacular; (3) regional vernacular; (4) 'dignified' Swabian; (5) Swabian-accented High German; (6) standard High German. Since North Germans would find even the regional vernacular hard to understand, the linguistic range is again wide. The social range is also wide. Villagers in remote areas are sometimes limited to 1 and 2, and effectively tied to the places in which they will live out their lives. The majority learn to use 4 and 5 where appropriate—e.g. in impersonal relationships, and for all forms of 'business'. Appropriateness may be precisely defined. A high school lesson begun in High German is likely to switch to dignified Swabian if exposition gives way to debate. Some facility in standard High German is necessary for those preparing to enter university, but most official matters are conducted in Swabian, and this is the 'highest' level that most will need to command. The purpose of the profile is to act as a parable for the potential use of 'dignified' Black English in American schools (Fishman and Salmon 1972). At its face value, it shows a communally agreed distinction between the linguistic expression of personal and impersonal relationships. The vernaculars retain vital communicative functions in the domains of family and friendship; they have connotations of 'emotional and primary experiences that none would forego'.

These examples have emphasized the institutional contexts in which a language or variety is normally used. They describe communities in which a wide repertoire exists, and the range of options open to an individual is closely related to his command of language. In principle, anything '*could* be said' in any language. In practice, that statement 'does not speak concretely to actual inequalities, for means of speech are what their uses make of them; they have been put to different ends, in different circumstances, and sometimes been caught up in the ends and circumstances of others' (Hymes 1972b, p. 322). Varieties in regular use in a speech community may serve distinct if overlapping purposes. Tanner's (1967) term *functional range* refers to their normal uses, or to the limits beyond which their use will be considered inappropriate. That range reflects the facts of social life in that community. 'The dimension of functional superiority and inferiority is usually disregarded by linguists, but it is an essential part of the sociolinguist's concern. It becomes his special and complex task to define the social functions of each language or dialect, and the prestige that attaches to each of these' (Haugen 1966, p. 928).

5. DIGLOSSIA AND DOMAIN

Functional differentiation between varieties of a language is the core of Ferguson's account of diglossia. The term describes the stable and complementary existence of High (H) and Low (L) forms of the same language in the same speech community. Its elucidation represented a reaction against descriptive linguists' neglect of socio-cultural setting 'in their understandable zeal to describe the internal structure of the language' (Ferguson 1959, p. 337). It is much more than a new name for an old situation. Though the original title of Ferguson's paper was—'Classical or Colloquial—One Standard or Two?'—he was *not* making the familiar distinction between standard language and dialect. The Low form may itself be fully standardized, imposed on or replacing local varieties. But the High form is superposed even on that. It is learned later, and formally taught. It is the main medium for literature, and the language of administration, law, religion, and the higher levels of education. The often widespread belief in its special beauty and complexity is partly the result of its standardization in grammars and literary tradition. It also reflects the prestige of the activities it serves. It is not used in ordinary conversation, even by the élite, and any attempt to do so 'is felt to be either pedantic and artificial, or else in some sense disloyal to the community'. The Low form is the 'home language', both literally and in the metaphorical sense of that language to which speakers revert when at their ease. The functional differentiation between the forms is therefore so sharp that it solves most decisions about which to use. 'In one set of situations, only H is appropriate . . . and in another only L, with the two sets overlapping only very slightly'. The functional range of the forms will obviously vary from one diglossic community to another; a personal letter would probably be written in colloquial (L) Greek and Arabic, and in Hochdeutsch (H) by Swiss Germans. But in general, though the suggestion moves outside the frame of Ferguson's argument, the forms are one way of 'realizing' linguistically two complementary sets of values—power and formality, solidarity and spontaneity. These values may also be realized through the more common standard-dialect distinction, or by fine details of stylistic choice. Diglossia is likely where literacy is limited to an élite, where positions of power are reserved for those either born to acquire the High form, or able to do so through an arduous training in a more meritocratic society (e.g. the Mandarinate in pre-revolutionary China). A democratic challenge to such linguistic and social stratification may involve raising the status of L so that H becomes a dead language, or so diffusing H that it becomes part of general usage with a full functional range.

Extending Ferguson's dual analysis, Fishman is similarly concerned to show stable links between language use and social functions. His concept of *domain* describes the 'institutional contexts' in which a language or variety is normally found. Their identification calls for 'wide and detailed socio-cultural knowledge', the careful mapping of the 'major clusters of interaction situations' within the community (Fishman 1972b, p. 441). Where do the boundaries come that separate one domain from another, and how distinct are they? How tight are the constraints on which language should be used in situations of a particular type? The answers to these questions will obviously vary with the complexity and specialization of the community's activities, and the extent to which interaction networks overlap. Frey's (1945) study of the Amish community in Pennsylvania described three languages in three main settings. English was the language of the school-room, enforced there by the wider society. 'Dutch' was used in the home and all everyday conversation. 'High German' was used for preaching and praying, its continued survival reflecting the determination to maintain the old ways. Five domains were derived from the use of Spanish and English by New York Puerto Ricans— those of family, friendship, religion, education and employment (Fishman 1972b, pp. 444–5). With some modification, these could also be used to describe trilingual switching in Sauris, and the changes from dialect to standard in northern Norway (Blom and Gumperz 1972). It might be tempting to look for the social equivalent of the High-Low dichotomy, but this would often lose sight of significant 'clusters of interaction situation' within the broad categories.

Fishman describes the derivation of domains and domain-appropriate usage from 'the data of numerous discrete situations' as a major task of descriptive sociology of language (1972a, p. 50). Successfully completed, it would show how systematic is the choice between and within languages, and how it could be explained in ways that 'combine factual accuracy and theoretical parsimony'. Like formal linguistic analysis, it relates to a level 'underlying' actual use through a process of deliberate abstraction. Domain is 'a socio-cultural construct abstracted from topics of communication, relations between communicators, and locales of communication, in accord with the institutions of a society and the spheres of activity . . . in such a way that *individual behaviour and social patterns* can be distinguished from each other and yet related to each other' (1972b, p. 442; italics in original). It provides a way of doing justice both to local circumstances and to higher-order regularities. Initial analysis might reveal 'patterns' of language use which ignore important situational variations. The account is then 'parsimonious', but 'factually inaccurate' or unrealistic. More detailed study is needed to 'save' the phenomena. In a representative anecdote, he describes a Belgian official who normally uses French in his office, Dutch in his club, and Flemish in his home. The domains seem distinct. Yet he speaks Flemish on occasions in the office. The identification of lower-order factors like setting, or topic, is then necessary to account for the switch of code. Domain is therefore seen by Fishman as 'integrating' large-scale and small-group research. The concept provides a convenient bridge to detailed consideration of 'context of situation'.

6. CONTEXT OF SITUATION AND THE ETHNOGRAPHY OF SPEAKING

Fishman describes 'situation' as the co-occurrence of setting, topic, and interlocutors related to each other in a particular way. Where the influences of persons, time and place are 'congruent' (e.g. talk between judge and barrister, in the court-room and while the court is in session), then the constraints on appropriate usage may be heavy. Including such 'social units' in the analysis will reveal systematic patterns of linguistic choice 'where only free variation or weak structure would be evident without their aid' (1971, p. 8). Linguistic options which are formally available are socially narrowed down in regularly occurring ways, and extending the scope of rule-governed behaviour to include them allows 'proper' usage to be predicted and explained.

Constraint is also resource; it has its uses. Norms of appropriate usage mean that the particular choice made carries within it some definition of the situation, a 'socio-symbolic' expression of the relative status of the conversants and their attitudes to each other (Fischer 1958). Alongside the referential function of speech lies what Hymes (1971) calls its 'stylistic' function, the accomplishment of communicative purposes by choice between or within languages and varieties. 'Rules' derived from regular associations between verbal and other social behaviour are *used* creatively to transmit 'social meanings', to maintain, modify or challenge the form of relationships.

In barest outline, the previous paragraphs refer to the critical distinction between *unmarked* and *marked* linguistic choice. Unmarked usage is 'normal' in the circumstances—i.e. given that particular combination of place, time and participants. It so conforms to expectations as to be part of the taken-for-granted background to interaction. Marked usage 'breaks the rules', but in recognizably meaningful ways. It can serve to define or redefine the situation. Both kinds of usage take their meaning from the *particular* circumstances in which they occur, which are unlikely to be accounted for solely under the heading of some domain. In his introduction to a book on 'communication in urban, black America', Thomas Kochman announces its intention not simply to describe communicative behaviours, but to reproduce as far as possible the contexts in which they are embedded. 'Recreating the structure of an event' would enable the reader to validate or discredit the writer's interpretation of it. He would also be able to make sense of speech incomprehensible out of context—e.g. the 'rappin' and stylin' out' of the book's title—and experience 'a sense of event, presence and action not often felt in a scholarly book' (Kochman 1972a, p. xii). This concentration on situated performance, and on detailed description from the 'inside', reflects a strengthening ethnomethodological trend in social science. But some of its elements can be found in the work of Malinowski, fifty years before. 'Context of situation' is his phrase, and it was later taken up by J. R. Firth. What they did with it is worth attention both for the intrinsic interest, and because it places more recent work in a perhaps surprisingly long perspective.

Malinowski too emphasized the detailed structure of events, a structure which could only be recreated by 'plunging into the lives of the natives', and acquiring the knowledge that underlay their communication. Without such long and painful learning, the observer was bound to lack 'that intuitive understanding which enables us . . . to handle the finer shades of meaning and . . . take part in the quick interchange between several people' (Malinowski 1935, p. xi). Where words 'stood for' objects and events in a direct-meaning relationship, they might be comprehensible from the *text* alone. This is true of most written communication, and of such specialized speech activities as lecturing. But Malinowski saw these as 'a very far-fetched and derivative function of language', which was primarily 'a mode of action rather than a counter-sign of thought'. Understanding this wider meaning depended not only on the words in their 'logical sequence', but on the whole situation of which they were a part (1923, pp. 97 and 307–12). This dependence is most obvious when the context 'gives the solution' to otherwise ambiguous utterances, allowing gaps to be filled in ways which are lost when the speech is uprooted. He did not insist that *all* meaning was inseparable from its context. It was, however, greatly extended and clarified by it, and in his field-work he sometimes tried to reconstruct the circumstances in which an utterance might have occurred.

The extent of such situational 'embedding' raises some difficult problems. It is hard to conceive of a conversation in which the speakers know (or guess) nothing about each other, and have no shared background knowledge to which they can refer. Any mutually meaningful discourse would then have to be constructed from scratch. It is very much easier to find conversation *so* embedded in its context as to convey nothing outside it. This distinction between context-dependence and independence is obviously a continuum. No speech is entirely 'free' of its situation, because part of its meaning will be implicit, supplied by the background knowledge of the participants. What is said is an index to larger networks of meaning. The more this local knowledge is presupposed, the more inaccessible speech will be to the 'outsider'. But how do participants relate particular utterances to particular features of the social context? More fundamentally, how do they recognize what kind of context it is? Their task is relatively easy when the context is a regularly occurring and labelled 'speech event' (e.g. playing the dozens). Most contexts are not like this, yet they cannot all be special cases. Categorization is likely. Where the categories are uncertain or ambiguous, how do the participants make known to each other what their definitions are, and how far do these definitions coincide? These questions are not raised by Malinowski. For example, what he called 'phatic communion' is 'a mere exchange of words', speech used to fill an awkward silence, or acknowledge someone's existence, or express some routinized goodwill. 'How are you?' is normally a greeting, not a question. But in some situations, a referentially meaningful response *is* required. How is this indicated and perceived? A further, linguistic, objection to Malinowski's approach has been that he fails to make clear what importance is to be given to the formal structure of language in transmitting meaning (Langendoen 1968, p. 19). But there can be no doubt at all about his 'socially realistic' emphasis. 'To us, the real linguistic fact is the full utterance within its context of situation' (Malinowski 1935, p. 11).

J. R. Firth shared with Malinowski a wide view of the knowledge needed to plan and understand speech. Both rejected a simple dyadic relationship between word and referent, insisting instead on 'a multidimensional set of relations between the word in its sentence and the context of its occurrence' (Robins 1971, p. 35). Where Malinowski tended to see context as the immediate concrete circumstances, what was 'going on' while the words were said, Firth included the personal history of the participants and the entire 'cultural setting' in which they interacted. This might be dismissed as 'little more than a convenient dumping ground for speakers' knowledge of their world' (Langendoen 1968, p. 50). Indeed, Firth never offered any detailed delineation, only an abstract representation of what the linguistically relevant environment might be. In time, he hoped to see a classification of the main 'components' of situation which would allow their inclusion as a normal part of linguistic description. This might seem an unmanageable task. So many social variables have their effect on speech behaviour that there are 'bagfuls of indicators' to do 'something correlational with' (Goffman 1964). Firth expected their description to be feasible because of the regularities in social life, the constraining of speech by 'typical' roles and situations. Like Malinowski, he saw language as a way of *doing* things and getting things done, as integrated with 'actual patterns of behaviour'. The approach suggests his own label of sociological linguistics. 'We must take our facts from speech sequences, verbally complete in themselves and operating in contexts of situation which are typical, recurrent and repeatedly observable. Such contexts of situation should themselves be placed in categories of some sort, sociological and linguistic, within the wider context of culture' (Firth 1957, p. 35).

As an example of the approach, it is worth looking briefly at his treatment of conversation. This he saw as a 'roughly prescribed ritual', partly *pre*determined by social 'regularities'; 'the roles and the lines are there, and that being so, the lines can be classified and correlated with the part, and also with the episodes, scene and act'. This may seem a typically misleading use of the dramatic analogy in describing roles, a ready-made 'script' being simply enacted. But prescription was also built up *during* the conversation. 'Once someone speaks to you, you are in a relatively determined context, and you are not free to say just what you please.' If that 'someone' is a social superior, or occupies a clearly defined role relative to your own, then the style of the conversation is considerably constrained. And even in the most personalized interaction, what 'you' say elicits referentially and linguistically compatible responses, 'shutting out most of the language of your companion' and leaving him with only a limited range of possibilities (Firth 1935; also 1957, pp. 28 and 93–4). This process of contextual elimination progressively narrows the options as the interaction proceeds. The brevity of the discussion makes it seem more determinist than it is. It implies, for example, a single 'content' and style, making no allowance for switches within the conversation which open up new sets of options. But it is unreasonable to blame Firth for completely neglecting the 'creative' use of language, and for presenting speakers as totally constrained by the given social situation (Langendoen 1968, pp. 3–4). Appropriate speech *is* speech that conforms to expectations, but some of these expectations arise in the course of interaction to *challenge* 'normal' usage.

In emphasizing the social functions of language, Firth was looking beyond the individual speaker in unique circumstances to typical situations and the speech styles appropriate to them. This interest in recurring sets of social constraints led him towards ethnographic description. Much later, what Hymes (1964a; 1971) calls an 'ethnography of speaking' explicitly enlarges the scope of the rules governing language use beyond sentences to communicative acts, events and occasions, and beyond correctness to appropriateness. From the observer's perspective, it again emphasizes the need to record *situated* performance, language in context. From the native speaker's perspective it refers to that extensive knowledge of the 'social etiquette' of language choice which must underlie effective communication.

Ethnographic description sets out what a culturally competent member knows in order to perform the roles open to him in the situations he is likely to encounter. Obviously, even the most detailed 'cultural guide' will not provide a detailed solution for every communicative problem. Indeed, if messages were as predictable as that, there would be little point in saying anything at all. Only by defining the parameters *within* which choice is made is it 'the task of an ethnographer of speaking to specify what the appropriate alternatives are in a given situation, and what the consequences are of selecting one alternative over another' (Frake 1964, pp. 127–8). What kinds of additional information would he provide for someone already 'technically' competent in a language? This question will be answered briefly as a preliminary to considering some 'components' of situation.

(1) Even a long conversation can be verbally explicit, most of what is relevant to its understanding being derived from the words alone. But most speech is not like this. Social context is relied upon to narrow down the referents of words which are an index to other implicit meanings. What is actually said is only 'a sketchy, partial, incomplete, masked, elliptical, concealed, ambiguous or misleading version' of what is being talked about (Garfinkel 1972, p. 317). Participants do not merely reinterpret what they hear, they extensively add to it from their cultural knowledge. The more this 'local' knowledge is presupposed, the more incomprehensible speech will be apart from its context and the particular relationship of the speakers.

(2) Hasan (1968) defines a *text* as 'a piece of language that forms an integrated whole rather than a collection of sentences', and analyses the linguistic means by which this coherence is obtained. The ability to recognize a series of utterances as a 'discourse', as similarly 'tied' together, depends partly on this linguistic knowledge, partly on recognizing the whole context of which the words form a part, and the boundaries of the various 'episodes' within it. 'Utterances are to conversation what sentences are to language'; like them in being subject to grammatical rules, they also have 'structural relationships to the interactional circumstances in which they occur' which determine what goes with what (Speier 1973). How the meaningful segments in a stream of verbal behaviour are announced and recognized is a major problem in communication (and in its analysis). It is made *relatively* easier when the units have specific cultural labels attached to them. Speech occasions, events and acts represent descending levels of generality in participants' perception of linguistically relevant contextual information. An 'occasion' describes a gathering of people with a 'right' to be there, at a place regularly associated with such interaction, and with the communicative roles and purposes at least broadly defined (e.g. a cocktail party, or committee meeting). An 'event' is more specific and more focused, like the round of introductions

at the beginning of a party; it may have a ritualized structure, and stereotyped opening and closing routines which define its boundaries. 'Acts' are conventional ways of 'doing things with words', like greeting a friend or asking a favour or telling a joke, in which selections may be made from a fairly limited cultural repertoire.

(3) These identifiable communicative units resemble Firth's 'prescribed rituals', in which the lines and parts are already determined. How is coherence obtained when there are no such specific cultural categories available? Firth described, very briefly, how order is achieved as a conversation proceeds—through stylistic rules of co-occurrence ('What you say raises the threshold against most of the language of your companion') and general rules of interaction (e.g. a question requires a response, or as Sacks puts it, 'The silence after my question is your silence'). Sacks' work on conversational structure attends in fine detail to the problems that must be solved to achieve order in everyday conversation. How does the speaker notify the addressee that there is going to be some communication? How does he indicate the appropriate hearers, and audience? How are the channels kept open? ('Uh huh . . .', 'Yes . . .', 'Mm . . .', 'I see . . .', 'You don't say . . .'). How is a 'fair' distribution of talk achieved? In dyadic conversation, alternation between the speakers is the normal practice. In a group, where 'one speaker at a time' is still the rule, how do participants know who is to speak next? If several begin together, who backs down? How does a participant indicate his readiness to take over ('That reminds me . . .', 'By the way,', 'Did I ever tell you . . .'). If one participant is telling a story, how did he 'get the floor'? If he allows some participation by others, how does he get it back? How much silence is acceptable, and whose responsibility is it to break it? Even this limited selection of problems indicates the complexity and subtlety of the conversational competence we acquire with the rules of the language.

(4) Problems like sequencing may be 'solved' in advance by strict rules relating to e.g. the seniority, sex and rank of the participants. Singly or in combination, these may 'cover' most communicative dilemmas, at least on public occasions. Within the bounds of grammatical correctness and referential intelligibility, particular linguistic choices are 'authorized'. To diverge from them risks having the message misunderstood, disvalued, or rejected. It is not being argued that *any* linguistic choice can be explained by relating it to some non-linguistic variable. Much of our speech shows 'socially-free' variation. If we say 'shrub' rather than 'bush', the sociolinguist is unlikely to comment. But if we refer to the colonel's 'lady' as his 'wife', the referential equivalence does not remove the social error. Emphasizing the existence of pre-

determined limits on what can be said, and who is to speak, and how, does not remove the need to show *how* the linguistically relevant social categories are recognized and interpreted in particular contexts.

(5) 'We exhibit our place in society, and we convey our feeling of formality and intimacy by linguistic variables that are grammatically optional and that also leave referential meaning unchanged' (Burling 1970, p. 134). The 'constraints' on choice are also opportunities for conveying social meaning. Knowledge of regularly occurring relationships between certain forms of speech and e.g. social status or role makes it possible to transmit important advance information about the kind of message to be expected, and how the speaker perceives himself, and himself in relation to particular others. All languages provide stylistic means of coding e.g. superiority, deference, formality and intimacy. And, beyond the scope of this book, is the huge array of paralinguistic and non-verbal communicative resources available to the culturally competent member (see e.g. Argyle 1972b: Crystal 1971: Hall 1963: Laver 1968: Leach 1972). For example, eye-contact, posture and physical distance are used to reinforce interaction by keeping the channels open, and to signal its imminent breaking off. Together with 'voice qualities', their importance leads Argyle to the surely exaggerated conclusion that speech is used mainly to solve problems and transmit referential information, while the 'silent channels' handle the immediate social relationship (Argyle 1972b: Argyle *et al.* 1970). In fact, the inter-penetration of verbal and non-verbal components means that neither is fully comprehensible apart from the 'total orchestration' of words, intonation, gesture, etc. Investigation of their *relative* importance requires detailed description of particular contexts, and of the cultural sensitivity to cues of different kinds. That last point is relevant to later discussion of communicative discontinuity in classrooms. Black students in American city schools often rely heavily on words 'modified by tone and emphasis, by non-verbal body movements, motions, gestures, shrugs, head movements, facial expressions, and the touching and holding of one person by another'. Such 'body language' may be both incomprehensible *and* disturbing to white teachers more accustomed to channel communication through words (Foster 1974, p. 117). And while many aspects of gesture and voice are idiosyncratic, conveying information most effectively to intimates, many are culturally coded in ways that can be used creatively to generate specific social meanings. Since the repertoire is more limited than that of verbal language, interpretation is more likely to be context-dependent (see Argyle 1972a, p. 41, for an attempt at a postural 'dictionary').

Ethnographic description refers to knowledge available to members of a speech community which is used, more or less consciously, to categorize persons, places and activities. It raises fundamental questions about the nature of rule-governed behaviour, how the rules are recognized as applicable by members, how they can be identified by an 'outside' observer, and how far the 'same' rules are used by members and observer to make sense of what they hear.

Much of the sociolinguistic research already described attempted either to establish social correlates for recurring patterns of linguistic choice, or to find corroborative linguistic evidence for previously mapped social situations (or situation-types). Approached from either direction, speech forms are seen as 'adhering to' behaviour patterns which are not primarily linguistic at all, the broader perspective revealing 'clearly delineable patterns' in what had previously seemed odd, erratic and unpredictable usage (e.g. Foster 1964: Fischer 1958). The assumption underlying such research is that selection among linguistic alternatives, all of which are formally 'correct', may be 'both patterned and predictable on the basis of certain features of the local social system' (Blom and Gumperz 1972, p. 409).

Some intention of *explaining* the choice is clear. What kinds of explanation are offered? What Wilson (1970) calls the normative paradigm is very evident in Fishman's work. Norms of appropriateness are seen as existing, outside the particular interaction, as a framework guiding choice. Participants treat specific situations and relationships as instances of some general category to which certain rules apply, and then apply them. They do so in the same, or compatible, ways, so that their definitions 'fit'. 'Proper usage dictates that only one of the theoretically co-available languages or varieties will be chosen by particular classes of inter-locutors on particular kinds of occasions to discuss particular kinds of topics' (Fishman 1972b, p. 437). Stable patterns of choice are identified into which the immediate interaction can be fitted—with due regard to 'local circumstances'. These domains and situations are abstractions, 'extrapolated from the data of talk rather than being an actual component of talk'. They are not descriptions of how the participants themselves would identify the constraints on their speech. Like linguistic rules, they represent knowledge inferred from regularities in behaviour; normally 'out of awareness', this knowledge might be 'recognized' by members if explicitly brought to their attention—e.g. by presenting them with speech inappropriate to its context and asking them what is 'wrong', and why (the method used by Fishman to investigate the 'construct validity' of domains). But Fishman's is essentially a view 'from the outside', concerned with 'normal' behaviour defined by rules abstracted from actual speech.

In their introduction to Fishman's paper on domains, Gumperz and Hymes (1972, pp. 435–6) insist on the contrast between it and Gumperz' own research in Norway. Here the analysis concentrated on the generation of regularities in behaviour from *within* the interaction— from 'a series of individual choices made under specifiable constraints and incentives'. The emphasis is on how the participants announce, recognize, maintain, modify or challenge the rules they apply to their interaction. The difference in perspective illustrates a continuous tension in social science between the structur*ed* and the structur*ing*, between the institutionally invariant and what depends on 'perception and implementation', the actors' recognition and *use* of the norms relevant to the particular situation. The first approach tends to regard the problem of social order as solved when the higher- and lower-order societal patterning is identified. The second is concerned with the *work* needed to produce that order, which is not a once-and-for-all achievement. It is also likely to emphasize the 'creative' use of rules, which are not seen as predicting *particular* 'surface' realizations of them but as general interpretative procedures which enable the speaker to cope with rapidly changing situations and 'generate' appropriate responses (Cicourel 1973: Moerman 1972). An essential part of the social scientist's task is to show *how* rules are applied to the interaction—how the abstract rule is related to actual behaviour and 'brought to life'.

The approach depends on a close match between 'native' and 'analytic' knowledge. Comparing the use of 'rules' by linguists and anthropologists, Burling (1969) argues that it does not matter whether these are extracted from observed behaviour, having no 'existence' apart from the analysis, or whether they represent rules the members themselves recognize and use. 'What matters is whether or not our rules somehow correspond to the data we seek to describe'—i.e. do they 'work' in the sense of distinguishing 'proper' and 'improper' behaviour, not as a 'list of specific instances but as *predictions* of the acceptable alternatives'. This would support Grimshaw's (1966) view of sociolinguistics as concerned with 'those reflections of social structure which are revealed in language', and as *not* concerned with either motivation or conscious behaviour. The approach may seem sensibly pragmatic. But it ignores the fact that information about the linguistically relevant social categories is obtained largely *from* the language used by participants, and that *how* they are relevant has to be made clear during the interaction. It also exaggerates the possibilities of prediction and underestimates the degree of variability in 'proper' usage. The possibility of some form of prediction can hardly be denied, for linguistic choice would otherwise have to be seen as random, or as arising out of an infinite number of *unique* contexts. Gumperz himself writes of 'stating the connection between language and social structure . . . in terms of regular rules allocating particular sets of forms to particular kinds of interaction' (1964, p. 138), an approach not obviously different from Fishman's. It was a path interestingly followed and then abandoned by Sankoff (1972) in his research in New Guinea. Initially, he used a predictive model in which language choice was accounted for in terms of three main variables, in order of salience and applicability: Is the interlocutor a fellow-tribesman? Is the situation formal? Is the topic religious? Such factors served to define the limits of acceptability, in the sense of ruling out some 'possibilities' while leaving the range of available options still open. The final choice might be *retrospectively* interpreted as conveying significant social meanings, in a perhaps ambiguous or fluid situation. Marked and unmarked usage is identified *during* the on-going interaction.

7. 'COMPONENTS' OF SITUATION: SETTING, PARTICIPANTS AND TOPIC

Social factors restrict linguistic selection 'as syntactic environments narrow the dictionary meaning of words'. Speakers take in clues from the situation, decide on appropriate behavioural strategies, and then translate these into 'appropriate verbal symbols' (Blom and Gumperz 1972, pp. 421–2). As we will see, recognizing these 'translations' of behavioural strategy is formidably difficult, but for the moment the difficulties are set aside. In describing the main social 'clues', a balance is needed between abstracting regular patterns of linguistic choice and doing so at a level too far removed from actual speech. Some observational framework is useful, and there are several models available (e.g. Ervin-Tripp 1964: Hymes 1967a). Which variables are included, and their relative salience, will obviously vary from one culture to another, and even from one context to another. The 'components' of setting, participant-status, participant-relations, and topic will be examined here—as examples of micro-sociolinguistic analysis and as a background for later analysis of classrooms as contexts for language use (Chapter 5). Clearly, there are *situational* 'rules of co-occurrence', so that the presence of one factor may imply or subsume another (e.g. the presence of a high-ranking participant limits the range of appropriate topics, and religious topics are normally discussed in religious settings). And there are culturally labelled speech occasions and events with specific constraints on topic, form and participants. 'Situation' can therefore refer to 'any constellation of status and setting that constrains the interaction' (Ervin-Tripp 1971a, p. 50), or to a *congruent* 'intersection of setting, time and roles' which mutually reinforce the constraints (Fishman 1972a, p. 22), or to a quite clearly defined cultural and communicative unit. Our concern here is with factors that can exert at least a potentially independent influence.

Setting

'Setting' refers to the locale rather than the action—to the stage, the set, the props, and the number and position of the 'cast'. The difficulty of identifying 'merely' spatial constraints is recognized. Yet in artificially controlled conditions, there is a long tradition of research into e.g. the effect of group size on the proportion of active participants in discussion, of the 'centrality' of members' positions on the number of messages they give and receive, and on the frequency of interaction between those placed in adjacent, opposite or diagonal positions (e.g. Kendon 1967: Mehrabian and Diamond 1971). Less contrived behavioural settings also 'channel' the flow of communication, inhibit verbal interaction or emphasize its impersonality, and locate the 'leader'. Physical barriers may keep potential interlocutors outside the culturally preferred range for intimate conversation, or in positions which symbolize the roles rather than the persons (e.g. a confessional box), and there may be a visible marking of communicative 'zones' for audience, peripheral contributors, active participants, and leaders (Barker 1968, pp. 49–51). Televised studio 'discussions' illustrate a spatially ordered hierarchy of talkers, as indeed does the traditional classroom with its 'dais' and rows of desks. Obviously, proximity may *create* interaction (Strodtbeck and Hook 1961), and it may *result from* previous interaction (Sommer 1969). More generally, spatial order and social relations and communicative channels are often closely linked, those of high status occupying (by mutual consent) a communicative position from which they can more easily dominate the interaction ('above the salt', 'at the head of the table', 'the platform speakers'). In less predetermined ways, the achieving of status within a group may be accompanied by 'a specific spatial orientation' (Moscovici 1967, p. 255).

Even these examples show the difficulty of separating 'setting' from *social* situation. It is much more than territory within which the participants happen to be located. In all cultures, the practice of classifying the environment into distinct locales often involves quite specific restrictions on the appropriate participants and activities, and those entering them are aware of the limitations on content and form. Setting is especially likely, then, to subsume other factors, or to be 'over-ridden' by them. In his research in Sauris, Denison (1968; 1971) noted its 'low selective power'; it was last in his listing of 'situational factors' in descending order of their correlation with language selection. Even the higher-order patterning summarized by domains *may* be spatially located; home, school and church provide the main settings for Amish 'triple-talk' (Frey 1945). But they are far more likely to be socially defined, a 'friendship situation' being perfectly possible in work, school or church locations. The Belgian officials cited by Fishman normally spoke French in the office because most conversation there was task-oriented. But if it moved to personal matters, then they switched to Flemish. Even where certain activities are associated with some 'primary' locale, where they are *physically* compartmentalized, they are rarely the only forms of communicative behaviour which take place there. People exchange gossip in church, and in front of market-stalls, and before therapy sessions. How is the normally appropriate talk begun, suspended, and ended? How do the participants make it known that the next utterances are not to be interpreted as everyday conversation? (Turner 1972). These questions shift the attention from setting to 'scene', from the ecological to the 'psychological' environment. Indeed, the basic 'ecological unit' of the 'episode' is defined by Soskin and John (1963) as—'an organised sequence of behaviours, occurring within a specifiable locale, and devoted to a particular activity'. As was mentioned earlier, the concepts of setting, situation and event refer to sets of constraints on speech arising from the ways in which members categorize their environment. They can be seen as progressively more complex and refined stages in the 'processing' of contextual information.

Participants
Participants may bring to their interaction a clearly defined status that sets limits around what can be said, by whom, and how. Status is used here to mean social identity, not 'institutionalized role'. It refers to attributes, ascribed or achieved, which consistently influence how an individual speaks, or is spoken to, because of *what* he is. 'How he speaks' means, in this context, what selection he makes from his repertoire of ways of speaking. The discussion is not now concerned with the size of that repertoire, or with speech 'indicators', but with speech that is more or less consciously adapted to the immediate cir-cumstances, especially to the speaker's perception of himself in relation to other participants in the interaction. It is concerned with who is talking to whom when the reference is not to unique individuals, but

to some commonly identified attributes which have a linguistic relevance.

Baby-talk is an obvious example of speech which is structurally and paralinguistically adapted to the addressee. Ferguson's (1964) research in six cultures showed a high level of conventional usage, and the persistence of some features over long periods of time. He also noted its more general use as an expression of protective feelings—to older children, pets, and lovers. Certain words or styles are often considered inappropriate in the speech of women, and in speech in the presence of women (Haas 1944). Where sex roles are sharply delineated, there may even be distinct varieties, without much overlap in their surface features (Trudgill 1974b, pp. 90–101). In industrial societies, the 'gentling' of speech in their presence is rejected by some women as sexist, and their own use of 'taboo' words becomes a significant egalitarian gesture. But as was mentioned briefly in Chapter 1, there is considerable evidence that they are more 'correct' in their speech, more sensitive to stigmatized features in contexts where they feel under scrutiny (Levine and Crockett 1966: Labov 1966a, p. 288: Trudgill 1974a, pp. 93–5). Often lacking the firm occupational identity of men, they may be more concerned with appearances. 'Working-class speech' also has connotations of toughness and masculinity which sometimes lead men to accentuate its features. High social rank is commonly associated with a consistent formality in speech, both given and received. In highly status-marked situations, the 'right' form of address may be precisely defined ('Your Majesty', 'Excellency', 'Mr President', 'Father', 'Sir'), and personal feelings tend to be 'properly' masked (Queen Victoria complained that Gladstone 'addressed her like a public meeting' while Disraeli spoke to her 'like a woman'; but Gladstone was simply overdoing what was appropriate, while Disraeli's informality was a deliberate personalizing of the relationship.) The right to speak first, and most, and to close the exhange, is often ascribed: to the king with his courtiers, an elder with young men of the tribe, a man in the company of women. And such prescribed inequality in the distribution of speech is often accompanied by unequal rights in determining form and content. As was mentioned earlier, it is almost impossible to say anything in Javanese without indicating respect or familiarity. This is the axis around which social behaviour is organized, and the entire etiquette system is 'summed up and symbolised' by the various stylistic levels (Geertz 1960). These express the basic structure of social relationships along the ascribed dimension of rank—i.e. their institutionalized and *relatively* invariable aspects. In fact, the relative status of the participants *is* sometimes uncertain, and it is sometimes obscured by other factors (e.g. a high-ranking politician's need to express his respect for a socially inferior audience of potential supporters). But whatever the uncertainty, some expression of how each ranks the other cannot be avoided. While all languages provide means of expressing e.g. deference and respect, they differ widely in how precisely these are coded, how generally they are coded (in choice of variety, stylistic level, or the selection of certain lexical or other features), and in whether a 'commitment' can be avoided or at least postponed. Thus Tanner (1967) describes how bilingual Indonesians sometimes switch from Javanese, with its enforced messages about formality and familiarity, to the relatively non-committal Indonesian, which provides a neutral starting-point in communicating with those whose status is uncertain. In similar situations of doubt, Japanese 'often try . . . to avoid using specific forms of address and self-reference' (Fischer 1964, p. 121). And the Apache do not speak at all 'when the status of focal participants is ambiguous'; there is then no firm basis for communication, the 'illusion of predictability' is lost, and silence seems safer than words (Basso 1972).

These examples make it apparent that what matters is usually the *relative* status of the participants, the facts of rank and familiarity that they must recognize in speech. *Who* they are may be so pervasively significant as to influence *all* the relationships in which they are involved. What is more likely to be significant is a particular *role*-relationship, which acts as a 'filter' through which verbal and other behavioural options are 'strained'. The roles may so dominate the interaction as to make other factors irrelevant, and they may sometimes be cast aside in favour of a more personalized relationship which relaxes the constraints. This casting aside is often *done* through speech, through a switch to the local dialect, or a 'lower' style, or a more intimate and equal form of address. In bilingual societies, the fact of the switch is *relatively* obvious, though its social meaning may require a careful reading of the whole context. In Paraguay, for example, Guarani is used by lovers *after* an initial Spanish-conducted courtship is successfully concluded. It is also used between close friends. Switching to it with an acquaintance may therefore announce a feeling of greater intimacy than usual, or the intention of moving the relationship to a new basis (Rubin 1962).

Modes of address, like other aspects of linguistic choice, both reflect and affirm how members perceive their relationship, and especially the social distance between them. In most of the studies cited here, they seem to do so essentially in terms of *hierarchy* and *intimacy*. This distinction is most familiar in the contrasting 'semantics' of *power* and *solidarity* (Brown and Gilman 1960), and most often investigated linguistically in relation to address. Whether power is derived from age, strength, wealth or rank, it implies the possibility of control and compliance. Expressed in pronominal choice, the superior uses the T form (second-person singular *tu, du, voi* etc.) and receives the V form (second-person plural *vous, sie, usted*, etc.). He may also graciously grant the right to reciprocate the T as a mark of temporary or even permanent favour. Both the non-reciprocal T-V, and an unequal right to decide on or initiate a change, indicate an asymmetrical relationship. The analysis recognizes the possibly reinforcing, possibly cross-cutting, influences of power *and* solidarity. There are two dimensions involved—a vertical one of above and below, and a horizontal one of closeness and distance—and it seems to be a sociolinguistic 'universal' that the same form is used to intimates and inferiors. Since it is obviously possible for people to be equal but strangers, unequal but intimate, which will prevail in a clash of criteria? In sharply stratified societies, solidarity is only likely between equals, and ascribed status governs relationships. As democracy progresses, the solidarity criterion becomes more salient; the T form is used to all intimates, regardless of status, and the formal V form to all strangers. Social distance is defined in relation to familiarity, not rank. On the way to 'democracy', there may be considerable uncertainty, and considerable differences within the same society. Slobin's (1963) investigation of Yiddish pronominal choice in Eastern Europe before 1939 showed the persisting influence of ascribed status and familial relationship as the most important criteria. More recently, it was the 'progressive' (and young) Indian who used T to his wife, and the 'progressive' French colonial who waived his right to non-reciprocated T in conversation with an African. The existence of such options provides the means of marking individual and situational nuances, and of manipulating or modifying the normally prevailing social distance. An employer may use and allow T as a gesture of relaxation, and revert to V to re-establish distance, or simply to 'return to business'.

This particular form of address provides an easily identified example of social constraints on speech, and of their use to 'do things with words'. Similar rules and possibilities may be related to the use of a particular language, or of colloquial style, or of 'honorifics'. In English, the use of first-name (FN), or of last name and title (TLN), are subject to much the same constraints, and carry similar social meanings. The one significant difference is that choice can be avoided or delayed (Brown and Ford 1961: Ervin-Tripp 1971a). Slobin *et al.* (1968) used the evidence of forms of address to comment on the structure of a business organization, and on the wider cultural context. Since achieved status is more important in American society, age was seldom a significant influence. Upper-management used FN to all, and rarely received it. At all levels, it was more likely to be received from subordinates than from subordinates' subordinates. Most forms seemed to be consistent across various work contexts, though middle-management were relatively flexible, and more likely to offer FN to superiors on levels they hoped to attain themselves. As in many other situations, use of FN when the recipient cannot return it can symbolize and even create an asymmetrical relationship. It can also create misunderstanding when speakers of the same language are playing this 'address game' by different rules. The 'upper-class' English use of *last* name only to equals will baffle Americans whose own early use of first name is seen as a premature claim to intimacy.

Denison (1971) suggests that some relationships are reflected largely in the kind of verbal interaction that takes place. His suggestion can be adapted to mean that the clearest evidence for the existence of a role-relationship rather than a personal one may be found in speech. Part of the next chapter considers the categorization of families as position- or person-oriented, and the possible linguistic consequences. And research already quoted has shown one language or variety being reserved, normally, for relationships in which the participants confront each other as persons rather than as occupants of some status or role which confines and 'filters' the interaction. In more finely detailed ways, 'stylistic' choice may do the same. Formality of speech may be 'proper' between doctor and patient as a symbol and reinforcement of affective neutrality. Formality in the commands of an employer, or army officer, makes the coercion supportable by impersonalizing it. An investigation of casual homosexual encounters found a prevalent silence which was more than a defence against being identified. Assuring anonymity and impersonality, it was 'a normative response to the demand for privacy without involvement' (Humphreys 1970, pp. 11–13). The use of casual or intimate speech to a relative stranger is one way of treating him tactfully as an insider. Conversely, to follow casual with formal speech can serve as a reproof, a reminder of relative status, and a means of moving a relationship which has become uncomfortably close back to a 'proper' basis of formality. And many relationships involve pressures for formality when outsiders are present, when there is a 'performance' to sustain. The sudden appearance of an 'audience' many transform the situation by re-emphasizing the *role-*relationship.

Topic

'Topic' is the manifest content of speech. It therefore involves constraints for relevance, and for the 'accuracy' and intelligibility of references to the 'world beyond words'. This is what the speech is 'about'—or, more realistically, what it is apparently about. Even in this obvious sense, it can involve stylistic constraints. In plurilingual societies, certain topics are often discussed in one language rather than another because of their cultural associations. In Indonesia, for example, politics are discussed in Indonesian and religious and other traditional matters in Javanese. In the 'high' context of Parliament itself, members revert to Javanese or Dutch outside the formal confines of the session (Geertz 1960: Tanner 1967). In newly independent countries, there are obvious pressures against discussing national affairs in the colonial language. Yet some topics may continue to be discussed in an international 'standard', either because those concerned received their special training in it, or because its use links them with the world-wide 'community of experts', or because the national standard lacks some of the necessary technical terms. Even where there are no obvious referential constraints, it may be felt as inappropriate, even disrespectful, to talk of some topics in the local dialect, or the 'low' style. This 'merely' social constraint has been the focus of some recent accounts of classroom language. It may be equally inappropriate to talk about local matters in the national language or standard dialect, attempts to do so being interpreted as an expression of aloofness. Blom and Gumperz (1972) found interesting evidence of unconscious topic-induced switching. University students returned to a Norwegian town for the vacation reverted to the dialect to maintain local ties and revive past friendships. Yet the intrusion of 'intellectual' topics in informal conversation brought frequent and sudden changes to the Standard which the speakers afterwards denied and even deplored. In Sauris, however, the German dialect was so entrenched in the domain of intimate relationships that when the necessary 'technical' items were lacking, Italian words and phrases were incorporated into a still German text (Denison 1968). Only where locals and non-locals were together was topic in itself a significant constraint.

As with 'setting', it is difficult to establish when topic itself is the critical influence on linguistic choice. Certain topics occur only in certain spheres of activity, with perhaps a limited range of possible participants. They are 'under the sway of one language or variety, and therefore perhaps under the control of certain speech networks' (Fishman 1972b, p. 440). A result of such regular association is that a change of topic can 'move' a conversation from one domain to another, so bringing into play different norms of appropriate usage.

As the Sauris example suggests, too narrow a definition of 'topic' makes the same mistake as that attributed earlier to 'socially unrealistic' linguistics—of overemphasizing the referential function of language, its use to convey 'factual' information about the circumstances of the speaker or his perception of the world. What speech is 'about' extends far beyond this. As we have seen, it carries 'social information' about e.g. the feelings of the speaker, his sense of importance, and how he regards the relationship in which he is involved. It may be a means of establishing the social inferiority of others or of getting them to do things. In the Black American speech events already described, the transmission of referential information is of slight importance. It is mainly 'artful talk', talk as performance and for display, and talk used to manipulate people and situations. In some variants, like 'signifying', the manifest content must be interpreted as a sign for quite different meanings. Rather similar uses of language are apparent in Frake's account of festive drinking in Subanun. Through the talk that accompanies the drinking, the speaker can 'express role relations' by the forms of address he adopts and achieve status by the quality of his performance. Early exchanges focus on the quality of the 'beer'. Conversation then shifts to gossip and current affairs, and ends in the creation of songs and verses in highly stylized form. In this very structured setting, the individual's social relationships are defined and extended. 'The cultural patterning of drinking talk lays out an ordered scheme of role play through the use of terms of address, through discussion and argument, and through displays of verbal art. The most skilled in "talking from the jar" are the de facto leaders of society' (Frake 1964, p. 132: see also Abrahams 1972b).

We saw earlier how Malinowski and Firth stressed language as a 'mode of action' rather than simply a 'counter-sign to thought'. Austin's (1962) distinction between performative and constantive (referential) utterances indicates a similar duality. And behind many functional approaches to language lies a basic dichotomy in its use— the *informative* (or ideational, or referential) and the *interpersonal* (or relational, or social). It is the basis of Bales' earlier analysis of group discussion under the headings of task-related and social-emotional talk (Bales 1950: also Halliday 1971: Soskin and John 1963: Barnes and Todd 1975b). As so often, a dichotomy can obscure the many-sidedness of social behaviour. Even the most 'propositional' of statements can express something of the speaker, and how he sees himself in relation to others in that context. It is much easier to find utterances with no referential content, as in Malinowski's phatic communion. Indeed, some accounts of 'lower-class' language present it stereotypically in almost this way—as a means of expressing emotion and not 'ideas', of reinforcing social relationships at the expense of any information about the unique experience of the speakers. But it seems more realistic to adopt a multi-functional approach to most of everyday speech, and look for the several and shifting purposes it serves.

Because the next chapter is mainly concerned with social class differences in the uses of language, the functional perspective is only touched on here. Bernstein especially argues the dependence of form upon function, and so raises fundamental questions about how precisely the 'appropriate' verbal realizations of meaning can be identified. They are outlined in concluding this chapter because they are so central to the sociolinguistic enterprise, the starting-point of which is defined by Hymes (1972b) as identifying social functions and then discovering the ways in which linguistic features are selected to 'serve' them. The task seems clear enough. First find the function, then find the structures that serve it. But how confidently can we identify items or patterns of linguistic choice as 'realizing' significant patterns of social behaviour? All languages provide means of coding social information. Sometimes this is done unmistakeably through the choice of a language, dialect, style or form of address, whether that choice is 'marked' or 'unmarked'. More often, interpretation depends on the context, for the 'same' information may be carried in many forms and there is no dictionary of 'social stylistics' to which we can refer. The difficulty of constructing one is apparent in Joos' (1962) description of five styles of speech— frozen, formal, consultative, casual and intimate. The labels are persuasive as a summary of participant-relations, but the efforts at *linguistic* diagnosis are unconvincing. Thus the two 'defining features' of a consultative style are that the addressee participates actively, and that the speaker does not assume that he will be understood without giving considerable background information. The first indicates a conversation rather than a lecture, and the second that the speech will be explicit. The identification is sensible, but hardly precise. Intimate speech 'avoids giving the addressee information from outside of the speaker's skin', and is marked by the abbreviation of expression made possible by a wide range of shared experience to which oblique reference can be made. Again, detailed linguistic correlates are not provided. Each style *may* have 'its own list of conventional formulas that we may call code labels', but Joos can offer only vague suggestions as to what they are. The present state of knowledge is perhaps reflected in Halliday's comment that behavioural strategies will be realized 'somewhere' in the linguistic system, grammatical options being systematic realizations of significant behavioural categories (Halliday 1971, pp. 169–72; 1973, p. 90). What *semantic* options are available is determined by the context of culture, as is the repertoire of means by which they can be expressed. They, and their 'realizations', can only be interpreted within a *particular* context or situation.

In these two chapters, I have outlined some main lines of enquiry in 'sociological' linguistics, and illustrated the range and variety of its concerns. This general review provides a background for more detailed examination of three inter-related areas of investigation—social class differences in speech, and in what language is used to *do*; the implications of these differences in the 'explanation' of educational failure; and the special characteristics of classroom talk, and their relationship to more general cultural and sub-cultural norms of speech behaviour. The first part of the book, then, provides conceptual and empirical vantage-points from which to describe in the next three chapters the communicative competence demanded in schools, and its resemblance to how communication is ordered and meanings are realized in other social contexts. I hope that this approach will show both the relevance of a sociolinguistic perspective to basic educational problems, *and* the contribution such applications can make to the mainstream of sociolinguistic enquiry.

3.

Language and Social Class: Evidence and Explanation

'Children from lower social class homes or minority ethnic groups usually speak a distinctive dialect form, and display retarded development on measures of language skills and general cognitive functioning' (Weener 1969, p. 194). The distinctiveness of social class dialects was considered in Chapter 1 and 2, without reference to *linguistic* inferiority though with some discussion of the *social* evaluation of linguistic difference. Bloomfield (1927) described 'illiterate speech' as no more haphazard than any other variety; its users had learned no less, but had learned something different. Over forty years later, Labov rejected the 'ungrammaticality' of everyday speech as a myth. When 'non-academic' speakers were talking about subjects they knew well, almost all their sentences were 'well-formed by any criteria'. His earlier research in New York had shown the marking and stereotyping importance of items of speech, stigmatized features being far more common in the performance of low-status groups. The socially constructed nature of their significance is apparent in the post-vocalic (r). In England, accents without it have more prestige. In New England, accents without it have less prestige. In New York, sounding it is generally more prestigious, but complications arise because this was not always so. An earlier (r)-less prestige accent has been gradually replaced by the form 'standard' in other parts of New England, and its use is therefore stratified by age as well as by socio-economic status, attitudes towards it being inconsistent in informants of more than middle-age. Clearly, there is nothing in such a feature that is good or bad but thinking makes it so. This is an easy example compared with the occurrence of multiple negatives, or the absence of the s-marker in verb forms. But here too, the kinds of investigation already referred to have emphasized that these are not 'errors', not random slips of the tongue. However important as a social handicap, they are no proof of linguistic deficiency.

This present chapter provides a transition to the explicitly educational concerns of the last part of the book, and most of the research to be discussed in it is overtly evaluative. Communicative deficiencies, variously defined, are seen as a major cause of failure in school. The *evidence* for profound social class differences in children's language, both in structure and in experience of its use, has been attacked for placing a gloss of linguistic 'respectability' over more traditional accounts of lower-class 'deficits'. The resulting 'confrontation' has raised fundamental questions of methodology and interpretation, in sociolinguistics and in the whole area of social science.

This review of the research is limited mainly to the contributions of sociologists, and to language development studies open to sociological interpretation. It is broadly chronological because of the scarcity of sociological work before the late 1950s, and the dominating influence of Bernstein (as inspiration and as target) since that time. The accumulated evidence shows a considerable consistency, or a number of recurring common themes. If critical disbelief is temporarily suspended, there is no doubting the accuracy of Cazden's summary, at least at the time it was made—'On all the measures, in all the studies, the upper socio-economic status children, however defined, are more advanced than the lower socio-economic status children' (1966, p. 190).

1. SOCIAL CLASS AND 'INFERIOR' ENGLISH

Early references to social class differences are either impressionistic sketches or summaries of environmental influences on language development which are 'translated' into social class terms. I have already quoted Wyld's (1920) description of 'Good English, Well-Bred English' as a *class* dialect rather than one associated with a region. Twenty years later, Fries included in his massive study of 'American English' an analysis of its 'standard' and 'vulgar' forms. His evidence came from letters sent to a government department by two contrasted groups of writers—college-educated professional people, and 'manual and unskilled' workers with no more than a basic secondary schooling. Since they were *able* to write letters *and* had chosen to do so, the 'lower class' sample was hardly random. Unlike much later research, however, it could be argued that he *had* controlled for topic and even communicative purpose as possibly independent sources of variation. All the letters were requests for official action (e.g. compassionate leave, exemption from military service), backed up by reasons why the desired action was necessary. And because such letters, to a stranger and an official, involve constraints towards formality and explicitness, Fries' analysis probably underestimated differences in the everyday speech of the two groups. Even so, his conclusion reads like a preliminary sketch for Bernstein's early 'profiles' of lower working-class language. 'Over and over again . . . it appeared that the differences between the language of the educated and those with little education did not lie primarily in the fact that the former used one set of forms and the latter an entirely different set . . . the actual deviation of the language of the uneducated from Standard English seemed much less than is usually assumed . . . The most striking difference lay in the fact that Vulgar English seems essentially poverty-stricken. It uses less of the resources of the language, and a few forms are used very frequently' (Fries 1940, p. 287).

If this relative poverty of usage was indeed a 'fact', it would suggest that communication across social class 'lines' might run into difficulties. The possible problems were outlined by Schatzman and Strauss (1955), from far more limited evidence than Fries made available. They studied the recorded narratives of ten 'upper-class' and ten 'lower-class' people, all recounting their experiences during a tornado to an interviewer who had not himself been present at the events described. Linguistically, their article is infuriating. No transcript material is given, nor is there any clear evidence for the 'striking' differences they claim to have found. These have to be taken on trust. Briefly, the lower-class narratives are said to be relatively 'unorganized', lacking any theme to which individual events could be related. 'Crude' chronological sequences were common, with 'then' and 'and' used to link loosely connected incidents. Apparent summary statements like 'and everything' or 'and stuff like that' were merely 'fillers', padding which added nothing to the meaning. Genuine generalizations were rare. Pronouns were often used without clear referents, making it difficult to follow the story, and this feature illustrated a general failure to take account of the listener's ignorance of the events being described. The linguistic conclusion can be matched with that of Fries. A limited exploitation of the resources of language led to incoherence and ambiguity.

The sociological commentary on this conclusion will be discussed later. And for all its methodological limitations, the study shows an acute awareness that inter-class communication 'risks being blocked by differential rules for the ordering of speech and thought' (Schatzman and Strauss 1955, p. 329). It was an awareness shared by few other sociologists at that time. McDavid (1946) blamed them for neglecting the rich data contained in the *Linguistic Atlas of the United States*. And in criticizing the *Atlas* for *its* neglect of sociological techniques, Pickford (1956, p. 223) admitted at least the possibility of mutual benefits. While sociology had not *yet* 'completed its analysis of class . . . it needs the help of linguistics; language certainly looks like being one of the clues'. And she praised one piece of linguistic research, as a possible straw in the wind, for its 'remarkable sociological awareness'. Working with very small numbers, Putnam and O'Hern (1955) found a high positive correlation between Warner's index of socio-economic status and their subjects' ratings of recorded negro speech. Their own 'objective' analysis revealed an 'extremely simple' grammatical structure in the lower-class samples, while their subjects too seemed to be going beyond accent to the 'degree of sophistication' in vocabulary and syntax in their evaluation of the recordings. But the evidence is slight, and the premature rush to generalize is a prophetic failing. Whatever 'clues' it might contain, there is a marked neglect of language by sociologists busily tracking down social class differences in so many other aspects of behaviour. Barber (1957), for example, argued that regional differences were far more important in such an 'open' society as America; those between social classes were 'subtle rather than gross', though still described as a matter of 'better' and 'worse' in both diction and grammar. Some notice was taken of their symbolic importance, and of the possible status-revealing cues they contained (Pieris 1951: Hertzler 1953). Yet Chinoy's text-book account of social stratification includes these 'status connotations', in one page, as the linguistic equivalents of 'mink or mouton', a Dior dress or a copy from the local department store (Chinoy 1961, p. 173).

One American sociologist, Allison Davis, took language differences very seriously indeed, in their extent and their consequences. His approach was part of a search at Chicago University for 'culture-fair' tests of intelligence. Davis argued that the predominance of verbal items in the standard tests gave them a pronounced middle-class bias because of the greater emphasis on verbal facility in middle-class life. Within this broad source of discrimination, individual test items were often unequally familiar in form or content. Either their vocabulary was drawn from socially restricted areas of experience, or their formal structure (e.g. 'A *is to* B as X *is to*. . . .') posed special problems to children unused to such stylistic abstraction. These problems were recognized in dealing with ethnic differences, but not in relation to the gulf between social classes. In practice, the new 'culture-fair' tests hardly altered the old pattern of group differences. But they foreshadowed more recent demands for culture-specific tests of intelligence and of language development (see pp. 121–2), and they rested on a clear view of language as 'a highly systematised form of cultural behaviour' (Davis 1948, p. 57).

What *evidence* was then available of consistent social class differences? Briefly, it was slight. It was also largely inferential. Environmental influences were an early focus of attention in research into language development (there is a detailed review in McCarthy 1954: see also Lawton 1968, pp. 20–38: John and Moskovitz 1970, pp. 167–80). Children brought up in orphanages were found to be relatively retarded in articulation, vocabulary, and in the 'organization' of their speech. They fell further behind as they grew older, even when comparisons were with children of unskilled manual workers. In one of the most ambitious of these studies, Goldfarb (1943; 1945) compared children who had lived in institutions for their first three years with others who had then been in foster homes, and he extended the comparisons into adolescence. The first group continued to be retarded in language skills, more 'unreflective' in their behaviour, and more limited in 'abstract conceptual development'. A later study in which unusual care was taken to match the groups beforehand for age, intelligence *and* social status showed that children from day nurseries used a wider vocabulary and more 'mature' sentence formations than those in permanent care (Pringle and Tanner 1958). Such research often highlighted the frequency and intensity of verbal interaction with adults. This was also used to account for the developmental 'lags' also apparent in twins, triplets and children from large families. Nisbet (1953), for example, found that the negative correlations between various test scores and family size were greatest on measures of verbal ability.

Some of this environmental evidence could be subsumed under social class headings, and so 'translated' into statements about social class differences. Indeed, in the absence of distinctively sociological research, the temptation to do so was often irresistible. And the results were highly misleading. Much of the 'relevant' research was concerned with extreme forms of social deprivation, seen as especially detrimental to language development. But while large families and broken homes *were* more common in low status groups, to take these and other gross environmental factors as equivalent to a summary of lower working-class 'conditions of life' was a distortion of research directed by quite different concerns. McCarthy's long review of language development research appropriately gives only two pages to 'occupational group differences'. The 'spatial' message is then contradicted by a reference to the 'considerable evidence of a marked relationship between the socio-economic status of the family and the child's linguistic ability' (1954, p. 586). What there was of it indicated, consistently, that middle-class children used longer sentences at an earlier age and had a wider vocabulary. The main explanations offered were the 'poorer' language models provided by lower-class parents, and their less frequent verbal interaction with their children. This summary of 'upper class superiority' was supported by Templin's extensive investigation of the language performance of 480 American children, which showed more and larger differences in relation to socio-economic status than to either sex or intelligence. The differences were most marked in the articulation of vowels and final consonants, in length of utterance among pre-school children and recognition vocabulary among those aged 6–8, and in grammatical complexity (Templin 1957: 1958). In her analysis of the language, intelligence was not consistently separated from socio-economic status as a source of variance. Most of the previous research had not controlled for it at all, making it extremely difficult to evaluate the results. There are other reasons too which limit their significance. All but one of the studies cited by McCarthy were of pre-school children. Their main concern was to establish norms of language development, and their main 'social' assumption was that the language of children from lower-class backgrounds was a less mature version of the language of their middle-class contemporaries. But very little of this research was directly and explicitly concerned with social class differences. Even in its total effect, it was quite insufficient to justify the conclusion that 'greater or lesser linguistic complexity is part of the matrix of class-associated behaviour' (Milner 1951, p. 107).

2. SOCIAL CLASS AND MODES OF COMMUNICATION

The most common social explanation for the linguistic superiority of middle-class children was their closer and more frequent contact with significant adults. Thus Milner's (1951) influential investigation of reading-readiness found that middle-class mothers seemed more likely to have meals with their children, to encourage conversation, and to read stories to them. Children whose mothers reported these activities as regular occurrences scored more highly on verbal tests. The argument was from the child's linguistic performance to his experience of what language had been used to do. A similar approach is apparent in

Bossard's (1945) study of meal-time conversations in thirty-five families. There were large differences in the amount of talk, the range of topics covered, the extent to which the talk was child-centred, and the strength of parental interest in 'enlarging the child's semantic grasp'. A qualitative social class difference was found in diversity of vocabulary. Properly cautious when the evidence was so slight, he 'tentatively' suggested that 'families at the lower social levels seem much more figurative in their language, less rational and less logical than other people' (in Bossard and Boll 1966, pp. 154–6). Despite that tentative note, the statement encapsulates two main failings of 'deficit' research—premature generalization, and quite unsubstantiated inferences from language to thought. More positively, the study is an early attempt to identify some linguistic consequences of different *uses* of language.

Allison Davis argued that social class 'structures the maze in which the child lives and learns', different conditions of life throwing up their own solutions to the problems which arose from them. The greater ambiguity and 'illogicality' which Bossard associated with lower-class language could be given just such a sub-cultural interpretation. Facility with words is not equally important at all social levels. And if most speech is between people who know each other well and have shared much of each others' experience, then the listener's 'semantic grasp' is quite likely to be taken for granted, with the speaker feeling no great need to be precise. This was the social explanation of linguistic difference offered by Schatzman and Strauss (1955). In a reference presumably to 'commonsense' rather than 'scientific' knowledge, they began their investigation from what they called a 'common assumption' —that important social class differences existed not only in 'literary style' but also in 'modes of communication'. The narratives they analysed indicated that the lower-class speakers had difficulty in taking other roles than their own in the events they were describing, and that they were less able to bridge the gulf in experience between themselves and their listener by providing explicit information. The evidence for the first 'failing' was a lack of variation in perspective, most incidents being centred on the speaker himself. The evidence for the second was the imprecision already mentioned, especially the many oblique references to persons and places which left their identity ambiguous. These speakers were recognized to have been on relatively unfamiliar ground in the interviews. But this very inequality illustrated the wider argument—that they were accustomed to talk at length only with those with whom they already shared 'a great deal of experience and symbolism'. In such conversations, they had no need to be 'self-conscious about communicative technique'. If they seemed in the interviews to be less well attuned to the needs of their listener, it was because they had much less experience of listeners of that kind. Far more accustomed to providing information 'on demand', even to strangers, the middle-class narrators provided lucid, coherent stories, and were far more sensitive to the precise questions they were being asked. Different 'modes of communication' were therefore seen as arising out of significantly different experiences of social interaction.

This article had a strong influence on Bernstein, whose own search for the cultural explanation of working-class failure in schools began at this time. The explanation was found at the outset of the search, and then minutely refined and elaborated. Different *modes of language* were said to be characteristic of middle-class and lower working-class children. Because of them, they related to objects and persons in distinctly different ways. For lower working-class children, these were not the ways of the school. The problem was not at all a matter of dialect, or of non-standard English, but of what language was habitually used to do. And the outcome was 'a culturally-induced backwardness, transmitted and sustained through the effects of linguistic processing' (Bernstein 1961b, p. 175).

Bernstein began his work with little to go on beyond 'some apt observations and a meagre theoretical literature' (Grimshaw 1966, p. 193). Since the theory was dominated by Sapir and Whorf, 'meagre' is an inappropriate adjective unless the reference is to work *directly* related to social class differences. Here the evidence *was* meagre, even at the level of illustration, and Bernstein admits it (1973a, p. 38). The most complete early statement of his 'theory of social learning' begins with a review of 'relevant research', most of which is quite *irrelevant* to the generalizations which follow (1961a, pp. 288–9). It was research of the kind outlined earlier, concerned mainly with language development in very young children and hardly at all with social class. For examples of 'working-class speech', he was confined to Bossard's family 'table-talk', Hoggart's vivid but impressionistic *Uses of Literacy*, and his own recordings of group discussion. The work of Schatzman and Strauss is also cited, and is later described as having excited him by its 'insightful and sensitive' descriptions of speech. The insight is certainly there, but the work suffers from the same weakness as Bernstein's own at this time—it is not made clear on what evidence 'lower class' speech is judged to be more 'concrete' or less 'organized'. And from this frail 'factual' base, Bernstein moved into confident generalizations about 'modes of speech' which are both described and accounted for.

Though he assumed too easily that the linguistic consequences could be readily indentified, the objection is not to his account of those constraints on speech which arise in a particular social relationship. This account is both sensitive and penetrating. But it was too often submerged in a crude social class dichotomy. Bernstein pointed out that a 'public language' was rarely found in its 'pure form', and that approximations of it would arise *wherever* certain conditions were met— wherever there was a wide background of already-shared knowledge, or identification *with* others took precedence over the expression of individual difference. To argue, then, that the lower working class was restricted to its use was to imply that *all* their significant relationships were of the same type—i.e. 'played out' against a background of common identities and shared meanings which made complex verbal procedures irrelevant. Lower working-class children's speech was described as consistently marked by the limited vocabulary and 'poor', 'limited' syntax of a 'public language' because it was consistently used to express the concrete, the here-and-now and the social, rather than the more individualized and verbally complex meanings made available to the middle-class child (Bernstein 1958, pp. 161–8: 1961b, pp. 167–70). They would feel no need, and have no need, for a finely discriminating use of language.

The early papers are described by Lawton (1968, p. 77) as exploratory, providing a 'general picture within a socio-linguistic framework' rather than a 'precise plan of the exact differences between the language of one social group and another'. Since no 'precise plan' was possible at that time, and is not possible now, their dogmatic style was quite unjustified by the available evidence. What additional evidence did Bernstein himself provide? He showed (1958) that the verbal I.Q. scores of a group of working-class adolescents were 'grossly depressed' in relation to their scores on a non-verbal test. Subsequent analysis of tape-recorded discussions showed the working-class speech to be more fluent and less hesitant (Bernstein 1962a). Pauses occurred at points of uncertainty, when speech had to be fitted to a specific context or referent. They were less frequent when much of the speech was ready-prepared (or 'ready-coded'), full of 'habitual combinations of words'. Working-class speech was more fluent because it expressed collective rather than individual experience. It was also more predictable. Grammatical analysis of the same data showed more of the characteristics of 'formal language' in middle-class speech—a wider range of adjectives and adverbs, more complex verb forms, more use of subordinate clauses to express relationships, and more self-reference (Bernstein 1962b). These results support the previous 'exploratory' statements, but the analysis was far too limited and linguistically haphazard to justify any indentification of distinct modes of speech. These seem to have been largely *inferred* as the possible linguistic consequences of the much better documented sub-cultural differences in socialization (Edwards 1974). And so an intricate web of theory was constructed around differences in *language* which were not then known to exist, at least in the forms for which Bernstein was offering his explanations.

The introduction in 1962 of the concept of linguistic 'codes' was an attempt to go behind the mere listing of attributes to 'the underlying regulative principles' (Bernstein 1973a, p. 26). Social structure was seen as transforming the possibilites of language into distinct codes, which in turn 'elicit, generalise and reinforce' the relationships necessary for their continuance (1962a, p. 31). *How* social structure was seen to stand between language and speech will be considered later in the chapter. My concern here is with the evidence that it did so. As should be clear, the codes were *not* abstractions from extensive data. They were constructs, polar dimensions towards which performance could usefully be seen as oriented. That orientation was clearly a matter of more-or-less, not of either-or. Socially induced preferences pointed the speaker *towards* one pole or the other. It would have been better to have written of 'elaborat*ing* and restrict*ing* codes, or better yet of elaborated and restricted cod*ing*' (Gumperz and Hymes 1972, p. 468). For in the writing, the theoretical dichotomy often became a dichotomy in performance. The construct was transformed into evidence. Thus Bernstein was prematurely believed to have 'shown'—i.e. *proved*, rather than argued—the existence of wide and consistent social class differences in language.

3. ELABORATED AND RESTRICTED CODES: A THEORY IN SEARCH OF EVIDENCE

In 1965, Bernstein summed up his speculations, in a more refined form but with the essential argument unchanged. The form of a social relationship 'acts selectively on what is said, when it is said, and how it is said'. Two codes, or speech systems, can be seen as 'regulating the options' which speakers take up. The codes differ psychologically in the extent to which they facilitate (or inhibit) verbally explicit statements of individualized meaning, and linguistically in the relative predictability of their vocabulary and syntax. A restricted code will be found *wherever* speech is 'refracted through a common cultural identity' which reduces the need to be explicit—i.e. among working-class *and* middle-class speakers. But while this social classification is recognized as 'an extremely crude index' of different ways of life, the lower working class is expected to be limited to the restricted code.

These ideas are so qualified in later papers as to become increasingly elusive, and the 1965 statement presents them in their most tangible form. At that time, the theory was beginning to guide an ambitious series of related investigations by Bernstein's Sociological Research Unit (their planning is described in detail in Brandis and Henderson 1970, pp. 1–16: Bernstein 1973a, pp. 27–36). Some of them were concerned with social class differences in the 'formal patterns' of language, and with their sociological interpretation. Others were concerned with different orientations to language use, especially in the 'critical contexts' of instruction and control. Together, they represent a research programme quite unusual in its dependence on a single theory. Before outlining the findings, that theory must be examined more closely. And the examination will concentrate on the concept of 'codes'.

(i) *Theory*

It is easier to begin with what the codes are *not*. They are quite distinct from linguistic competence. Restricted code is in no way a synonym for 'linguistic deprivation' because its user has the full range of linguistic options available to him. Because of the context in which he speaks, and perhaps the *type* of context with which he is most familiar, he makes a relatively limited and therefore predictable selection from those 'resources'. The outcome is not sub-standard English. It is not non-Standard English either. The codes should not be confused with social dialects because there is nothing in a dialect to inhibit explicit statements of individual feeling or opinion. While dialects are identified by their formal features, and by *who* their speakers are, codes are identified by the kinds of meaning they transmit and by *what* the words are used to do.

The codes *are* sets of 'planning procedures' underlying linguistic choice. They represent differences *at the level of meaning*. An elaborated code arises where there is a gap or boundary between speaker and listener which can only be crossed by explicit speech. A restricted code arises where speech is exchanged against a background of shared experience and shared definitions of that experience. It 'realizes' meanings that are already shared rather than newly created, communal rather than individual. The speech is 'context-dependent' because participants rely on their background knowledge to supply information not carried by the actual words they use. The meanings are 'particularistic' because they are only available to those who have that background knowledge.

Because they referred to 'planning principles' underlying speech rather than to speech itself, the term 'linguistic codes' was profoundly misleading. This Bernstein later realized, preferring '*socio*-linguistic' as a more appropriate label. But there are deeper sources of confusion, beyond the remedy of a new name. The codes 'exist' only in the mind. They are 'nothing more than' verbal planning activities at what Bernstein calls the 'psychological level' (1965, pp. 160–1), and are observable only in the choices which they 'regulate'. The extreme difficulty of 'matching' structure and function was considered in Chapter 2. But Bernstein argued boldly that types of social relationship generate particular forms of meaning which then 'activate specific grammatical and lexical choices'. The formal patterns of speech are 'activated' by a 'semantic component' which controls not one feature or another, but whole sets of co-occurring choices. Now analysis of literary or conversational 'style' also depends on identifying items which 'go together'. Thus De Camp (1969, pp. 162–4) suggests some of the simultaneous changes that might be recorded if the feature (+ pompous) was included in the generation of a passage of speech. Certain linguistic choices would then be 'triggered', and others 'blocked'. This analogy is *empirically* gloomy because the identification of 'styles' has not got very far. It may be *theoretically* misleading because Bernstein is concerned with 'deeper' matters, Labov's (1969b, p. 12) reduction of elaborated codes to 'mere' stylistic elaboration being a travesty of the argument. Nevertheless, their 'existence' depends on the regular appearance of those 'formal patterns' they are said to regulate. If the patterns cannot be found, it is difficult to see what is left of the concept.

Early characterizations of the codes contain lists of items (e.g. 'simple' verb forms, 'socio-centric sequences') which are clearly seen as going together. Linguistically a 'rag-bag', they are a *sociologically* consistent attempt to describe what context-dependent speech might be like. And they imply that speech can only be explicit, and so 'transcend' its context, if it has certain specified formal features. This is a position from which Bernstein has since retreated. He has criticized the term 'linguistic codes' for suggesting a one-to-one relationship between syntax and meaning, and he has admitted that the code descriptions are themselves context-dependent i.e. that the indicators of a restricted code in one context may not be so in another (1973, pp. 193–4). These are significant concessions. The first is a common-sense recognition that there are many ways of conveying the 'same' meaning, and many meanings possible in the 'same' sequence of words. The second is described by Coulthard (1969) as a 'frightening proposal', presumably because of the amount of research needed to recognize the codes in all their changing guises. Both points are illustrated in one of the most carefully argued studies carried out by Bernstein's Research Unit. Turner analysed children's speech when they were describing a 'control situation' involving a broken window and an irate owner. Working-class children made relatively more mention of threats, a form of control realized largely through subordinate clauses ('If you do that again, you will be in trouble'). Since subordination was *generally* more prevalent in *middle-class* speech, the finding suggested 'the importance of tightly controlling for linguistic control when investigating social class differences in grammatical categories'. This comment might be interpreted unfairly as meaning— 'Construct the contexts which give you the results you expect'—and less unfairly as suggesting that the indicators of a restricted code in one context might be indicators of an elaborated code in another. Turner's main argument is extremely important. It is impossible to make sense of social class differences in speech without looking at 'the contexts which control the meanings'. Explicitness is a matter of meaning, and not of 'good' or even 'complex' grammar. 'There may well be a correlation between explicit communication and grammatical complexity . . . but grammatical complexity is certainly not a necessary condition for explicit verbal communication.' The task remains that of relating the 'syntactic alternatives which speakers take up' to the meanings which they express. But it is best to *begin* with the 'semantic categories', because these may be realized in many ways (Turner 1973, pp. 186 and 141).

The confusion arising from Bernstein's *syntactic* descriptions is apparent in his references to predictability. A restricted code is consistently described as more predictable, and in its 'pure' forms this may be so. In the ritualized exchanges of the wedding service, or even the conventionalized openings of a cocktail-party encounter, form and content are closely prescribed. A participant who 'knows the code' will literally know what is coming next. There is a high level of lexical and structural prediction. But outside such constrained contexts, 'structural predictability' is a gross exaggeration of the relative 'simplicity' associated with a restricted code. The options 'open' to the speaker are still so diverse that they can neither be anticipated by the listener nor contained within any meaningful *statistical* prediction ('in this context, there will be x% "subordinate" to "main" clauses'). If the term has any meaning at all, it *is* at the semantic level. Indeed, the very definition of a restricted code emphasizes the background of *already shared* meanings to which implicit reference can be made. It is plausible to suggest that a conversation between close friends will contain few semantic surprises. It is plausible that their speech will be highly 'condensed' and often unintelligible to an outsider. It is far more dubious to try and identify *specific* grammatical choices, and totally misleading to suggest speech so extensively 'pre-packed', so full of clichés and 'social counters', as to be literally predictable. A relative predictability of *meaning* should not imply its relative simplicity. There is no need for a speaker to be explicit about what his listeners already know, and his words may bring to the mind a wealth of shared experience. In such a context, there is no question of the communicative inadequacy of a restricted code. Yet scattered through Bernstein's writing are references to 'constraints' on the elaboration of unique experience which are quite illogical even within his own frame of argument. It is precisely *because* the speaker does not intend this elaboration that he makes his 'restricted' choice. A restricted code 'does not help to put into words his unique purposes, beliefs and motivations' because it *does* help him to transmit meanings that are 'communal' rather than unique. He does *not* 'subordinate his behaviour to a linguistic code' (1965, p. 152). He subordinates his *speech* to the transmission of appropriate meanings.

As their linguistic realizations are broadened and diversified, the codes take on a more profound but shadowy form. They become more elusive still in Bernstein's later and emphatic distinction between speech codes and speech variants. Variants are sets of linguistic choices evoked by a specific context, by the 'dictates of the local relationship'. A code is both 'deeper' and more general, 'a regulating principle controlling speech realizations in diverse social contexts' (Bernstein 1973a, pp. 29–30; also 1970a, p. 118; 1970b, p. 346). If the distinction is 'critically important', so is the relationship between them, and this Bernstein has been unable to clarify. In a dubious analogy, he defines variants as 'surface structure', codes as 'transmitting the deep-meaning structure of the culture or subculture'. The analogy faces the same criticism as that directed at Chomsky, that 'deep structure' is beyond observation, beyond proof or disproof, and so outside the domain of social science. In so far as they 'exist', the codes are 'visible' in the kinds of context in which meanings are realized in elaborated or restricted ways, and in the relative *frequency* with which these realizations are apparent. They seem to represent probability statements about how meanings will be realized which are based on summary statements about how they *have been* realized in certain 'critical areas' of experience. Thus lower working-class children are no longer seen as limited to a restricted code. They do the same things less often. In specific contexts, they express individualized meanings in verbally explicit ways. But because of their predominant experience of language use, they see the need to do so less often. There is a restriction on the contexts in which elaborated speech variants will be employed. Though their speech is less flexible, the question is no longer of assigning them to a single code, but of 'the scope of their repertoire of coding' (Gumperz and Hymes 1972, p. 466).

The dangerous dichotomy has receded, and the social class determinism has been somewhat relaxed. What, then, is left of the codes? In recognizing the importance of context as 'a major control upon syntactic and lexical selections', Bernstein has to admit the difficulty of finding 'any general linguistic criteria for the isolation of the two codes'. Only when speakers can 'freely determine' their choice can it be taken as evidence of habitual patterns of selection. Such 'freedom' seems an example of socially unrealistic linguistics. It is hard to see how the researcher could ever discount the 'intervening' influence of context. And *how* he allows for it is admitted to vary from situation to situation. Similarly, evidence of restriction to a restricted code would require so many samples of speech, 'each analysed in the light of each context according to the explicitness and specificity of meaning', as to be a task without end (Bernstein 1973a, p. 30). When would a switch from restricted to elaborated speech indicate flexibility *within* a code, and when would it indicate a change of code? At what point would the frequency of code-switching make the whole concept of codes redundant? The increasing emphasis on speech variants suggests their tacit disappearance. Accepting that 'degrees of context-dependence ... are variable' and that there are no 'absolute' means of diagnosing one code or the other, Hasan suggests the possibility of 'an array of varieties of codes rather than just two highly idealised ones' (1973, p. 285). Such an 'array' seems to diversify the concept out of existence. A theory of differences in meaning has been unrealistically specific about the linguistic 'realization' of meaning. The codes are not 'useful' as a summary of differences in form. But as will be argued later, they may still be useful in interpreting social class differences in the kinds of meaning which language is most often used to express.

(ii) *Evidence*

As should be apparent already, the scope of Bernstein's theory is immense. Beginning with a search for the cultural explanation of educational failure, he turned to the investigation of deep relationships between social structure and symbolic orders. And he has blamed some of his critics for not appreciating the scale of the enterprise. Even in that part of it which concerns us here, the speculations range widely. The purpose of his Sociological Research Unit was to put them to the test. This demanded several distinct but interwoven strands of evidence. Were there consistent social class differences in linguistic choice? Could these be related to the 'planning procedures' summarized in the codes? Were there social class differences in orientation to the possibilities of language, and in how it was used in certain areas of experience? Could significant features of children's speech be related to their different experiences in these 'critical contexts'? And accompanying the attempts to answer these questions, an Experimental Language Programme to improve communicative competence was devised and evaluated (see p. 144).

My concern here is with the evidence for different patterns of linguistic choice, and with the usefulness of the codes in their description and interpretation. It is obvious that simply finding differences, even consistent differences, would not do. The theory offered definite criteria of relevance. According to Bernstein, it could support 'only very general expectancies of grammatical choice' at the time he carried out his own research (in Turner and Mohan 1970, p. x). In fact, some of these expectancies were firm, if extremely ill-defined— e.g. 'the short, grammatically simple, syntactically poor sentence which is the typical unit of a public language'. The terms 'simple' and 'poor' make no sense linguistically, and they imply deficiencies in 'knowledge' which are irrelevant to the theory and contrast strongly with his frequent denials of any concern with linguistic ability. The later code characterizations are a mixture of crude generalizations about 'complexity' (e.g. the restricted code 'is epitomised by a low level and limiting syntactic organisation') and quite specific 'expectancies' which have elaborate edifices of sociological interpretation built on them (e.g. the more frequent use of the pronoun 'I' by middle-class speakers more accustomed to the individualization of experience). The greater 'fluency' of working-class speech was taken as evidence of its simpler and relatively cliché-ridden character (Bernstein 1962a). Coulthard (1969) is rightly critical of this use of hesitation in speech to indicate *structural* complexity rather than problems of lexical choice, and of Bernstein's (1962b) grammatical analysis for turning slight differences into evidence of discrete planning procedures. While admitting that the code indicators were a matter of relative frequency, not of presence or absence, Bernstein argued that different frequencies of occurrence across a range of measures produced an *overall* difference in the patterning of speech. This is plausible if the differences are large, or consistent across many samples of speech. No such evidence was then available.

The haphazardness of the early analysis is recognized by Bernstein himself (1973a, p. 18). It illustrates the danger mentioned earlier—of a narrowly utilitarian borrowing from the other discipline resulting in 'loose linguistic sociology without formal accuracy'. The same comment can be made of other research at that time which was closely based on the theory of codes. Lawton (1968) found significant social class differences in the speech and writing of twelve- and fifteen-year old boys, closely matched for verbal and non-verbal ability. Middle-class essays were longer, suggesting an easier transition from speech patterns that were themselves relatively elaborate and explicit. The working-class boys used fewer passive verbs, fewer complex subordinate clauses, and a less diversified vocabulary. Simple content analysis showed them to use fewer abstractions and more concrete examples in argument. Robinson (1965a) also found working-class boys to be using a more limited and predictable vocabulary. Both studies offered some support to Bernstein's 'intuitions', but they also raised questions about contextual constraints which he had largely ignored. Lawton found that a 'functional' shift from description to abstraction had consistent effects on linguistic choice, though middle-class boys made the greater adjustments. His discovery that he could 'force' the working-class boys towards more elaborated responses in highly structured communicative tasks suggested the danger of generalizing from a single context. Robinson (1965b) tested the possibility of code-switching by varying topic, receiver and communicative purpose. 'Informal' letters written by twelve-year olds showed many of the expected social class differences. But in 'formal' letters, these were insignificant. Here, constraints for explicitness seemed to 'override' differences in more everyday uses of language.

The lack of linguistic respectability in this research was remedied in the work of Bernstein's SRU by its use of Halliday's Scale-and-Category Grammar. This provided a precise and standardized descriptive framework. Such 'respectability' could have been bought at the price of considerable sociological irrelevance. But the Grammar met all the needs of a theory concerned with 'the social structuring of relevant meanings and the form of their linguistic expression' (Bernstein 1973a, pp. 267–8). It had been constructed with the needs of other disciplines in mind, and it was concerned, not with 'the native speaker's knowledge of the language, but with what he does with it'. It was used in the research programme both to characterize the 'overall' patterning of speech and in the detailed analysis of particular items and units. That programme involved altogether over 400

children, from two socially contrasted London boroughs, whose speech
was recorded before they began school and again two years later. This
may suggest more extensive speech data than is the case. Because of
the demands of their factorial design (the matching for sex, ability,
social class, and mothers' scores on a 'Communication Index'),
several studies used the same subjects, and some of the same data was
subjected to repeated analysis. The apparent accumulation of evidence
is, to some extent, a repetition of evidence. Nevertheless, the main
findings provide some justification for Bernstein's early 'explorations'.

In their response to questions involving description, narrative and
explanation, middle-class children were found to use speech that was
less 'concrete' and more 'precise'; they apparently took more account
of the needs of the listener, and in describing how a game was played
they were less likely to 'list the ingredients' and more likely to offer
general explanations (Rackstraw and Robinson 1967). The relative
'concreteness' was a heavily emphasized feature of a restricted code. It
was also associated with a low tolerance for ambiguity. Expressions of
tentativeness and uncertainty seemed to be more highly correlated with
social class than with verbal ability, a finding attributed to the greater
likelihood of middle-class children being socialized to look for alternatives and so experience the 'burden' of choice (Turner and Pickvance
1971). Two other studies made intra-class comparisons between
children previously identified as using a restricted or elaborated code
(Robinson and Creed 1968: Coulthard and Robinson 1968). Though
performance on tests of visual and verbal discrimination seemed more
closely related to ability than to the speech assessments, there were
some indications that restricted code users did less well on tasks
requiring 'a constrained precision of language'. More interesting than
the results of this research is the use of scores on a few linguistic
measures to assign subjects to one code or the other. The co-existence
of further 'critical' features is taken for granted. This economical
method was also used by Cook-Gumperz (1973). In her research into
maternal methods of control, only limited analysis of the mothers'
language was practicable. A small number of criteria were taken as
justifying the larger label, the frequency of socio-centric and ego-
centric sequences being described as an especially convenient 'shorthand
way' of distinguishing the codes. This assumption of co-occurrence
seems highly premature.

A restricted code was essentially the language of *implicit* meanings.
This was the central 'fact' which acted selectively on grammatical and
lexical choice. By definition, then, the special attributes of persons and
objects would not be picked out. Within the Scale-and-Category

framework, analysis of the nominal group showed how aspects of linguistic choice could be related to the sociological theory. The group consists of a 'head', which may be modified or qualified. The head is normally a noun or pronoun. Modifiers occur before it (e.g. *the* man, *ten* men, *the tall, thin* man) and qualifiers after it (them *both*, men *with sticks*). Since pronouns are rarely modified and almost never qualified, the choice of a noun as head opens up the possibilities of elaborating and differentiating meaning. And to simplify considerably (if only because precisely chosen 'head' nouns may do the job as well) the more extensive the modification and qualification, the more differentiated the meaning is likely to be. It is 'largely through the use of modifiers and qualifiers that the uniqueness of an entity may be made explicit in language' (Hasan 1973, p. 264). Analysing stories told by five-year old children, Hawkins (1969) predicted and found that the middle-class group made relatively less use of pronouns and more of nouns. In their response to various descriptive and explanatory tasks, middle-class children were described by Henderson (1970a, pp. 47–8) as showing 'more concern to make explicit classifications of persons and objects, and more precise ascription of attributes'. Simply, they used more adjectives and nouns, and a greater variety of both. They also showed greater flexibility in their choice according to the demands of particular tasks.

These studies still depended on frequency counts of various features and a sociologically relevant interpretation of their total effect. Hasan's (1968) analysis of types of reference provided a *direct* measure of context-dependence. The cohesion of a 'text' depends on unambiguous references, 'backwards' (anaphorically) to what has already been mentioned and 'forwards' (cataphorically) to what is about to be mentioned. Pronouns are a principal source of possible ambiguity. Anaphoric reference ('They sat down and then *he* . . .) and cataphoric reference ('*He* was the man who . . .') are verbally explicit. But in everyday conversation, reference is often 'outwards' to what is visible but not mentioned by name, or to background information not carried in the words. Such exophoric reference is embedded in its *context*. The importance of this aspect of speech to the whole concept of codes is emphasized by Hasan. It indicates the *causal* nature of the relationship being argued between social structure and linguistic choice. Where the proportion of exophoric reference is high, the information encoded in the items is assumed to be already available to the listener, who will use this background knowledge to remove any ambiguity. Both the feature and its interpretation are important in considering Hawkins' (1969) research. The working-class children used more pronouns *and* more exophoric references in making up a story about a set of pictures, so that objects and persons were often ambiguously identified. But the nature of the task seems highly significant. The pictures were still visible to the children and their listener while the stories were being told. Bernstein comments that they may not have *perceived* the need to be explicit in that context (1970b, p. 346). But there *was* no need to be explicit, since the background information was clearly available. Indeed, *ignoring* the presence of the pictures could be seen as communicatively insensitive, or as an example of that 'habitual elaboration' often associated with middle-class speech (see p. 118). In my own research, stories were elicited from a similar set of cartoons and then retold from memory on a later occasion. The second, visually unsupported, versions contained far fewer exophoric references.

The general importance of task differences will be considered later in the chapter. It appears in an interesting form in one of the few contradictions of Bernstein's earlier work to come out of the SRU programme. Hawkins (1973) investigated his suggestion that working-class girls might use more elaborated language than boys because of their more complex roles within the family. He did so by analysing hesitations in the speech of children asked to 'make up a bedtime story'. *Working*-class girls proved to be the most fluent, and working-class boys the least fluent, of the four groups studied. There was no evidence that fluency was associated with any inferiority in the speech. In an interpretation which at least makes more appeal to common sense than Bernstein's, fluency was associated not with grammatical 'simplicity' and redundancy, but with verbal facility and confidence. But it was a confidence in *that* context. The working-class boys seemed especially ill at ease with the task, one detached from any accompanying physical activity and perhaps 'outside their competence' (Hawkins 1973, p. 246). The implication is clear that a different task might have transformed the results.

Despite their general consistency, the findings of the whole SRU programme are difficult to evaluate. This is party because of the overlapping of results mentioned earlier, partly because of the lack of evidence independently collected but still within the framework of the theory. Some American investigations of social class differences in linguistic ability relate their results to Bernstein's despite a quite different orientation (e.g. Loban 1963, p. 89). More relevant support is offered by Tough (1970), who found that the more 'socially favoured' nursery-school children used a wider vocabulary, more nouns, more 'complex' verb forms and less exophoric reference. A more recent study repeated with written language Bernstein's own comparison of public school boys and craft apprentices, but included technical topics deliberately intended to favour the working-class group. Linguistic analysis was concentrated on the nominal group, especially on the 'heavy' modification associated both with technical writing (as a register) and with elaborated code. An overall working-class 'deficit' was wiped out on those topics where the need for elaboration was recognized and so produced a sharp increase in complexity (Rushton and Young 1974). In my own research with eleven-year-old children, I found no significant social class differences on most of the measures used in comparable studies. The lower working-class children made no less use of nouns relative to pronouns, of complex verb forms, or of dependent clauses. Their vocabulary was not obviously more limited, nor their grammar 'simpler', nor their style more 'concrete'. Over the whole interviews, they did make more exophoric reference and they used fewer modifiers and qualifiers. But where constraints to be explicit were heaviest, the group differences were greatly reduced. There was no evidence of 'coding principles' over-riding the demands of the immediate communicative tasks (Edwards 1976a; 1976b).

Despite that impressive programme of research, it is still open to question how far distinct patterns of linguistic choice can be described within the framework of the codes. And it is still possible to contrast the breadth of the early generalizations with the narrowness of the evidence. Indeed, the accumulation of evidence has been accompanied by increasing qualification of the thesis itself. The research showed social class differences in children's language which could be subjected to elaborate sociological interpretation. Detailed analysis of the nominal group and of pronominal reference provided linguistically respectable means of describing the relevant evidence and perhaps the most convincing indicators of 'restricted' speech yet suggested. But there is no adequate evidence for what Bernstein continued to call occasionally 'the' two codes, or for their 'verbal manifestation . . . in mutually exclusive formal patterns' (Hasan 1973, p. 262). Some patterning might be expected from the 'semantic compatibility which arises from the deep-meaning structure of the code', and it is this 'semantic' consistency which Bernstein seeks to establish when he asks— 'What is responsible for the simplification and rigidity of the syntax of a restricted code?' (1973a, p. 169). Strictly, *he* is, since the codes are his constructs and this is how he defines them. And what follows that question is a list of attributes as crude as those in the early papers. Yet as we saw earlier, he now accepts the difficulty, even impossibility, of identifying any general criteria for the codes, and the necessity for contextual interpretations of linguistic choice. Commenting on the apparent lack of significant social class differences in the speech of the mothers studied by Robinson and Rackstraw (1972), he is 'inclined to think that if the semantic styles differ, we might reasonably expect differences in their linguistic realisations' (Bernstein 1973b, p. 6). The tentativeness of the statement contrasts sharply with those confident lists of what the realizations 'are'.

The final importance of the SRU programme may well lie less in its findings than in 'the questions which have been opened up and the procedures used' (Bernstein 1973a, p. 8). But in academic life as in everyday life, a situation defined as real acquires its own reality. The codes provide 'radical' sociologists with a vivid example of the re-ification of constructs, the transformation of speculations into 'facts'. Bernstein has commented on his surprised awareness in 1964 of the frequency of ritual references to his work. In these references its ambiguities were generally discarded, leaving a 'hard' core of new 'knowledge'. Deutsch, for example, wrote of the restricted code as 'the major speech form of the lower class', denying any opportunity of advancement to those who lacked 'the necessary verbal strategies' (1967, p. 179). And in a caricature of the theory, Jensen (1968, p. 105) described lower-class language as a 'mainly incidental emotional accompaniment to the here-and-now', bereft of any real information about objects or ideas. Such premature acceptance of a complex hypothesis as 'proven' justified Cazden's (1966) warning that Bern-stein's work was so often cited and so rarely analysed as to bring the danger of a pervasive linguistic stereotype. This danger has made it a main target of recent attacks on the 'myth' of verbal deprivation (see pp. 132-9). In this country, it has been attacked psychologically for the huge inferences from thought to language (Herriott 1970, pp. 52-5), politically for its 'caricature' of working-class life and language (Rosen 1972), and linguistically for the limitations of the analysis and the fundamental confusions in the concept of codes (Coulthard 1969: Jackson 1974).

These last criticisms have received such close attention in the previous pages that little mention has been made of the studies of language and socialization which were a large part of the SRU pro-gramme. Bernstein's 'larger concern' was with the problem of *how* culture is transmitted and sustained. His answer, essentially, was that 'social structure becomes the child's psychological reality' through the shaping of his acts of speech. This shaping referred to the ways in which language was used to mark out and organize his world. The approach has a value independent of that frustrating search for the 'specific' linguistic realizations of meaning. Without necessarily detailing what their linguistic consequences might be, or even presuming that they could be consistently identified, it could be argued that important functional differences in language both reflected and maintained wider social class differences. Much of the SRU's work was concerned with this area of enquiry. Separating it from the findings already outlined distorts both the individual studies and the integration of the whole programme within a single 'conceptual frame'. But it also emphasizes the importance of that research despite the elusiveness of the codes, and it allows reference to other sociological accounts of how different conditions of life lead to a different sense of the possibilities of language.

4. SOCIAL CLASS, LANGUAGE AND SOCIALIZATION

Any language is capable of conveying any meanings relevant to its users. This doctrine of potential equality does not mean that language is equally important in the life of all societies, or that it is used to do the same things. The point was well made by the anthropologist Franz Boas in his rejection of any causal relationship between 'primitive' language and modes of thought:

> It seems very questionable how far the restriction of the use of certain grammatical forms can really be conceived as a hindrance in the formulation of generalised ideas. It seems much more likely that the lack of these forms is due to the lack of their need . . . Primitive man . . . is not in the habit of discussing abstract ideas. His interests center around the occupations of his daily life, and where philosophic questions are touched on, they appear either in relation to definite individuals or in the more or less anthropomorphic forms of religious beliefs . . . The fact that generalised forms of expression are not used does not prove inability to form them but . . . that the mode of life of the people is such that they are not required; they would, however, develop just as soon as needed.   (in Hymes 1964, p. 18.)

Boas' line of argument is clearly *from* social structure *to* language. And despite other misleading connotations of 'primitive', it provides a valuable corrective to many accounts of 'lower-class' language. The optimism of the final sentence contrasts sharply with the bleaker versions of deficit theory, and would provide a useful 'text' for parts of the final chapter. Attention is firmly fixed on what language *is* used to do, without any ascribed limits to what *could* be done if demands were different.

Studies of socialization include what the *group* requires its members to know, and how the *individual* learns the ways of his world well enough to function effectively within it (e.g. Inkeles 1966). In any diversified society, that 'world' may be a sub-culture. Different 'basic conditions of life' then bring appropriately different responses. These may include a different value placed on language in interpreting and acting within a particular environment, and a different sense of what uses of it are most necessary and rewarding. The critical social class differences may not lie in *patterns of* linguistic choice, but in *systems for* language use.

In the study of different 'modes of communication' referred to earlier, Schatzman and Strauss (1955) explained the narrative superiority of their middle-class subjects by their greater familiarity with the task of transmitting information to strangers. Lower-class accounts were 'concrete' and often disjointed. The speakers assumed a shared perspective too readily, making little allowance for their listener's ignorance of the events. Coming from communities in which most talk *was* between people who knew each other well, they could not adjust to the absence of background knowledge. Interesting though this study is, it is also a rarity. Few sociological investigations of social class differences focused directly on either the uses of language or the value placed on it. References had to be heavily inferential. Reliance on inference in so varied and central a part of human life has been criticized already, and what follows is intended only as illustration, *not* as a summary of 'facts'. Many middle-class occupations involve the manipulation of symbols, and many demand skill in dealing with strangers and with whole series of brief encounters. 'Street-corner' society also places a high value on 'artful talk', and some of *its* occupations (e.g. 'conning') depend on it. But as a simple generalization, manual occupations do not normally require extensive task-oriented speech. Manipulative skills are learned and then repeated, leaving little need for the verbal elaboration of problems and solutions. The existence of an *individual* career-line, a series of upward moves dependent on his own efforts, has been part of the explanation for the greater individualizing of experience supposed to characterize middle-class life. While such a career often involves competition between colleagues, manual work on the other hand is often done in groups into which individual efforts are merged. The resulting importance of collective action encourages the use of language to maintain group relationships and solidarity. There is an ambitious attempt to trace the effects of different occupational experiences in Kohn's study of parental values. Again, it is not directly concerned with language, but can be 'suitably' re-interpreted. Was work mainly with objects, or with persons and symbols? How heavily was it supervised? How much was it a matter of routine? Did security or success depend on individual or collective effort? From their experience in these four critical 'dimensions', parents acquired their sense of what was important for their children to learn (Kohn 1963: Kohn and Schooler 1969). Working-class mothers placed relatively more emphasis on neatness, conformity to rules and obedience to authority. Taking 'respectability' for granted, middle-class mothers gave priority to curiosity, consideration for others, and self-control. Such variations were 'entirely appropriate' to different conditions of life, and represented different formulas for survival. Some of the linguistic implications are clear. Where obedience is what matters, communication can be terse. Where the aim is self-control, the elaboration of feelings and reasons is essential. The difference is *not* one of relative punitiveness, but of making meanings individual and explicit. Working-class mothers were less concerned with internalized standards of conduct because they were more likely to see life in terms of externally imposed roles. And Kohn attributes to a pervasive sense of powerlessness and insecurity their tendency to 'exclude or minimise considerations of subjective intent' (Kohn 1959, p. 366). He can be criticized for concentrating too much on experience at work. Behind many other accounts of the group-centredness of working-class life are the additional factors of a common occupational status, a high density of housing, and a low level of geographical mobility. In such a community, relatives were also neighbours, and work-mates acquaintances of long-standing. Most interaction was between those familiar with each other's lives, and able to trade on a large store of common knowledge. Such closeness brought strong pressures to conform to traditional behaviour and ideas, if only to provide some sense of security in a life felt to be largely outside the *individual's* control. The 'resulting' conformity, fatalism, and tendency to 'live for the day' are strongly emphasized in the 'scientific' literature (for a convenient example, see Klein 1965, pp. 487–516). More popular accounts may balance the warmth and co-operativeness against the anti-intellectualism and suspicion of the new (Hoggart 1957), or present a black picture of total conventionality of thought and expression (Seabrook 1967). Language is seen to be used predominantly to maintain close relationships, and to reinforce rather than question the order of things. The main intuitive objection to these accounts is the way they confine the infinite variety of language within a strait-jacket of limited use. The overwhelming empirical objection is the lack of such extensive recording of language use as would be needed to fill in those crude outlines.

Bernstein's early portrayals of working-class 'life and language' are similarly crude thumb-nail sketches. They too describe language as used mainly to emphasize similarities, and to control behaviour by defining roles (1958, p. 166: 1961b, p. 167). The critical attributes 'generating a particular (restricted) form of communication' are later summarized in terms of community relationships, work relationships, and family role systems (1973a, p. 165). The summary is theoretically confusing because there is no indication as to whether the various attributes are to be seen as inter-active or merely cumulative, whether all must be found together, and whether all are functionally related to the code or possibly incidental accompaniments. It is empirically dubious because behind the abstractions lies the powerful image of a 'traditional' working-class community, with its assumed combination of closeness, solidarity and conformity. Bernstein himself doubts its relevance to modern conditions of relative affluence, increased subjection to the influence of mass media, and a growing challenge to the traditional role of women. And he has been fiercely criticized for making no differentiation within the lower working-class in terms of 'history, traditions, job experience, ethnic origins, residential patterns, levels of organisation, or class consciousness' (Rosen 1972, p. 6). A critic of the blanket generalizations might well point to the tradition of articulate political protest in some mining areas, or to the high regard for eloquence ('artful talk') associated with industrial South Wales. He might refer to substantial evidence in doubting whether the same normative systems are shared by the 'rough' and the 'respectable', the 'status-assenting' and the 'status-dissenting', the 'proletarian' and the 'privatized', even in that third of the population which Bernstein has seen as denied access to an elaborated code.

While recognizing that conditions now exist 'for the emergence of less communalized and more individualized relationships' in the lower working class, he still sees social class position as the most formative influence on work- and family-roles, and so on the generation of codes. *Why* he does so provides some answer to criticisms of his work for neglecting the distribution of material resources (Byrne and Williamson 1972), or the power basis of the class structure (Rosen 1972). Manual work offers relatively little role discretion, and security depends on *collective* acts of assertion. In a wider sense, an elaborated code is 'normally' associated with 'a stratum seeking or already possessing access to major decision-making areas of the social structure' (Bernstein 1962a, p. 33). It is because social class gives 'differential access' to the sense that the world is 'permeable' (i.e. open to change) that it 'controls access to' elaborated codes which are by definition expressions of questioning and challenge. Restricted codes are described by

Robinson as 'an integral feature of feudalism', helping to maintain a stable and passive subculture. But in arguing that 'working-class consciousness' may require command of an elaborated code before their situation can be articulated and communicated, he reverses the 'proper' relationship between social structure and language (Robinson 1971, p. 90; 1972, pp. 158–9). It is not the absence of the code which prevents the consideration of alternatives. It is because alternatives do not seem available that speech is predominantly used to state things as they are. Bernstein himself has seen in Civil Rights and Black Power movements in America a powerful influence on language *because* the challenge to the passivity of the old sub-culture demands the articulation of alternatives.

The argument so far has concentrated on possible social class differences in language use. Bernstein shares with Kohn a wish to show how such differences are transmitted from one generation to the next. Both describe parents as emphasizing forms of behaviour which are important to life as *they* see it. Both try to integrate an account of what parents do with what children learn, and both see different patterns of mother-child interaction as arising out of social class position and producing significantly different learning environments. In Bernstein's analysis, the class system acts on the 'deep structure' of communication. It is through talk that the child discovers the nature and requirements of his world. He learns to look at and talk about things and events as others do, and so to act with them to 'produce and perform social order' (Cook-Gumperz 1973, p. 7). The 'focusing and filtering' of his experience within the family is seen as a 'microcosm of the macroscopic orderings of society', and a fundamental part of how the class structure affects the distribution of 'privileged meanings' (Bernstein 1973a, p. 198). As the child learns his language, so he learns which uses of language are most necessary and rewarding in coping with *his* environment. The words he uses are inseparable from his experience of words as means of getting things done, of social control, of learning, of mediating personal relationships, and of developing self-awareness (Halliday 1969). Important social class differences are seen to exist in how far language is relied on to differentiate and organize experience —in how much it is used, and how it is used. The 'genes of social class' are carried through modes of communication that social class itself promotes. Different conditions of life lead to different normative systems which in turn create different family relationships and methods of control. These orient the child to different patterns of language use, which then reinforce the conditions of their own existence. Through the ways in which meanings are realized in certain 'critical contexts' of socialization, the structure of society becomes the structure of the child's experience.

The contexts most closely studied in the SRU programme were those of control and instruction. Underlying the enquiries was Bernstein's emphasis on the individualizing of meaning. The main 'condition' for the emergence of a restricted code was a relationship based on 'an extensive set of closely shared expectations', a common cultural identity which reduced the need to 'verbalise intent'. This 'condition' was more likely to be found in working-class areas. And in Henderson's (1970b) research, middle-class women placed relatively less emphasis on talking with friends for affective and role-defining reasons, and relatively more on the exchange of ideas and the acquisition of information.

Control was an especially significant context because of the association of restricted codes with *role*-relationships in which individuals relate to each other largely because of *what* they are, their unique attributes being submerged in the general categories. In so-called 'positional' families, roles are ascribed and their boundaries well-defined. Interaction between parents and children is governed by status, and the justification for a command is inherent in the relationships and the norms that regulate it ('Do it—because I say so . . . because little girls don't behave like that'). Individual feelings and intentions are rarely considered. In 'person-oriented' families, roles are less ascribed and so less stable. It is assumed that lower working-class families are predominantly of the positional type (Bernstein 1973a, pp. 176–85: Cook-Gumperz 1973, pp. 49–56). To investigate this assumption, three broad types of control were distinguished. *Imperatives* are simple commands, with no reasons given. *Positional appeals* refer to the relative status of controller and controlled. The recipient is reminded of what is expected of people like him, and his place in the social order is announced and reinforced. *Personal appeals* refer to the unique characteristics of the situation and the participants. They may be affective, appeals to the feelings of child or adult, or they may involve a logical chain in which the action is related to possibly distant consequences or to some explicit principle of behaviour. Either way, they carry more explicit information, and generate not only more talk but more talk of particular kinds. The child is made more sensitive to his own and others' feelings, and he learns how an item comes under a relevant rule *and* how it is both like the rule and in particular respects different from it.

Hypotheses about social class differences were tested by asking mothers what they *would* do in various 'disciplinary' situations. Consistent differences in their responses would suggest different 'implicit theories' of control. Middle-class mothers reported more linguistically mediated and personalized controls, and especially more cognitive appeals. There was some slight evidence that they switched their strategy more often according to the immediate context. But the main conclusion was that they 'transmit knowledge of social rules, not only by explanation, but through shaping their explanations in the light of the particular attribute of the problem, context and child; whereas it appears that the working-class mothers are more concerned with constraining the child, offer less explanation and are more likely to be oriented towards general rather than particular attributes of the problem, context or child' (Cook-Gumperz 1973, p. 104). Analysis of their children's responses showed smaller, but a similar pattern, of differences. Making a content-analysis of those cartoon-based stories mentioned earlier (p. 99), Turner (1973) found working-class children more likely to mention threats and commands, and less likely to refer to feelings and obligations in ways that were both specific and explicit.

Other research has also taken modes of control as the most salient social class difference in socialization. Kohn (1959) emphasized the difference in priorities—whether the main concern was with obedience or self-control, the consequences or the motives of behaviour. The Newsons described middle-class strategies as emphasizing reciprocal rights and obligations rather than appeals to authority, and as relying on verbally explicit generalizations from specific events to some relevant principle (J. and E. Newson 1970, pp. 469–83). And the basic distinction between status- and person-oriented control was used by Hess and Shipman (1965; 1968) in their investigations of the 'socialisation of cognitive modes in children'. Their very similar analysis produced very similar results. Lower-class mothers were more likely to report the use of imperatives which simply announced the rules. Middle-class mothers were more likely to appeal to subjective feelings or logical consequences in ways that were verbally explicit and left the child some room for reflection and choice.

This same theme of individual autonomy and 'discretion' dominated research into the instructional methods of parents. Middle-class mothers more often reported buying toys 'to help the child find out about things', and less often to 'show affection' or 'keep him occupied' (Bernstein and Young 1967). They were more likely to prepare their children for an active pupil role, presenting learning as something to be actively sought out rather than passively received (Jones 1966). In a study of how language was valued in different areas of socialization, middle-class mothers placed a greater emphasis on its use in personal relations, and working-class mothers on its use in teaching skills. Within the 'skill area', there was a greater working-class emphasis on showing 'how to do', and less on 'how things work'; less autonomy seemed to be allowed the child in his learning (Bernstein and Henderson 1969). As a more detailed area of enquiry, what happens when the child takes the initiative, and asks 'Why'? Is he answered at all? At length? Is the answer closely related to the question? Does it state the facts, and close the enquiry? Or does it open the way to further questions? Again relying on reports of how they *would* respond, Robinson and Rackstraw (1967) found middle-class mothers apparently more willing to answer their children's questions, to provide more information in their answers, and to refer less often to an inescapable order of things (e.g. 'Because they do, that's why'). In a follow-up study of the children's mode of answering, there was a greater middle-class tendency to offer detailed information, to match it closely to the specific question, and to refer to cause-and-effect relationships rather than simple regularities or appeals to authority (e.g. 'Because it's naughty'). The learning opportunities offered by the mother in her responses were cautiously suggested as a determinant of the child's verbal behaviour (Robinson and Rackstraw 1972).

All this research was based on mothers' reports, a source of evidence which may well indicate 'best intentions' rather than actual practice. The research of Hess and Shipman is interesting for its direct observation of mother-child interaction in an instructional context. Their work will be considered more fully in Chapter 4, but it shares with Bernstein's a view of social class as 'a useful but gross variable, a statement of probability that the child will encounter certain types of experience' (Hess and Shipman 1968, p. 92). The critical aspects were similarly defined as the extent to which he was offered alternatives in thought and action from which to develop a capacity to discriminate and make rational choices.

The consistency of the SRU results under the headings of control and instruction led to the development of a Maternal Communication Index which could be used to discriminate, between and within social classes, in 'orientation to the relevance of language'. A low score would be recorded by a mother who seemed to have discouraged her child's attempts at conversation, evaded awkward questions, was unconcerned with the 'educational' value of play or toys, and used mainly imperative or positional forms of control. The components of the Index were closely inter-related. It discriminated usefully within the working-class sample—e.g. those with high scores were more likely to stress an active partnership between home and school than to draw a sharp boundary between the two, and they were also more likely to have children with high verbal ability scores. But over the whole sample, there was a close association with social class. It seemed to show 'radical differences in the use of language for purposes of explanation and control, and in the willingness of mothers to respond to communication initiated by their children' (Bernstein and Brandis 1970, pp. 105–6). Through the realization of meanings in these areas of experience, sub-cultural differences were 'made substantive'.

5. SOCIAL CLASS AND LINGUISTIC PROFICIENCY

Bernstein has often denied having any concern with linguistic ability, or making any contribution to 'deficit theory'. He *is* concerned with the uses to which knowledge of language is put, and with socially constrained choices *within* the available resources. Much contemporary research, however, even when it cites his work for support, *is* explicitly concerned with ability. Reporting the results of his longitudinal study of children's language, Loban found 'nothing which controverts Bernstein' in his own evidence of lower-class deficiencies (1965, p. 128). There was 'a persistently parallel variation between language *proficiency* and socio-economic status' which suggested that it was 'culturally as well as individually determined' (1963, p. 89).

'Proficiency' is open to very different interpretations. It may refer to articulation, vocabulary, grammar, or all three of these; to receptive or expressive skills; to 'absolute' deficits or developmental 'lags'; to competence or performance; and to communicative deficiencies with or without profound cognitive implications. Whatever 'level' of deficiency is identified, its cultural explanation tends to emphasize the range and variety of the child's experience, the quality of the language models available to him, and the nature of the feed-back to the forms and functions of his own speech. Some of this explanation is difficult to separate from what has already been discussed, except that it is mainly offered under the labels of 'psychology' and 'child development' rather than of sociology. It is similarly concerned with how 'the structure of the social system and the structure of the family shape communication and language' (Olim *et al.* 1967, p. 415). What follows is not intended as a complete review, but as an indication of the main varieties of evidence and interpretation. These will be presented largely on their own terms, reserving some serious objections to the evidence for the last section of this chapter.

A relatively limited range of active vocabulary has been a frequently reported characteristic of 'lower-class' language (Cohn 1959: Templin 1957: Loban 1963). The data is especially vulnerable to criticism of the narrowness and artificiality of the sampling of language, but it is also a 'deficit' easier to reconcile with linguistic theory than are revelations of 'poor' syntax. It might be accounted for by applying sub-culturally Sapir's definition of vocabulary as 'a complex inventory of all the ideas, interests and occupations that take up the attention of the community' (1949, pp. 91–2). The more necessary it is to distinguish within an area of experience, the more specific will be the labels used. What has not been experienced, even vicariously, will not be labelled at all because there has been no need to do so. Receptive or 'passive' vocabulary reflects the whole range of the user's experience, and expressive or 'active' vocabulary the range of familiar experience— those objects, activities and ideas encountered in everyday life for which labels are readily available. The repetitious use of common words by 'lower-class' children has been attributed to their narrower range of experiences to classify and organize (Deutsch 1965: Raph 1965). Their parents are also said to be relatively content with loose and undifferentiated labels, and so to exert less pressure for precision and for learning how various objects may *properly* be classified under a single label (John and Goldstein 1964: Kessler 1965).

Statements of *grammatical* deficiency raise fundamental questions about whether they refer to competence or performance, to what *is* done or to what *can* be done. As was argued earlier, no language or variety is less rule-governed and more random than any other. Bernstein's use of 'poor' and 'inaccurate' to describe the typical syntax of 'public language' (and, supposedly, of all lower working-class language) was linguistically absurd. Yet 'strong' versions of deficit theory have sometimes argued a low level, or even an absence, of systematic structure in lower-class language. The summary which follows represents, not unfairly, a travesty of social science and of responsible academic writing. Among the 'conspicuous deficits' ascribed to such language are 'grammatical patterns full of errors', a predominance of present tenses and incorrect tense forms, and meagre use of prepositions and conjunctions to express relationships. 'Sentences are largely incomplete', short, and made up of a simple clause or of a string of simple clauses linked by 'and' (Raph 1967, pp. 205–6: see also Bereiter and Engelmann 1966, pp. 34–6). Only consistent evidence from the most extensive and varied sampling of language could have justified such a summary. Without it, it is the crudest of stereotypes.

More reputable research has charted social class differences in the rate of linguistic development, showing either the same goals achieved at different ages or a more limited lower-class progress in the same direction. Two studies of young children's acquisition of morphological rules showed *no* significant social class differences. The first tested their application to nonsense syllables so as to make verb, plural and possessive forms (Shriner and Miner 1968), and the second their use as clues to identify the form-classes of items in a made-up language (La Civita *et al.* 1966). Their conclusion that the dynamics of language development were fairly uniform is vitiated by serious methodological weaknesses—a wide and uncontrolled age range in one, and a blurring of the social class contrast in the other (La Civita) by a large overlap between the groups. A series of investigations using word-association tests to measure linguistic maturity produced some predictable and some surprising results. Paradigmatic responses (i.e. matching nouns with nouns, verbs with verbs, etc.) were taken as indicating more 'advanced' development towards 'acquiring fundamental concepts about words' (Entwistle 1966, pp. 69–70). Urban children were found to make more of these responses than rural children of the same age, though the gap was made up in time. Social class differences within these broad categories were slight. Later research in a large city showed white slum children to be *more* advanced in this respect than their suburban, first-grade contemporaries, with black slum children at least holding their own. This was a striking exception to the usual 'lower-class' inferiority in whatever was being measured. But by third-grade, the 'normal' order of superiority had been restored (Entwistle 1968a; 1968b). The initial advantage of the slum children was explained by their heavy vicarious exposure to speech through un-restricted access to television, and their direct exposure to relatively simple language models. Their early 'maturity' in basic skills was at the expense of more sophisticated skills. And even at first-grade, suburban children did better on the less developed form-classes (adjectives and adverbs) and on individual words that were uncommon in everyday speech.

It is the difference in more 'sophisticated' skills that is emphasized by Martin Deutsch, and 'confirmed' by his research programme at the New York Institute of Developmental Studies. Convergent, 'restricted' use of language by socially disadvantaged parents was reflected in a limited use of the resources of language by their children. The differences lay in variety, not quantity—not in how much they said, but in how they said it. Even at first-grade, their speech was simpler in syntax and less rich in modifiers and descriptive terms (C. Deutsch 1967). By fifth-grade, the gap had increased, and 'the speech content and range of vocabulary and verbs tended to identify the social class membership of the subjects' (Deutsch *et al.* 1967, p. 186). Very evident in this research is a hierarchical ranking of speech systems in terms of their cognitive consequences. The social class differences seemed especially marked in more 'complex' language forms, and in tasks involving categorization and abstraction rather than 'simple' labelling and enumeration (John 1963: John and Goldstein 1964: for a similar emphasis on abstract language, see Jensen 1968: Golden and Birns 1968). Language was seen as especially sensitive to the various deprivations of 'lower-class' life. Children were likely to have fewer objects to handle, label, and relate. They usually received less individualized attention, and had less reason to see in language an essential means of finding out about the world and enquring into their own and others' feelings and ideas. The quantity and quality of language directed at the individual child were likely to be relatively limited. A similar environmental profile appears in much of this literature, and can be illustrated in one of its more extreme versions. 'The language spoken in the home . . . is typically poor in quality and quantity. It is not used to express subtle feelings or to extend ideas or thoughts. With inadequate stimulation from people and experiences, there is little to talk about. Much of the communication is by nonverbal means' (Gerber and Hertel 1969). What a wealth of participant observation is misleadingly implied by those 'facts' of lower-class life! In fact, it remains unclear whether 'mere' exposure to language is sufficient to develop the basic structures of that language, and how far the quality of the models matters, and in what form feed-back is necessary and most effective. Through what they hear, and what they say themselves, children develop and test notions about the meaning of words and how they are put together. The acquisition of vocabulary may benefit from something like direct instruction, from the correcting of mistakes and an insistence on precision. But there is little evidence that parents correct the grammatical 'errors' and experiments of their children, or that it would be effective if they did. A detailed account of language acquisition is beyond the scope of this book, but one general point is clearly relevant. Simple exposure to language may be enough to develop basic morphological and grammatical rules. This is obviously not true of competence in its wider, 'communicative' sense. Some of the time in all families, and much of the time in some, the child's talk will be ignored, or receive only a token response, or be responded to in ways that are affectively rewarding but involve no extended verbal interaction. How, and how often, it *is* reinforced will have an important influence on his responsiveness to verbal channels of communication, and to the importance of language in certain tasks and areas of experience.

Many of the differences outlined imply deficiencies. They also suggest that difficulties will arise in communication across social class 'lines'. These can be investigated by using cloze procedure—the random or systematic deletion of words in a passage of written or recorded speech which decoders have to fill in. Their response can be analysed for their 'absolute' (same word), grammatical (same form-class), or semantic (equivalent meaning) accuracy. Peisach (1965) found that middle-class children were more effective at guessing gaps in middle-class speech, and no less effective than lower-class children with lower-class speech. Working with Negro girls, Williams and Wood (1970) found that the gaps in working-class speech were more accurately filled, suggesting its greater redundancy, and that middle-class girls were generally more efficient at prediction. The significance of the method arises from the fact that in everyday speech, any sustained communication is rarely heard word for word, and that gaps are supplied (predictively and retrospectively) from familiarity with the vocabulary and syntax of the speaker. It can be criticized because comprehension of the whole message may be only loosely related to the accuracy of this filling-in. Some studies have therefore involved direct tests of comprehension. Krauss and Rotter (1968) used abstract figures, deliberately chosen because they were hard to describe, which children had to transmit to a partner. Lower-class seven- and twelve-year olds were less effective as encoders and decoders of the descriptions. Heider et al. (1968) found a similar inferiority, though the lower-class children also used a more effective informational style when directed to be more explicit. This additional result indicates the problem of distinguishing cognitive from motivational differences.

With some significant exceptions, the research reported in this section and the last adds up to a bleak portrayal of differences hard to dissociate from deficiencies. The results will be summarized, not as proof but as a convenient starting point for a more critical examination of the evidence, and of reasons why it is still *dangerous* to 'propose conclusions at this stage of our knowledge' (John and Moskovitz 1970, p. 173). The 'authority' for what follows lies in the preceding pages.

The language of lower-class children 'is' impoverished because of a relatively limited exploitation of the resources of language. It 'is' marked by a limited, less varied vocabulary; a high ratio of pronouns to nouns, and to all other words; less differentiation of meaning within the nominal group; more frequent 'errors'; relatively simple grammar, with fewer complex verb forms and types of subordination. This language 'is' therefore more fluent and predictable; less well organized and complex; more concrete and anecdotal; less likely to express uncertainty and fine shades of meaning; less capable of expressing abstractions; less informative about persons, events and ideas; and more implicit and context-dependent.

6. THE STATUS OF THE EVIDENCE

Such an accumulation of evidence might suggest that the 'facts' are now known, and that we can turn whole-heartedly to their explanation and remedy. But the data base is far less solid than it appears. If many researchers produce similar or compatible results from independent investigations, we may be impressed. If some largely restate the work of others, the 'facts' gain spurious force from repetition but are not multiplied. If all of them use similar research techniques and methods of analysis, there may be a compounding of errors. A reality is constructed, and it will be increasingly difficult to challenge or even detect the assumptions underlying the evidence. Much of the research summarized has been attacked as 'pathological' in perspective, transforming what are merely differences into deficits and so propagating a 'myth' of verbal deprivation (see pp. 131–41). These criticisms are not presented in the hope of 'demolishing' the evidence outright. But they do represent a case for extreme caution in describing, interpreting and generalizing differences in something as complex and fluid as language.

A good deal of social scientific evidence arises from what Barker (1963) calls 'behavioural tesserae', carefully contrived and controlled situations remote from 'real life'. The dilemma in language research has been especially acute. Systematic recording is likely to define a context in which more than minimum attention is paid to the words, yet the observer is likely to be interested in 'everyday' speech which 'disappears' as he approaches. Where a variety is stigmatized, a striving for 'correctness' makes the very target of research inaccessible (Bailey 1966, p. 6). Investigating Jamaican pronounciation in London, Wells (1973) argues hopefully that his 'friendly non-censorious attitude' and the fact of recording in his informants' homes outweighed the constraints of a questionnaire evidently concerned with speech and a researcher who was white, a stranger, and spoke with an RP accent! A main feature of Labov's New York research was its evidence of sharp shifts of 'style' from careful talk to contexts in which the speaker's attention was sufficiently diverted from the forms of speech to allow the vernacular to 'emerge'. And in his later research with black adolescents, he followed the same path as Barker's 'ecological psychology', and tried to obtain 'the language of members integrated into the peer group in spontaneous interaction with one another' (1969a, p. 716).

Clearly, a researcher cannot analyse what *might have been said*. But he should consider how far the context might have 'created' his data. Plumer (1971, p. 280) describes the problem as 'whether to use a test that reveals optimum or representative performance'. There is a curious confidence in this remark. Even to identify 'representative' usage demands a huge quantity and diversity of data; the 'optimum' seems for ever out of sight. Rather less ambitious questions should be asked instead. Was the speech so constrained by the situation or the task that generalizations beyond that context would be misleading? Were there occasions to use those features, the presence or absence of which were thought to be significant? Only then might it be claimed that a speaker 'does not have a given form in his system because of his consistent failure to use it in a context where other members of the (speech) community do so regularly' (Labov 1971, p. 167). Otherwise, its absence may indicate a lack of facility, or an unawareness that it was 'needed' or appropriate in that context. Such systematic and extensive eliciting of speech has been rare, and some accounts of verbal deprivation rest on a premature assumption that what is not done is never done, or *cannot* be done.

McCarthy's (1954) review of research into language development includes three pages on the effect of 'situation', and a salutary warning against taking limited samples of speech as representative of the speaker's ability. The *social* situation in which speech is recorded has continued to be a neglected source of variation in performance (Cazden 1970). Even the *quantity* of speech is obviously influenced by the speaker's sense of involvement—by whether he has something to say, and someone to whom he wishes to say it. How far was he at ease with the researcher, interested in the communicative tasks facing him, and experiencing no 'semantic' difficulties that might be wrongly interpreted as evidence of *linguistic* deficiencies (he may have lacked enough to say, rather than the means of saying it)? Such questions were asked about their own research by Strauss and Schatzman (1955). What did the interview mean to the respondents, and how did their differential responses affect its structure and course? It was almost certainly an unfamiliar experience for the lower-class subjects, unaccustomed to 'instant' communication with strangers and facing, in effect, a *different* task.

Two major research problems are involved here. First, the interviewer is himself part of the situation, the integrity of which makes it impossible simply to 'control' its various components. An interview is a collaborative event, dependent on a measure of co-operation and rapport that cannot simply be assumed. Even working-class adults are likely to define it as a formal occasion because of the social distance between themselves and the interviewer. Where the gap between speaker and listener is wide, either in 'power' or in experience, speech which stays close to what is immediately visible and a matter of common knowledge is a way of playing safe. It offers some guarantee of shared referents, and reduces the risk of contradiction and error. The apparent 'concreteness' of such speech can then be seen as a *socio-linguistic* phenomenon, the 'realization' of sharp differences in status or background knowledge. Children face an especially unequal communicative relationship, and one in which they may well see themselves as 'on trial'. There is some evidence that lower working-class children give brief responses to interview questions unless actively encouraged to elaborate them, while middle-class children expand their answers as a matter of course (Williams and Naremore 1969). Unless it *is* a 'habit', elaboration is a 'cost' more likely to be borne in situations which are valued or enjoyed, and when condensed forms of communication are obviously inadequate. Standardized probes can therefore penalize some children, leaving them 'free' to limit their responses. Additional 'social-emotional' reinforcement may be necessary to establish rapport (e.g. Henderson 1970a, p. 23), and they may be 'pushed' towards more elaborate and explicit language where the need for it is made apparent (e.g. Lawton 1968, pp. 138–49: Heider *et al.* 1968). Such departures from 'objectively' standardized research procedures recognize that the 'same' situation may be seen in very different ways by those involved in it.

The second, larger, problem is the gulf mentioned earlier between 'artificially induced' and 'real-life' behaviour. Following through the research implications of his emphasis on *situated* meaning, Douglas (1971, p. 16) argues that because human actors 'act in accord with their constructions of meanings for the concrete situations they face . . . experimentally induced acts cannot be taken as representative of everyday acts'. Taken to extremes, this would bury most research under a plethora of context-specific statements from which no generalizations would be possible at all. But much of the evidence on language 'deprivation' *has* been collected by researchers unfamiliar and perhaps threatening to those they were studying, and it *has* represented an extremely narrow sampling of language. Any experimental setting takes the child from his 'normal' tasks and relationships, and from 'the meanings he normally creates and receives' (Bernstein 1973a, p. 276). But where the object of study is as diverse, fluid and context-dependent as language, the implications of this are especially serious. For example, most of the 'deficit' evidence involved language used for *referential* purposes, a function said to be relatively unimportant in working-class speech; there is an obvious circularity here, a building-in of the 'appropriate' proof. In the virtuoso displays of 'artful' street-corner talk described earlier, referential information is slight and the metaphorical power considerable. No school-room or 'laboratory' setting is likely to reveal or even hint at this power. This illustrates a problem generalized by Houston in her distinction between 'School' and 'Non-School' Register. For speakers of 'uneducated English', black or white, the first may be 'careful' speech but it will not be their 'best speech' (Houston 1969, pp. 601–2: 1970, p. 953). Yet it is what they are likely to use when interviewed alone, when interviewed by someone seen as 'authority', and when in a 'school' setting (Labov 1969b: Williams and Naremore 1969). The results will gravely underestimate their 'normal' level of performance. There is an analogy with ethnographic accounts of cognitive processes, where skills not revealed by experimental investigation are apparent in coping with the problems of everyday life. An 'ethnographic base-line' then provides some check on 'the meaningfulness of the experiment to the subject' and a way of testing whether 'cultural differences in cognition reside more in the situation in which different cognitive processes are applied than in the existence of a process in one cultural group and its absence in another' (Cole *et al.* 1971, pp. 217 and 233). What we are concerned with here is not a 'universal' difference between 'experimental' and 'natural' behaviour, but the possibility of *differential* effects on the performance of children from various backgrounds.

'Still unresolved is the degree to which social status contrasts may be assigned to variability in the attitudes of the respondents when responding to truly common stimuli, or to variations in the meanings of the stimuli to the respondents' (Lesser *et al.* 1965, p. 9). This is a comment on research into intelligence and its components, but it sounds a general warning against the traditional assumption ttah laboratory-like controls are sufficient to remove bias in the colleciotn of data. If there are social class differences in how *tasks* are categorized in terms of the language appropriate to them, then the tasks used to elicit language need careful scrutiny. Templin noted (1958) how complexity of expression 'fluctuates with the opportunities for the use of elaborate sentences'. If children are asked, for example, to describe simple scientific experiments, then the task may 'create the need for . . . subordinate clauses', and especially for 'if . . . then . . .' constructions (Moffett 1968, p. 180). If they are asked to describe pictures, their response may be markedly affected by their familiarity with, or interest in, the particular picture chosen, and the detail of their description by whether the picture is still visible when it is given (Cowan 1967: Brent and Katz 1967). These are sources of task variation applicable to any group of subjects. But the effects may also vary across social class (or ethnic) lines, and so be discriminatory. Two examples of this were mentioned earlier—working-class boys' distaste for a story-telling task which affected their fluency, and a greater working-class use of exophoric reference when there was no obvious need to be explicit (see pp. 99–100). A further example raises the general problem of how to elicit 'spontaneous' talk. Deutsch used mechanical toys which lit up or moved as long as the child kept talking, and 'died' when he fell silent. This is described as 'a relatively unstructured speech reinforcement situation'. In fact, it encouraged repetition, stock phrases, and other such methods of maintaining the flow. Quantity was all-important. One middle-class child is quoted as telling a story well-known to him, so producing speech which was complex and coherent and scored highly—yet which is also, in Bernstein's terms, habituated speech in a restricted code (Deutsch *et al.* 1967, pp. 178–87).

As we saw earlier, some research has suggested a relative rigidity in lower working-class speech, and an increase in social class differences as the 'complexity' of the communicative task increased (e.g. Deutsch 1965: Henderson 1970a). Other research shows the differences diminishing where the task constraints are most stringent (e.g. Robinson 1965b: Edwards 1976b). These two examples from my own research are not given to 'prove' a point, but to illustrate the possibility of eliciting from lower-class children a level of performance often denied them, both in overall 'quality' and in relation to specific features such as e.g. 'complex' verb forms and expressions of tentativeness and uncertainty. They suggest, I think, at least a relaxed interview situation, and some involvement in the communicative task:

If I saw a friend stealing, I think I'd tell of them to put them in the right, and not go on stealing . . . I'd say what I think is right. You're only going to lead them into danger otherwise. I think it's bad if you steal. I think it's very serious, cos if you keep doing it in your school-days, you're going to keep doing it more and more when you get bigger. And then you'll just keep getting put in prison, until you die. And then it'll be no use to you, the thing that you stole . . . They'd probably call me a tell-tale, so I wouldn't easily know what to do. But I think I'd do what was best for them, and tell of them.

When you're doing Ouiji, you know, you can get terrified. And there was this cotton-wool. And it was just an ordinary block of cotton-wool. And then it took the form of a—you know, the shape of a man, with one eye open and one eye shut. And it grew fangs, things like that. It formed something every night, when we were in bed. And one day we were getting so frightened of it that Martin just went and dismantled it . . . And after that, we were doing Ouiji and we asked the ghost if it was mad, you know. And it just went mad. And the glass smashed. So we put all the glass in this container, we put the lid on, and we buried it. And when we came to dig it up next day, it had already been dug up. And the headstone we'd made had been ripped. It had been ripped, and the thing dug up.

Even as illustrations, these extracts indicate the danger of seeing the results of language research as properties of the subject independent of the setting.

Objections to the *collection* of evidence on verbal deprivation are briskly summarized by Ervin-Tripp (1971b, p. 35)—'Most tests use communicative settings which are middle-class, middle-class inter-viewers, middle-class kinds of tasks, middle-class language, and middle-class scoring criteria.' Criticisms of its interpretation arise mainly from a basic argument that systematic, rule-governed departures from Standard Language are wrongly described as omissions, even 'errors'. Speech is fitted into a single 'standard' mould, and deficiencies are 'created' out of what are merely differences. The main lines of the argument were followed in discussing social dialects (Chapter 2), and will be considered more fully in that part of Chapter 4 concerned with the 'myth' of verbal deprivation. Briefly, no dialect is any less systematic than another. So-called 'errors' are the result of following different rules. Strong evidence of this has come from the unconscious acts of 'translation' which occur when children from one social class or ethnic group are asked to repeat, word for word, sentences spoken in another dialect (Osser *et al.* 1969: Jordan and Robinson 1972: J. Baratz 1971). Responses each way are different, but predictably and consistently so. For example, 97% Negro children asked to repeat— 'I asked Tom if he wanted to go', responded with—'I ask Tom did he wanna go'; 78% white children exactly reversed the translation (J. Baratz 1969b). Both groups recognized other forms than those they habitually used. *All* children are regularly exposed to standard forms, in school and from the mass media, and it is essential to separate receptive from productive competence (Troike 1969: Weener 1969). They understand far more than they say. This is part of the argument that the extent, and certainly the 'depth', of dialect differences have been exaggerated. They are largely a matter of frequency, and it is rarely possible to say with confidence that standard features are not in the linguistic system at all. It is more 'a case of different probabilities of occurrence in specifiable social and linguistic contexts' (Cazden 1972, p. 192). There is a further false (or premature) assumption that if some grammatical distinction is not encoded in standard form, it is not encoded at all. A single 'standard' measuring rod is manifestly unfair to children from ethnic or other minority groups, who need tests oriented directly to their speech community or to features (e.g. possession, location, passivization) common to different language systems (Ervin-Tripp 1971b: Williams 1971b: Wight and Norris 1970). Otherwise the tests are measures of acculturation, not of basic linguistic skills. The children are not being asked how well they have learned *their* language, but how well they have learned something else.

The interpretation of linguistic evidence demands an appreciation of the infinite diversity of language. Its collection demands an appreciation of possible situational constraints on the language produced. When that situation is as obviously constrained as a test, or an interview, then Labov's 'methodological paradox' is very evident. The researcher may be interested in 'habitual' speech, but he records it for analysis in a context which excludes real informality. Speech produced 'on demand' will lack most of the subtleties of everyday speech, greatly limiting the devices by which meanings are normally conveyed. The researcher should surely retain an acute sense of humility as he contemplates that fragment of a person's speech that constitutes his data.

4.

Language and Educational Achievement: Perspectives on 'Verbal Deprivation'

Over thirty years of research have brought a detailed charting of the 'social determinants of educability'. 'Class chances' can now be defined with some precision through varieties of 'state-rate' analysis—the association of social conditions with the frequency of some level of attainment. The far more difficult search for the mediating variables proceeds essentially on two levels. How does the structure of social experience develop and reinforce certain skills and values? Which skills and values are 'strategic' for educational success? Even while recognizing the complex inter-relationship of influences, it is tempting to look for a 'prime mover', a *main* cause. And at both levels, language has seemed to many to be at the heart of the problem. It is the main means of communication. It 'inter-penetrates' experience. And it expresses 'highly acculturated styles of thought and ideational modes for solving and not solving problems' (Deutsch 1965, p. 79). The child's use of language *reflects* his social experience—his experience of order and disorder in his immediate environment, of the relating of present action to future consequence, of his own questioning of his world and of others' questioning of him. It also *affects* the ordering of his experience, and his capacity for self-analysis and self-control. He is made more or less familiar with the forms and functions of language that predominate in schools.

Critics of 'deficit theory' often place an equally heavy emphasis on language differences as symptom and source of educational disadvantage. For example, Stephen and Joan Baratz (1969) offer 'a simple cultural explanation' for the difficulties facing lower working-class children, especially those who are black. They arise from disregarding the pluralistic nature of modern society, and so refusing to *accept* cultural differences without making value judgments upon them. Linguistic intolerance is part of a wider intolerance, but the general insensitivity is most evident in standard responses to non-standard language. In this respect above all, the existence of 'monocultural schools in a polycultural society' may be 'the first and most damaging inequity foisted upon the poverty child' (Williams 1971a, p. 5). It allows the responsibility for school failure to be shifted from the insensitive institution to the victims of that insensitivity. The obvious forms of positive discrimination—more staff, more material resources—are seen as irrelevant to what is essentially an educational problem.

I sympathize strongly with this approach. But though the comment may seem surprisingly restrained in a book concerned with language, I also believe that linguistic differences have been exaggerated as a prime cause of educational failure. More accurately, they have too often been detached from wider consideration of social conditions and social relationships (a criticism impossible to level at Bernstein). For all the evidence of 'verbal deprivation', 'there is nothing that compels us to cut into the cycle of language and poverty at the language segment rather than the poverty segment' (Plumer 1971, p. 299). It has been a persistent myth that the royal road to equality starts from the classroom. Even in a linguistically stratified society, more open access to the 'standard' language will provide only a slender 'ladder' if other social facts remain unchanged; the main barrier to opportunity is poverty (Cassidy 1969). Too much emphasis on 'simple cultural explanations' may imply panaceas, and so distract attention from the general distribution of resources within the society (Byrne and Williamson 1972: Jencks *et al.* 1973, pp. 255–63). As was argued earlier, research into the linguistic consequences of family modes of control has often neglected to ask what 'alternatives' were realistically available to the child, and how the parents are themselves influenced by their sense of autonomy or powerlessness in the wider environment. If their predominant sense is of an insecurity beyond remedy by their own actions, then the use of language to challenge the status quo and explore alternatives is likely to seem a luxury in the tough business of coping with daily life. In the framework of Bernstein's argument, a restricted code maintains a stable sub-culture and transmits traditional meanings. In the short run, it may seem functional for those in repetitive jobs and those denied participation in an 'affluent' society. 'Possibilities which could become aspirations unsupported by the means to achieve them are not conceived . . . Children are not encouraged to ask a variety of questions outside the parents' competence to answer' (Robinson 1971, p. 91). It would follow from this that an elaborated code is a disturbing force. If its use was to be emphasized by teachers of lower working-class children, the activity could be described as highly subversive! The same argument was advanced by Bernstein with the relationship reversed. The new self-awareness of Black radical movements necessitated the 'elaborated' symbolic manipulation of their world. Language arises out of and then reinforces particular conditions of life and the view of reality generated by them. A transformation in way of life must transform the use of language as the main means of organizing experience. The study of language in relation to educational failure cannot be detached from the wider social context, nor from the forms of social relationship which predominate in schools.

Three approaches to 'verbal deprivation' will be considered in detail in this chapter. The distinction between them is less sharp than the lay-out will suggest. Indeed, there is more overlap among them than some of their respective advocates would readily admit. Admitting the simplication, then, the first approach concentrates on linguistic abilities. Though it includes a variety of research assumptions and methods, it shares some view of a working-class 'deficit', a relative 'poverty' of language. Its text could be taken from Martin Luther King's ironic comment on the eve of the 1965 Selma March—'Those of us who are negroes don't have much. We have known the long night of poverty. Because of the system, we don't have much education, and many of us don't know how to make our nouns and our verbs agree.' Such 'deficiencies' both reflect and reinforce social disadvantage. The second approach represents a radical confrontation with both the evidence and the explanation of social class differences in language. That 'lack of agreement' between nouns and verbs is not the result of ignorance, but of knowledge of a different set of rules. Verbal deprivation is a 'myth', created and sustained by the authority of a social science which transforms differences into deficits, and then justifies remedies for 'weaknesses' that are not 'really' there. The third approach offers a more distinctively sociological perspective, emphasizing the functions of language and the critical discontinuities between its predominant uses in home and school. It can be seen as a more sophisticated statement of even more intractable 'deficiencies', or as an invaluable stimulus to studying the 'insensitivities' of the classroom in relation to the socio-linguistic competence of working-class children.

All three approaches assume that 'the speech patterns of each social class are part of its all-pervading cultural behaviour' (Hertzler 1965, p. 366). They disagree profoundly on how these patterns are to be described and explained, and therefore on what their educational implications might be. Very different definitions of what constitutes the 'problem' lead to very different remedies, and to sharp contrasts in where the main responsibility for so much educational failure is seen to lie.

1. VERBAL DEPRIVATION AND THE DEPRIVATION OF MEANING

The first perspective reveals 'deficits', explicitly recognized as such. They may be identified as linguistic—'knowing less language'—or as a lack of experience in certain uses of language. Either way, environmental explanations are offered for the 'resulting' differences in performance, and there is usually some reference to the 'cognitive poverty' of lower-class life.

As was argued earlier, the 'less language' approach is open to fundamental theoretical objections once it extends beyond the confines of vocabulary. Empirically, it would need support from *far* more evidence than is now available—or is easily conceivable. Even for the 'facts' we have, the notion of deficient linguistic *knowledge* is grotesquely simple. Deficient experience of some *uses* of language is easier to argue, and to 'prove'. Indeed, it will be a theme running throughout this chapter, though appearing in very different forms. Its most stark appearance has been in some of the psychological contributions to 'deficit theory'. These have tended to provide sociologists with a negative frame of reference—a target to attack, and an invitation to display their own more profound view of culture and of 'cultural deprivation'. Rather than attempt a general review, this section will concentrate on three influential examples of the approach, and on how the problems appear from these vantage points. I hope to avoid the temptation to set up a falsely soft target.

Deutsch and his associates saw language as especially sensitive to the stimulus deprivation 'characteristic' of lower-class life (see pp. 113–14). The research programme which justified this conclusion was an attempt to discover 'how the structure of experience as mediated through particular environments influences the patterning of cognitive processes' (Deutsch 1965, p. 79). What was in doubt was not the learning ability of lower-class children, but *what* they learned—especially what training they had received in coping with abstract ideas. To provide a means of specifying which aspects of the learning environment were significant, a Deprivation Index was constructed from those background variables which were both socially patterned and related to reading-readiness. They included the traditional 'gross' variable of family size, and more subtle measures of the child's conversation with adults, and his participation with them in 'cultural activities' (broadly defined as *any* event likely to stimulate an exchange of information and opinion—e.g. a visit to a theatre, zoo or baseball game). The focus of the research was on 'the *quality* of linguistic interaction in cognitively and motivationally stimulating settings' (Whiteman and Deutsch 1968). Hess and Shipman (1965: 1968) also saw social class as 'a discrete array of experience and patterns of experience' with discernible linguistic and cognitive outcomes. The most educationally relevant difference was whether children were offered alternatives in thought and action, and so encouraged to adopt an active, exploratory approach to learning, or whether they were presented with pre-determined solutions which inhibited curiosity and rationality. The argument moves through four stages. Behaviour leading to educational failure is learned in early childhood. The main shaping force is a lack of 'cognitive meaning' in the interaction of mother and child. The form of this relationship shapes language. And language shapes thought and styles of problem-solving. A deprived environment did not lack warmth or affection, but it *was* lacking in encouragement to use language to enquire, discover, and reason. 'The meaning of deprivation is a deprivation of meaning' (Hess and Shipman 1965, p. 885; see also Olim *et al.* 1967: Olim 1971). The same cognitive emphasis is evident in the third, and most extreme, example of 'deficit theory'. Here the supposedly limited range of sensory experience in lower-class life is denied. There is no *verbal* deprivation either as long as attention is confined to the social and affective uses of language—its use to control behaviour, express emotion, and reinforce shared knowledge. What is lacking is its use to describe, relate, compare and analyse (Bereiter and Engelmann 1966, pp. 31–2). In an extraordinary leap into the unknown, the attitudes and life-styles of minority groups are portrayed as so uniform that they can be transmitted without explanation or detailed exposition. Language 'is', for the socially deprived, a mainly un-reflective social accompaniment to the routine, unchallenged activities of everyday life.

In this last example, the consequence of deprivation is a severe limitation on linguistic resources, and not merely a limited exploitation of 'fully-developed' language. This is the 'core deficit'. Disadvantaged children are 'retarded most in the areas that count the most'. Restricted in their ability to manipulate symbols, and so to reason, they have not learned how to be taught (for a similar approach, see Brottman 1968: Blank and Solomon 1968; 1969: also Jensen 1967: Freeburg and Payne 1967). *If* the diagnosis were correct, the recommended remedies follow logically from it. If linguistic knowledge is missing, fill the gaps. If certain structures essential to logical thinking have not been learned in the home, teach them. To do otherwise would compound the disadvantage. It is necessary, for example, to develop systematically the ability to discriminate colours, use prepositions for the precise location of objects, make simple 'if . . . then . . .' deductions, and handle polar opposites ('if it is not . . . it must be . . .'). Linguistic and cognitive structures are seen as inseparable (Bereiter and Engelmann 1966, pp. 48–50). The underlying argument is the same as Hertzler's (1965, p. 43)—that 'thinking is never more precise, complex or extensive than the language of the thinker'. But this assumption raises especially formidable difficulties where the linguistic evidence of 'primitive' thinking is as totally insensitive to dialect differences as that on which Bereiter and Engelmann built their remedial programmes. The programmes are planned to provide the 'missing' skills. For establishing and maintaining social contact, 'restricted' forms of language may be sufficient. But the ability to 'carry on a dialogue through which information is accumulated and used—a dialogue with others or with oneself—would seem to constitute the very core of verbal intelligence' (Bereiter and Engelmann 1966, p. 39). The diagnosis follows logically from the symptoms, and the remedies from the diagnosis. But the symptoms have been crudely identified and interpreted, and there is little support in modern linguistic theory for such sequential, highly structured tuition in a 'poorly learned' *native* language. 'When a richly supplied cafeteria is available, no carefully prescribed diet is necessary' (Cazden 1972, p. 138), and the linguistic 'malnutrition' which authorized the diet has yet to be proved.

It is less clear in the other examples whether the social class differences described are differences in what *can* be done, or in what *is* done most readily and with greatest ease. Certainly the diagnosis is more subtle, and the remedies range more widely. But the critical differences are still seen as existing where educationally they matter most—'in abstract and categorical use of language' (Deutsch 1965, p. 85). It is here that the negative effects of social disadvantage are most apparent. Lacking essential learning strategies, or at least unfamiliar with them, children find much of their school experience meaningless. Some of the by-products of these deficiencies are social. Not recognizing the difficulties pupils face, teachers often set their expectations too high and make their disappointment too obvious. When 'instruction is geared to the listening habits and patterns of middle-class speech', pupils' awareness of their 'grammatical ineptness' may lead to a persistent reticence, an unwillingness to communicate very much at all

(Deutsch *et al.* 1967, p. 178). But beyond such social misunderstandings are cognitive consequences, identified by Deutsch in ways found again and again in the 'deficit' literature. Lower-class children are described as more impulsive and less reflective in problem-solving, more 'relational' and less 'analytical' in their thinking, more likely to be immersed in concrete details and less able to generalize (Hess and Shipman 1965; 1968: Jensen 1967; 1968: Cohen 1968: Krauss and Rotter 1968). Indeed, similar cognitive profiles can be found in earlier, less language-oriented accounts (Miller and Swanson 1960: Riessman 1962). The later argument usually rests on direct 'translations' from language to thought, and there is an obvious circularity in it. The evidence for differences in perception or cognition *is* difference in linguistic expression; in the absence of other, non-verbal indices, the causal relationship between the two can only be inferred. Differences which are interpreted as evidence of underlying cognitive patterns may be differences in verbal facility, or in the preferred (or most readily available) mode of expression. The linguistic resources may be there, but they have been used less often to process information or exchange ideas in those ways, or in that context.

The various learning strategies prevalent in different cultures can be described without advancing any notion of linguistic or cognitive 'primitiveness'. American Indian children tend to learn skills by being *shown*, not told. They watch, practise privately, and perform in public only when reasonably proficient. Schoolroom demands for immediate public statements of what has been verbally transmitted make them uneasy and resentful (Dumont and Wax 1969: Dumont 1972: Philips 1970; 1972). An 'exploration in experimental anthropology' among the Kpelle tribe of north-east Africa showed a similar absence of explicit teaching, and a consequent difficulty in formulating problems verbally (Cole *et al.* 1971). This research is particularly interesting because it shows a very high value being placed on verbal skills in other spheres of interaction. The results of such anthropological research have been quoted frequently by those adopting an 'appreciative', non-evaluative approach to *sub*-cultural diversity. But however 'appreciative' they are, they may still uncover a *relative* disadvantage when those from one kind of social background move on to unfamiliar ground. The Kpelle study compared performance on Western-type tests with ethnographic evidence of 'the intelligent adaptive behaviours that people engage in every day'. But in arguing the relevance of the research to understanding the difficulties faced by minority groups in American schools, a cautionary note is sounded. 'The problem of transferring skills applied on the streets to the classroom is not solved by demonstrating the existence of the skill on the streets. The child must be taught how to apply those skills *in the classroom*' (Cole *et al.* 1971, p. 234). In that context, the criteria of relevance and success may be significantly different. The same relativist judgment can be made of school tasks in general. Thus Cohen (1969, p. 838) reserves the term 'deprivation' for *quantitative* characteristics of pupils' repertoire of skills and information—for times when they *can* reasonably be said to *know less*. 'Cultural difference' refers to *qualitative* characteristics of that repertoire, to acceptable variation rather than differential adequacy. But equivalence may be denied or disowned by those who define what is appropriate. Cohen herself argues a basic discontinuity between the 'conceptual style' of the lower-class, which she calls 'relational', and the 'analytical' style predominant in schools. This school style is also seen as having pervasive social correlates which contribute powerfully to the bewildering impact of schooling—e.g. the emphasis on concentration, independent work, precise time-schedules and a 'cool, impersonal, outer-centred approach to reality organisation' (1969, p. 830). Interestingly, some of the critics of any notion of verbal deprivation argue a rather similar cognitive *difference*, a lower-class preference for inductive enquiry over the deductive process of working from explicitly stated propositions (Cazden 1972, p. 193: Kochman 1972b, p. 246). And the broader interpretation of 'discontinuity' is central to the argument of Deutsch, and of Hess and Shipman. If social class categories represent 'statements of probability that the child will encounter certain types of experience' (Hess and Shipman 1968, p. 92), then experience of language being used *to* him for purposes of instruction, and *by* him for finding out and solving problems, is seen as what the lower-class child has largely missed. There is the gulf between *what* he has learned in his home, and *how* he has learned it, and the communicative demands made on him in school. He may be quite unprepared for vital aspects of the pupil role—for prolonged listening, for understanding verbal instructions, for answering questions and regarding adults as a source of information and answers, and for adopting an active approach to problem-solving (Deutsch 1967, pp. 78–9). The wide definition of what is lacking leads to an equally wide-ranging statement of the remedies required. Broadly, the approach involves filling the 'experiential gaps', providing those 'missing' experiences likely to stimulate new or more effective uses of language. What is needed may *include* 'special training in such areas as vocabulary development, general ease in self-expression leading to lengthy but meaningful verbalisation, greater exactness in sound discrimination, and in precision in the use of language' (Deutsch *et al.*

1967, p. 227). But the main means of 'compensation' provide and emphasize experience of language to analyse, explore and explain. The socio-linguistic relevance of the approach will be considered in detail in section 3. In rejecting the idea of *linguistic* deficit, Hess has argued that language *follows* social structure, and that changes in the context that evokes speech will be far more effective than working directly with vocabulary or grammar. And where Bereiter and Engelmann base their remedial language programme on a pre-structured and teacher-controlled sequence of tasks, Deutsch calls for a school context 'in which the verbal matrix would be reflected in a person-orientation rather than a closed-end status orientation, the child encouraged to ask questions, seek reasons, choose alternatives, make his own active inquiries so that he can better inter-relate his experiences' (1967, pp. 78–9).

2. 'DIFFERENT, NOT DEFICIENT': THE 'MYTH' OF VERBAL DEPRIVATION

Behind programmes of 'compensatory' education lies the authority of social scientific theory and data. Behind language-remediation pro-grammes directed at lower-class children lies a view of 'verbal deprivation' which its critics reject as linguistically absurd, as sympto-matic of a general rejection of cultural diversity, and as yet another attempt to explain away the failure of the schools. Some criticisms of the evidence for deprivation have already been examined. They are part of a wider controversy which can only be touched on here (see Edwards and Hargreaves 1976). Briefly, 'deficit theory' is said to rest on a 'social pathology' model of cultural difference which channels both the collection and interpretation of data. It involves assumptions about the superiority of 'standard' forms of behaviour, and so about the legitimacy of imposing standard templates upon *non*-standard behaviour. A disadvantage arising from a difference is not the same thing as a deficit. It is made to look like one because the assumed superiority of mainstream culture justifies a normative approach to cultural diversity. The resulting 'deficits' are created by the measures used, and by the socio-centric assumptions underlying them. Yet the behaviours so labelled are functionally adequate in their context (S. Baratz 1970: S. and J. Baratz 1970: Leacock 1971, pp. 24–7).

This defence of cultural relativism is a powerful one. But it raises its own difficulties. It is immediately necessary to specify the context within which behaviour is being described, and the standpoint from which any judgment of its 'adequacy' is made. The difficulty is high-lighted in the study of language. Standard or 'normative' measures impose narrow definitions of 'correctness'; set to find what is missing, the researcher is likely to ignore what is said, and to record what is not. The 'different but not deficient' approach has been invaluable in showing the range of systematic variation within a language, and the equivalent structural complexity of social dialects. But its practitioners sometimes fail to distinguish between an *absolute* linguistic inferiority, which there is every reason to reject, and an inferiority relative to some of the communicative demands and expectations encountered outside the particular sub-culture. The 'pathology model' is blamed by the Baratzes for 'forcing the misguided egalitarian into testing a racist assumption that some languages are better than others'. But Standard English may be 'better' in some contexts, for some purposes. Its use may avoid eliciting unfavourable stereotypes, manage im-pressions more favourably, and facilitate interaction with strangers. 'The objection is surely not to *any* evaluation of speech, but to a non-specific, decontextualised use of "better", with all its possible cognitive and "moral" connotations' (Edwards and Hargreaves 1976). When their own argument moves from broad principles to details, critics of deficit theory often make such relative assessments themselves—the Baratzes, for example, describing Black English as a handicap in 'attempts to negotiate with the standard-English speaking main-stream'. It is important, then, to look closely at the various educational implications of this emphasis on language *differences*, and at how the problems appear from this perspective.

Emphasis on the 'fully-developed' nature of non-standard language leads naturally to a rejection of the dire cognitive consequences attributed to its use. Whatever their social significance, 'there is simply no evidence that certain formal characteristics interfere with the learning of anything except other formal characteristics' (Horner and Gussow 1972, p. 172). All the 'basic tools' of thought are already there, their apparent absence being the result of a deep failure to recognize them in non-standard forms. It is this failure which allows the 'evidence' that black disadvantaged children lack the *concepts* of e.g. plurality, or possession, or past-time, to be completely discounted. A much-quoted example is the importance Bereiter gave to the absence of the conditional 'if' ('I asked Alvin if he wanted to go') when the NNE translation ('I axed Alvin did he want to go') carries the same logical structure. There is no justification, certainly in our present state of knowledge, for equating any form of overt language with particular modes or levels of thought (John 1971: Houston 1970).

And that 'concrete-abstract' polarity referred to in the previous section is objectionable on several grounds—its residue of earlier attempts to differentiate the thinking of 'primitive' and 'civilized' man; the neglect of the complex and abstract conceptual abilities demonstrated in the fact of learning *any* language; the arbitrary definition of 'abstract' which ignored, for example, the high use of metaphor also supposed to characterize lower-class language; and the premature acceptance of different *verbal* styles as evidence of underlying cognitive processes (Drucker 1971). Even before the full confrontation with verbal deprivation evidence was underway, Cazden (1966) doubted whether non-standard speech could be considered as anything more than a *social* handicap. In the full flood of radical criticism, Labov argued that 'negro children in the urban ghettoes receive a great deal of verbal stimulation, hear more well-formed sentences than middle-class children, and participate fully in a highly verbal culture: they have the same basic vocabulary, possess the same capacity for conceptual learning, and use the same logic as anyone else who learns to speak and understand English' (1969b, p. 2). The statement shows a triumph of good intentions over evidence, a willingness to match the gloomy guess-work of deficit theory with optimistic guess-work from the other side. What Labov more properly emphasizes is that the *cognitive* superiority of Standard English is unproven, that it remains to be shown which aspects contribute to complexity and precision of thought, and which are matters merely of *stylistic* elaboration. He might have reinforced his scepticism with an argument used earlier about 'High' varieties in diglossic situations—that their association with prestigious activities makes them *seem* more beautiful or more logical. If intellectual instruction is normally given in Standard English, a convention may well seem a necessity, and a correlation be taken as a cause (see pp. 46–7). It will then be difficult to take seriously those who talk in markedly non-standard ways. When Labov denies that there is any basis for 'attributing poor educational performance to the grammatical and phonological characteristics of any non-standard dialect of English' (1969b, p. 1), he is proclaiming the principle of linguistic equality at the structural level. How teachers and others *respond* to those characteristics may still contribute to educational failure.

'A cultural relativist position affirms the functional utility of behavioural differences, and recasts the solution to our current social problems in terms of acculturation, and not integration or separation' (S. Baratz 1970, p. 64). New patterns of behaviour must be learned from the familiar cultural base, the old patterns being respected and used. Again, the general argument is highlighted in its sociolinguistic form. Awareness of *different* speech systems alerts teachers to the possibility of 'interference', and checks the ignorant disvaluing of non-standard forms. An obvious practical implication is the unfairness of charting language development with only standard measures (see pp. 121–2). The association of dialect with deficit is then the 'product of a circular argument which first defines linguistic competence in Standard English terms and then proves that dialect speakers are incompetent' (Wight 1971, p. 5). Scoring procedures for some standard intelligence tests are also biassed towards the grammar of standard English. There have been attempts, not always with significant results, to redress the balance by translating a test into non-standard form (e.g. Quay 1971), and to find communicative settings, tasks, language and scoring procedure compatible with the experience of different cultural groups (Ervin-Tripp 1971b). Their main importance so far has lain in their recognition of a possible gulf between what the child has learned outside the classroom and what he is expected to know when he enters it, and of the school's responsibility to move some of the way to bridge that gulf.

A practical application of this approach has been the use of vernacular material when children are learning to read. Refusal to do so provides one 'simple cultural explanation' for educational failure, and willingness to do so illustrates the possibility of working *with* what the child already knows. The example has been most striking in relation to ethnic dialects (J. Baratz 1969a; 1971: Wight and Norris 1970). In learning to read, the black child faces the common task of learning a new set of symbols and how they relate to the spoken word. If the language of the books is very different from what he uses himself *and* from what he normally hears, he faces a double task of decoding and 'translating'. Obviously there is no simple one-to-one relationship between the spelling and the sound. This is true for all children, and teachers allow for it. The special problems arise when non-standard versions are not seen in this way—when a reading or a spelling is an accurate rendering of a word *as the child knows it*, and yet is rejected as an error. If the teacher is culturally and linguistically insensitive, and such 'errors' are frequent, the child may come to feel that there is something terribly wrong with his language, and with himself. *Using* the dialect in the early stages of reading has the double advantage of reducing the strangeness of the task, and granting the child's language some admittance to the classroom. The concessions needed are not extreme. Since he can understand more of the Standard than he can use, and will probably expect to find it in the specialized activities of reading and writing, it will be enough to retain the sentence patterns of the dialect. Vocabulary and spelling can be conventional. What follows is part of a story devised by Stewart (1970, p. 129) 'from the language these children actually use':

> It's a girl names Shirley Jones live in Washington. Most everybody on her street like her, 'cause she a nice girl. And all the children Shirley be with in school like her too. Shirley treat all of them just like they was her sisters and brothers, but most of all she like one boy name Charles. Shirley she be knowing Charles 'cause all two of them in the same grade, and he in her class . . .

Such use of the dialect is a means to an end, which is acculturation into the mainstream in respect of this critical skill. It is followed by the use of 'transition' readers for the move from vernacular to standard. The aim is to add to the vernacular, not replace it. Indeed, if reading and writing materials were restricted to Black English (or Creole), it would help to make black and white speech repertoires discontinuous, and so reinforce social distance. A similar approach is taken in the 'Breakthrough to Literacy' scheme, in which the breakthrough is both to the written medium and to standard dialect. This project is concerned with *social class* differences, and its inspiration is Halliday's 'social perspective' on language use. The language the child brings with him to school is seen as a central resource from which he should not be insensitively cut off. As a first step, children create their own sentences from basic words written on cards. Story-books are then built up from samples of their speech in such a way as to be 'sociologically indeterminate' in content and form (Mackay *et al.* 1970, p. 142).

This is a highly specialized area of enquiry but it raises some important general issues. If there is a case for vernacular and transition readers, is there also a case for vernacular and transition curricula, teachers, and teaching styles? If the answer is 'yes', but only as an intermediate stage, then this could be seen as a more subtle version of the old assimilationist policy. If the answer is a long-term 'yes', extending throughout schooling, it would indicate a wish for educational and cultural segregation or, putting the point more favourably as Kochman (1972b) does, an explicit acceptance of cultural pluralism. Most critics of deficit theory want some 'negotiation' with the mainstream to take place, and seek a reconstruction of means rather than of ends (e.g. S. and J. Baratz 1970). The use of vernacular teaching materials is one step in this direction, and its practical effectiveness is so far uncertain. It seems likely that the structural contrasts between the child's speech and the written material presented to him are less important than the attitudes arising from them. 'If the Baratz-Stewart materials do result in faster learning, one reason might be their effects on teacher attitudes. If teachers believe the child has a language and culture of his own that they themselves do not fully understand, they are less likely to treat him as "deficient" . . . Therefore research on the effects of (such) materials should include some sensitive indices (perhaps of the Lambert speech-guise type) of changes in social attitudes towards dialect speakers . . .' (Ervin-Tripp 1971b, p. 57). The same point can be made in relation to assessment in its broadest sense—teachers' daily response to their pupils, and the expectations which they make apparent. As was argued earlier, children whose habitual speech may be very different from the 'Classroom Register' may be adept at 'code-switching'. In doing so, they may sometimes over-correct or show stylistic inconsistencies which are then taken as evidence of errors or of generally unsystematic speech. And while that 'Classroom Register' may be their most 'careful' level of performance, it will not be their 'best'. Premature assessment of their linguistic ability may have the most far-reaching consequences. Even in relation to reading, it has not been proved that understanding *written* language is significantly affected by dialect usage, and where the dialect is itself highly valued, it seems to present no particular problems. What *does* create the problems is the teachers' failure to respect linguistic difference, and their consequent expectations of failure.

The same *social* emphasis should be given to general difficulties of comprehension across dialect 'lines', between pupils and between pupils and teachers. At the level of simple referential understanding, these might seem obvious. Sustained communication is rarely heard word for word, and meanings are frequently anticipated or 'retrodicted' from the context. The ability to do this successfully will depend on previous experience of communications of that kind, and will be affected by marked dialect differences. But as we saw, there is little evidence that pupils face serious problems at *this* level of understanding. Much more striking is the evidence of unconscious 'translations' from one dialect to another, and of the receptive competence which these demand (see pp. 121–2). What has not been tested, to my knowledge, is teachers' understanding of pupils' speech. Indeed, their daily experience of language may be so much less varied that they lack that receptive competence they tacitly expect of their pupils (Troike 1969). At the most obvious level of accent, I encountered a difficulty in the first football trial I took in a London school, when I recorded more aspiring players from Form 1I than there were boys in the form. To my untutored Welsh ear, 1A and 1I were identical, both sounding as 'eye'. Accounts of Black Vernacular in America and of Creole in English schools have identified similar 'objective' difficulties in hearing the right word which are quite distinct from the mutual attitudes and evaluations of speaker and listener—e.g. the frequent simplification of final consonant clusters and a loss of the post-vocalic (r) and (l) which blur the distinction between pass and past, wind and wine, sore and saw etc., and the loss of inflections which make the understanding of tense, case and gender more dependent on the linguistic context than is usual in standard English. These difficulties are important, especially where a teacher's frequent expression of incomprehension may deter the child from saying very much at all. But they are less important than the evaluations that may be based on them, or justified by them. In Labov's somewhat melodramatic statement, too many teachers hear in Negro Non-Standard English not a dialect different from their own, but 'the primitive mentality of the savage mind' (1969b, p. 27). The same comment might be made about any markedly non-standard speech; equating it with conceptual deficiencies can provide a 'theoretical' basis for prejudices already held.

What evidence is there that this happens? Williams (1970) asked inner-city American teachers to evaluate recorded speech samples from socially and ethnically differentiated children. Sounding 'low class' was associated with the raters' perception of a general lack of confidence in the speaker and his use of non-standard features. Ratings of speakers' status could be reliably predicted from such indicators as incidence of pausing, verb forms, subject-verb agreement, and the articulation of such phonemes as (th). These subjective judgments corresponded closely to assessments made independently by trained linguists. White teachers tended to equate race with social status because they seemed to equate non-standardness with both low social class and linguistic ineffectiveness. This stereotyped response was so prevalent that speech was seen as making a critical contribution to teacher expectations and so, through the operation of the self-fulfilling prophecy, to pupil achievement. Two other studies in which Wallace Lambert participated follow from his preoccupation with speech as a 'conspicuous indication' of cultural group, and so of the characteristics conventionally attributed to it (see pp. 28–30). Recordings of children's speech were combined with their photographs, drawings, and essays as 'evidence' from which student teachers rated various qualities. Speech provided highly significant cues to how intelligent, self-confident and socially privileged the children were thought to be, and even to whether they were considered 'good students'. This research used very inadequate speech samples—a passage read aloud after two trial runs, which surely emphasized the test-like nature of the occasion and risked that social class bias discussed in the last chapter. The teachers were also being forced to make instant judgments they would normally suspend until more evidence was available. The results are therefore less interesting than the suggestion, needing much more extensive research, that teachers may base their academic evaluation of children on what is strictly irrelevant information (Seligman *et al.* 1972). Frender and Lambert (1972) used still more constraining tasks, and they themselves criticized the narrow sampling of speech (in their defence, they also note the extreme difficulty of recording 'spontaneous output' while also controlling for content). Speech ratings by linguists were compared with the school grades and I.Q. of ten-year old boys from four English schools in Montreal. The aim was to find evidence as to whether speech style could be seen as mediating teachers' expectations, and whether 'the speech variables could increase the amount of variance in school performance over and above that explained by the more traditional predictors'. There were moderate correlations between I.Q. and favourable ratings of pitch, fluency and 'confidence' of intonation, but no significant relationship between standardness of pronounciation and school grades when intelligence was controlled. The lack of evidence of social discrimination in this research is not surprising, since all the subjects were lower working-class. A wider social range would surely have made a more interesting and relevant study. But in the longer perspective of Lambert's work, lower-class speakers were generally rated as less 'competent'—no less 'kind' or 'humorous', but as relatively lacking in intelligence, confidence and ambition. 'This selective perception of class-marked speech suggests that the low status speaker runs a greater risk of being taken for a good-natured clod or an honest peasant' (Frender and Lambert 1972, p. 245).

If this is true, it could be argued that schools should concentrate on the Pygmalion aspects of linguistic disadvantage. The dialectologist Raven McDavid adopts just this approach, writing of teachers' obligation to give their students sufficient command of 'the English of educated people' to achieve the economic and social position to which their intelligence and ambition 'entitled' them. Irrelevant barriers would then be removed. Those speech forms most likely to elicit stereotyped responses should be identified and made the target of specific remedial action. This would imply no general disvaluing of the speaker's cultural background. Teachers themselves would have enough linguistic knowledge to avoid making irrelevant judgments themselves, and they and their students would be allies against those who would 'do the student down' unless he acquired the additional skills to evade their prejudices (McDavid 1966: 1969b). The argument might seem to trivialize the problems of 'verbal deprivation'. But it properly emphasizes the entirely *socio-political* superiority of Standard English. It is because he assumes *cognitive* deficiencies in non-standard speech that Bereiter (1965) urges fundamental remedial action before the child starts school, whereas a 'stylistic' facility in Standard English needs only to be acquired 'some time' before he leaves the education system. His critics confine their attention to the social implications of linguistic difference. Because 'upward mobility is impossible for under-dogs who have not learned middle-dog barking, we must teach it to them for use in their excursions into the middle-dog world' (Sledd 1969, p. 1313). Such teaching would be for highly context-specific purposes—e.g. for those occasions when it is important for the speaker not to arouse negative reactions which might lead to the disvaluing of himself or of his message. Whether profound or superficial from a linguistic perspective, differences which are socially stigmatized should be placed under the speaker's control, to be 'monitored' when he chooses. In terms of an earlier discussion, they should be markers rather than indicators. It is a matter of addition, not replacement—a matter of extending the verbal repertoire.

Sensibly utilitarian as this approach may seem, and sensibly empty of unproven statements of cognitive deficiencies, it is itself open to some objections. The necessary 'lessons' would certainly be rejected by those who *intend* to speak in ways which symbolize their ethnic or social class identity. If part of the 'problem' is to get people to do what they *do not* do rather than what they *cannot* do, then there will be powerful intervening influences of group loyalty and affiliation. Allen (1969) points to an obvious motivational difference between learning a second language and learning a second dialect—that students may not recognize, or may reject, the 'need' for the latter. How is the teacher to indicate that need without seeming to criticize the speaker and his community? The problem is acute if he thinks he already uses the standard dialect, or if he denies the authority of the definition of standardness. In the conference session at which Allen developed this argument, there was an interruption from a black member of the audience, 'outraged and insulted' by the discussion and insistent on the autonomy of Black English. There were some adroit responses from the floor—Stewart denying that linguists meant anything evaluational by the term non-standard, and Labov complimenting the protester for the sociolinguistic competence displayed by the 'appropriate' standardness of her outburst (Alatis 1969, pp. 198–202). But that outburst at least drew attention to attitudes towards language differences in the dominant culture. McDavid himself seems to see his standard-dialect 'lessons' as a short-term tactic, emphasizing as the larger strategy the need to accept the legitimacy of all dialects (1969a, p. 100). This in turn could be seen as part of a wider acceptance of cultural diversity. From another standpoint, however, the approach can be seen as merely a palliative. Even if the removal of status-revealing clues were both eagerly sought after and successfully accomplished, it would achieve little unless accompanied by complementary changes in the rest of the speaker's environment. If opportunities remain closed to 'people like you', the fact that you speak as you do will rightly seem unimportant beside the basic facts of how power and wealth are distributed. Indeed, it is tempting to argue that changes in speech will follow anyway the decision to 'make one's way' in the world (Plumer 1971). Directing attention to ways in which the response to differences in speech *makes them into* 'deficiencies' has been an invaluable area of research and argument. But defining the 'inferiority' of ethnic and social class dialects in socio-political terms also directs attention to deeper sources of inequality and discrimination.

What linguists call contrastive analysis shows up the intrusion of features from one speech system into the speaker's performance in another. The intrusion may show itself in accent, vocabulary or grammar. But verbal communication depends on far more than these. The earlier discussion of possible dialect barriers to understanding was concerned solely with referential meaning—i.e. could the listener directly identify *what* was being talked about. Much of Chapter 2 was concerned with *social* meaning, with the ways in which choice among referential equivalents can be used to e.g. express feelings and define a social relationship. In this area of enquiry, 'what is at stake is not logic, rationality, reasoning power, but what we think of each other and of ourselves' (Hymes: in Cazden *et al.* 1972, p. xxxl). There has been very little research in classrooms into the systematic com- munication of hostility, respect or deference, and into *how* it is understood and often misunderstood. The speech used by pupils *and* teachers can provide stereotypical cues to other assumed attributes. It can also create and maintain social distance, leading to a disvaluing of the speaker's world because of the way he speaks, or his disvaluing of the experience of others because of the way they speak to him. Speech may be a way of asserting difference. On the teacher's side, the neighbour- hood dialect may be brusquely excluded from the classroom, or seen as in permanent need of correction. On their side, pupils may emphasize non-standard features so as to assert their own cultural identity against his. Even without such deliberate intent, their ways of speaking may make it difficult for them to give accounts of their actions and attitudes which satisfy their teacher, or even make sense to him. The emphasis here is on ways of speaking, or more broadly, of communicating. They include not only formal features of speech, but intonation, pitch, volume, speed of delivery, facial expression, stance and gesture (e.g. Byers and Byers 1972). One recent description of the 'culture-shock' frequently experienced by teachers and pupils in American inner-city classrooms begins the chapter on verbal communication problems with a quotation from Genesis—'Come let us go down, and there confuse their language that they may not understand one another's speech.' The reference is to *all* aspects of verbal communication, and the aim is to make teachers of ghetto adolescents more sensitive to double meanings, different meanings, intended and unintended insults (Foster 1974, pp. 117–72). There is detailed material too on such Black speech events as 'signifying' and 'playing the dozens', so that the teacher can recognize what kind of exchange is taking place, identify its ritualized forms, and realize when an exchange has explosive possibilities. More general still is the information on the importance in ghetto society of acting tough verbally, of putting on a verbal display, and of 'putting whitey on'. The reference has broadened to the whole area of communicative competence, and to possible discontinuity between what counts as appropriate communication inside and outside the classroom.

Sociolinguistic analysis has extended the meaning of 'interference' to include systems *for* language use—to knowledge about when to speak, and what about, and at what level of formality and explicitness. 'When a child from one developmental matrix enters a situation in which the communicative demands are defined in terms of another, misperception and misanalysis may occur at every level' (Hymes 1972a, p. 287). In its wider meaning, a speech community is made up of those who share the same *ways of speaking*, and of interpreting speech. In this wider sense, teachers and pupils may be communicative strangers. Thus an apparent inability to answer a question may arise from a different understanding of what constitutes a question, or an appropriate answer, especially when that answer has to be given 'in public' and in the 'proper' form. Educationally relevant evidence of such differences was cited earlier. Passive listening is not normal in negro audiences and congregations, the extent of the verbal participation often creating a dialogue between speaker and listeners (Powell Williams 1972: Kochman 1972b). The audience is not only more expressive, but individually and physically so. If classroom etiquette requires the student to be still, and denies him the right to participate until officially authorized to do so, then what is normal behaviour in other contexts may appear to the teacher as a deliberate challenge to his authority. American Indians similarly blur the boundary between active performer and passive audience, and it is for the individual to decide how far he wishes to participate. In a classroom insensitive to such cultural differences, children may be bewildered by demands for prolonged reception interspersed with sudden demands for verbal contributions (Philips 1970; 1972). Communicative competence also refers to how the child perceives and categorizes social situations, and differentiates his ways of speaking accordingly. We know nothing about how such categorizations are learned, and little about sub-cultural differences in the judgments made e.g. about when formality or explicitness is appropriate. Children from some social groups will be *socio*-linguistically disadvantaged if the speech contexts in which they are most at ease are largely alien to the classroom, and if the purposes to which they normally put language are missing, or pointedly ex-cluded. As was argued earlier, the principle of linguistic equality is a recognition of equal *potential*. Opponents of deficit theory do not argue that non-standard varieties are simply different ways of saying the same things, or of 'doing' the same things with words. Beginning with the 'time-honoured dictum that all languages are adequate to meet the needs of the communities that speak them', Horner and Gussow (1972) see the problem of social class differences in language as lying mainly in patterns of use. How close a match is there between the *uses* most relevant to the demands of home and neighbourhood, and those encountered in the schools?

3. 'RADICALLY DIFFERENT SYSTEMS OF COMMUNICATION'

In many accounts of verbal deprivation, Bernstein's work has been freely quoted as supporting evidence. For example, he is said by Bereiter and by Jensen to have 'shown' the limited, 'illogical' nature of lower-class language and thinking. Not surprisingly then, he has been fiercely attacked by critics of the concept. Describing his views as 'filtered through a strong bias against all forms of working-class behaviour', Labov questions whether the elaborated code is anything more than an elaborated style, lacking any cognitive superiority (1969b, pp. 4, 12). Caught in the cross-fire, Bernstein has rejected the interpretations of both sides. In fact, he has faced both ways at different times. Though he has blamed critics and exponents for misunderstanding him, he *has* argued a profound educational disadvantage, arising from the social conditioning of language use, which is not easy to distinguish from a deficit. He has also rejected any notion of *sub-standard* language, and maintained his radical credentials with a strong attack on compensatory education. Both his theory and the evidence for it have already been examined in detail. What is important here is the changing nature of the communicative discontinuity which he has identified.

In relation to his *early* writing, the denial of any contribution to deficit theory is disingenuous. Lower working-class children were confidently described as less sensitive to words as mediators of feelings and ideas, less curious about their environment, and more 'rigid' in their thinking. They were less able to communicate exact logical distinctions, or relationships needing to be precisely formulated. They were progressively pointed towards description rather than analysis. Simply, they were less equipped to learn (1958, pp. 160–5; 1959, pp. 312–13; 1961a, p. 303). The account was 'especially depressing' because it suggested that the lower-class child did not merely lack critical skills, but had 'learned a self-perpetuating code that effectively bars him from acquiring them' (Bereiter and Engelmann 1966, p. 32). And in a paper written principally for teachers, Bernstein *was* deeply depressing. Certain ways of thinking were facilitated through the social shaping of children's speech, and some were not. 'To ask a middle-class child to qualify verbally his individual experience, generalise, order a verbally presented problem, is to ask him to develop: to a working-class child, it is a demand for change' (1961b, p. 175). The inference of a relative cognitive poverty seems to align him, at least at this stage of his work, with the deficit theorists whose company he has so often denied. Indeed, the overlap with the work of Deutsch, and of Hess and Shipman, is considerable. Though the implied adequacy of the 'documentation' is misleading, what follows is not too distorted a précis. 'As documented by Bernstein, the language environment of lower-class children is likely to differ sharply from that of middle-class children. Adults, for the latter, use language to extend the child's experience . . . For lower-class children . . . a harsh, limiting, inconsistent language . . . develops passivity, inhibits curiosity, and militates against adequate adjustment to school' (McCandless 1969, p. 815). That interpretation could be supported again and again by quotations from his early writing. Yet he has claimed consistency in his statements that 'code restriction does not constitute linguistic or cultural deprivation', only a social constriction of choice from the 'same' linguistic resources. In the very paragraph in which that claim is made, code restriction *is* equated with 'educational deficit . . . from a specific psychological viewpoint' (in Gahagan and Gahagan 1970, p. 117). The last phrase defies understanding, for the argument ends at that point. *What* is that 'specific psychological viewpoint'? Indeed, the larger enterprise was to show how social class was 'made substantive', how subcultural differences in socialization shaped the cognitive development of children and so their ability to benefit from school.

The cognitive correlates of a restricted code were investigated in several SRU studies (e.g. Robinson and Creed 1968). These raise all the questions discussed in Chapter 3 about how the communicative tasks were perceived. Social class differences in e.g. explicitness may have arisen from different definitions of the task, and the kind of meanings appropriate to it. If so, they did not represent an intractable deficiency, but were open to situational manipulation. It may be true that for the habitual restricted code user, 'the subtleties of private emotion may be felt but not raised to the level of specific verbal meanings', or that 'precise logical relationships' are not expressed (Gahagan and Gahagan 1970, pp. 12–13). And the explanation for this *may* lie in verbal ability. But this is emphatically not what Bernstein's later theory suggests, in either its sub-cultural or social-psychological aspects. The determinism of the early papers has been profoundly relaxed through the switch in emphasis from speech codes to speech variants. In the analysis of sub-cultural influences, this directs attention to 'critical contexts' of socialization. In the analysis of situational influences, it directs attention to 'the dictates of the local relationship'. A restricted code is not taken to mean that expressions of uncertainty or individualized meaning will never be used, or are not 'available', '*only* that there is a restriction on the contexts in which they are used'. That 'only' is heavily stressed. The implications of this approach were the basis for the experimental language programme devised in Bernstein's Research Unit, which combined some formal 'training' (or 'drill'), attempts to develop greater sensitivity to speech, and a wide range of communicative tasks which the children would see as requiring explicit and elaborated language. The overall purpose was to provide the kind of cognitive demands made on the middle-class child at home which led to his flexible use of language, and so bridge the gulf between what some other children had experienced and the communicative demands made on them in school (Gahagan and Gahagan 1970, pp. 37–50, 109).

The lower working-class child is no longer seen as wholly 'denied access to' elaborated codes. But his experience of them is likely to be relatively limited, or he may be oriented towards their use in rather different contexts. In this sense, educational failure is still explained in terms of 'radically different systems of communication'. A restricted code is entirely suited to some contexts and some purposes, and carries 'its own aesthetic'. Problems arise when those accustomed to its use move into contexts in which other communicative demands are made. In particular, 'it directs the child to orders of meaning and relevance that are not in harmony with those of the school' (Bernstein 1973a, p. 166). Why this 'is' so raises important questions about the sub-culture from which he comes, and about the kind of meanings and roles which are assumed to predominate in schools. I have never been convinced that the contrast is as sharp as Bernstein presents it. Descriptions of *both* sides of that relationship have been greatly simplified and over-generalized. The sub-cultural descriptions have been criticized already. What seems useful here, as a transition passage to the last chapter, is to consider briefly the references to schools.

Bernstein's argument is *not* reducible to a matter of stylistic elaboration because of its emphasis on the functions of language, and the kinds of meaning being transmitted. The 'discontinuity' which he identifies is not 'linguistic', but what he calls 'cultural' and might have called 'sociolinguistic'. The lower working-class pupil is described as having had less experience of elaborated speech variants in two areas of experience obviously relevant to school, those of control and instruction. He has learned to look to adults as the source of directives, but not for the reasons for their orders, or the principles by which he should control his own behaviour. He faces problems in school because he is not used to feeling a personal responsibility for his actions, or to lengthy probing of his motives, or to subtly-phrased and indirect commands. He has special difficulties in learning because his curiosity has been less often rewarded, his questions have less often been answered in ways directly relevant to them, his awkward questions have been more often evaded, and his attention has been drawn less often to the general principles underlying concrete examples. Above all, he has had less experience of being offered alternatives to explore, and problems to solve for which the solutions are diverse or uncertain. He will be ill at ease with the universalistic orders of meaning which are emphasized in schools.

There are two main directions from which this summary can be questioned. Are the lower working-class children like this? And are schools like this? The school end of this discontinuity of experience is described with infuriating vagueness. Justifiably enough, the main efforts of the SRU went into the intensive investigation of family roles and relationships. The orientation of the lower working-class child was towards 'closed' roles and particularistic meanings. Schools, however, 'are predicated upon an elaborated code and its system of social relationships' (1973a, p. 212; also 1970a, p. 117). Does this mean *all* schools, at all age levels, in all degrees of selectivity, in all varieties of expressive or instrumental orientation? There is an interesting contrast between the 'global' assumptions about schools in Bernstein's writing on language, and the carefully differentiated analysis to be found in his writing on organization and curriculum (Bernstein 1967; 1971). If disbelief is suspended, the idealization takes the following shape. In formal education, principles and operations are made verbally explicit. They are freed from their immediate context, and from the implicit background knowledge made available by a shared cultural identity. Such universalistic meanings can be self-consciously examined, the grounds for them scrutinized. Though at some risk of insecurity and even alienation, alternative realities can be contemplated. Meanings are therefore provisional, open to change. They can arise only from relationships that are themselves open to change—which are personal and achieved, not positional and ascribed. Entering such an environment, the lower working-class child steps into a symbolic system which provides few links with his life outside (Bernstein 1970a, p. 120). Yet all this would not be true of the highly ritualized, hierarchical school; or the 'closed' school: or the school where what counted as knowledge was strongly 'classified' and 'framed'. Selecting some 'traditional' characteristics of schools (such as are described in Bernstein's own writing), it could be argued that meanings are too often 'given' as part of a natural order which cannot be questioned; that children are too rarely encouraged actively to enquire, experiment, and 'create their own world on their own terms in their own way'; that the boundary between teacher and learner is too clear, the latter having too little discretion; and that the individual child is so submerged in the pupil role that meanings relate not to him but to the category in which he is fitted. The counter-argument is as tendentious and over-generalized as the original target. But when Bernstein describes, in relation to the critical contexts of socialization, the underlying system of communication which is regulated through a restricted code, it is tempting to see some schools as fitting that picture without undue distortion. In so far as they do, their lower working-class pupils should, in Bernstein's own terms, feel perfectly at home. An underlying restricted code is found where communication is 'realised through forms of speech where meanings are implicit, principles infrequently elaborated, qualified or explored, infrequently related to the specific experience of the child or the specific requirements of the local context, where alternative possibilities are infrequently offered, where questioning is less encouraged' (in Gahagan and Gahagan 1970, p. 116). If *some* schools resemble this description, then extending their working-class pupils' range of control over language (crudely, 'teaching them' an elaborated code) will require new roles, functions and communicative tasks more demanding than the traditional classroom routines. Otherwise there will be too *much* continuity between home and school experience of language. That suggestion must be tentative because we know so little about the forms and functions of classroom language, and about how the sociolinguistic rules relevant to them are learned and applied.

In the long tradition of research into the social determinants of educability, the school has remained a largely 'neglected variable', or complex of variables. To its demands, tacit and explicit, pupils respond selectively in terms of their previous experience. That selective response has directed the attention of researchers to the home, and to sources there of 'cultural', and communicative, discontinuity. But it is also essential to examine the demands themselves, and the problems they cause for many pupils—problems not always necessary to the main instructional purposes of schools. The theme of the next chapter is an extension of Cazden's (1970) comment on the neglect of context in language research. 'When a particular child makes or fails to make a particular utterance in a particular situation, look at the character of the situation as well as of the child.'

5.

The Language of the Classroom

As long as children are expected to write . . . upon subjects which afford them no opportunity for imitation of what has been well done in speech by their teacher . . . they are not likely to express themselves well. And when the subjects are such as deliberately throw them into the atmosphere of their out-of-school life, it is almost certain that they will express themselves in the language of the home and the street which, teachers constantly assure us, is ever in conflict with the language the school is trying to secure.

(Board of Education, *Report on the Teaching of English in Elementary Schools*, H.M.S.O., 1929.)

One of the reasons for the resistance of children to the middle-class norms is that their teachers advocate a language, and an attitude towards language, which is quite remote from everyday life . . . Almost everyone agreed that the speech of their high school English teachers was a remote and special dialect which had no utility for everyday life. (Labov 1966a, pp. 493–4.)

My last teacher, you could talk to him . . . we used to have giggles; he seemed to be the same sort of class as us; he wasn't stuck up. He was born in an area like this, and he talked like myself. He was a right Herbert. Whereas the others, any little thing you slipped up on, they'd give you a right rucking, the ladies especially—they talked posh, real English. Everything pronounced right, with a la-di-da accent. They probably went to high school themselves, where a lot of people do talk like that.

(Ex-Secondary Modern School pupil: in Peter Willmott, *Adolescent Boys of East London*, Penguin, 1969, p. 90.)

These quotations are a tendentious selection, chosen to exaggerate a theme. A frequent stylistic gulf between teachers and pupils, with all its social connotations and consequences, might be expected from arguments advanced earlier in the book. Classroom language is likely to be superposed over other varieties. At least in secondary schools, it is likely to be formal, aligning the classroom with the 'public' world of business and the professions. It is also 'formal' in Joos' sense. It is designed to *inform*, with few assumptions being made about the background knowledge of the hearers. It may descend quite often to the 'consultative' level, so allowing them to participate more actively. But for much of the time, the 'formal code labels' tell the pupil that 'he must wait until authorised to speak' (Joos 1962, p. 25). The kind of information being conveyed requires a high level of abstraction and impersonality. And the teaching of particular subjects depends on a hard core of essential specialized vocabulary, with a larger layer of more conventional subject-usage. The classroom, then, is a special kind of context for language use. For many, both teachers and taught, 'it has been a total inhibitor of the natural voice' (Creber 1972, p. 111).

The domains of school and home are sharply segregated in that official Report of 1929. Almost fifty years later, the Bullock Report (1975) recommends that the teacher 'should start where the child is, and should accept the language he brings to school'. The goal is a gradual *extension* of his communicative powers to meet new demands and situations, and the problems of linguistic discontinuity are sympathetically described. But while the school's 'civilising mission' is no longer insensitively proclaimed, a considerable stylistic gulf is still assumed.

There is no mistaking what follows for the 'language of the home and the street'.

> They were called city states because they were complete in themselves. They were governed by themselves, ruled by themselves, they supported themselves . . . These states were complete in themselves because the terrain between cities was so difficult that it was hard for them to communicate. Now because these people lived like this in their own cities, they tended to be intensely patriotic towards their own city. Now what's patriotic mean?
> (Barnes 1969, p. 55.)

Of course, there are no norms of appropriateness which 'require' such aridity of expression, and we can feel the teacher's relief as he emerges from his expositional maze. But there *are* reasons why he should expound, ask questions, and evaluate the answers, and why this talking is done in a style considerably removed from that of everyday life. In this chapter, some of the reasons are considered, in ways which apply to the language of classroom perspectives developed in other parts of the book. I hope that the discussion will provide both a useful example of applied sociology of language, and a useful approach to the study of classroom interaction.

1. SUBJECT REGISTERS AND 'CLASSROOM REGISTER'

Speech 'registers' are identified by the formal properties which make them stylistically distinctive, and by the activities and situation-types with which they are causally associated. Davies (1969) suggests a clear-cut division of labour in their study, sociologists 'presenting' different situations to which linguists attach systematic descriptions of the language used. Such descriptions are difficult because of the amount and diversity of data needed, the *range* of appropriateness in most registers making it too easy to mark out the linguistic 'boundaries' prematurely. Nor are the two 'sets' of correlated features easily brought together. We are often intuitively aware of a 'language of' (for example) religious services, and careful analysis might give shape to 'impressions of types of grammatical structures' which are felt rather than defined (Thorne 1970). But many situational categories are simply assumed to have some predictable linguistic identity which 'locates' them. At an extreme of verbal restriction, Halliday (1964) mentions the 'register' of bidding at bridge, which is so ready-coded in vocabulary and structure as to leave little room for dialectal or idiolectal variation. He also mentions the 'registers' of household chores and golf, which normally involve no more than the intrusion of specialized items of vocabulary into more general conversation. It trivializes the concept when a register is suggested for any *socially* defined activity without regard to its formal characterization. There is an obvious danger too of a merely circular argument, so that the register of politics 'is' the language of politicians talking *in role* about political matters. Such talk will have a preponderance of register-irrelevant material, which is true of almost any register; it *may* have very few features indeed which are not shared with civil servants and some business groups. In general, register is 'a slippery and unsatisfactory' area of enquiry, and one in which 'theory would do well to wait for practical analysis to catch up' (Davies 1968, p. 111: Crystal and Davy 1969, p. 62).

Subject registers

There are good reasons for caution in any predominantly *linguistic* discussion of school-subject registers. The best of these is that we know so little about the language teachers use. Even when describing written exposition, 'the language of' chemistry or economics is a metaphor, and may easily exaggerate the linguistic distinctiveness. Obviously there will be a proliferation of highly specific labels in areas of special concern, terminology being 'a complex inventory of the ideas, interests and occupations that take up the interest of the (academic) community' (Sapir 1949, p. 95). There may also be a high frequency of some sentence structures, like the prevalence of passive verbs and 'X+Y= (or→) Z' constructions found in chemistry texts—e.g. 'A large amount of hydrogen is made to combine with nitrogen to make ammonia' (Davies 1969: see also Barber 1962: Crystal and Davy 1969, pp. 251–3). But similar 'deep' structures would certainly be found in other scientific writing, and similar 'realizations' of description-cum-explanation might be almost as common in e.g. psychology or economics. Many such characteristics, however distinctive of the 'frozen' style of academic writing, would not be expected in the 'consultative' style of spoken exposition. Yet we know almost nothing about the adjustments teachers make to their 'subject language', about how far the 'language of' (for example) *history* teachers is an abridged or 'colloquialized' version of the 'language of' *historians*. The phrase itself was described as a metaphor, with misleading implications of discreteness. There seems no reason to extend far beyond vocabulary the differences between a teacher using the English language to teach chemistry, and his next-door colleague using it to teach economics. But even in stylistic analysis, the number of significant or distinctive features may be small, especially if the intention is to describe those unique to (or uniquely frequent in) a particular register. They may be entirely items of vocabulary and still have a critical importance if the focus of attention is their *social* significance. The earlier discussion of argot and jargon (pp. 22–6) can be extended, from this perspective, to include the 'special language' of subjects.

Any 'special language' is both 'an instrument of effective common action . . . and the means and symbol of group loyalty' (Lewis 1947, p. 49). This double function can be related to the distinction Rosen (1967) makes between the 'linguistic intellectual' and the 'linguistic conventional'. The first term refers to denotation, to words which are essential for precise and rapid communication between fellow-specialists, and which make discriminations for which everyday language (and other forms of academic language) have no need. The second refers to connotation, to the associations a word has for the insider, and the way it reinforces his sense of at least temporary separation from the everyday world. It marks the 'psychological reality' of the specialist group.

Because their concerns are sufficiently arcane to justify it, some subjects have a wide vocabulary of special terms so obviously different from everyday meanings that there is no risk of confusion. Subjects like history and sociology offer reflections on human affairs in a form partly special to themselves, partly drawn from the *general* currency of academic discussion, and partly resembling normal 'educated' usage. It is this 'semi-technical' usage which causes the greater problems— those words which have their usual meanings overlaid with special significance. It also raises more readily a question that can be asked of all academic language. Only by using the symbols common to his specialism can the academic communicate to his group, typifying experience in the same ways as they do. We can 'locate' him intellectually 'by ascertaining what words his functioning vocabulary contains, and what nuances of meaning and value they embody' (Wright Mills 1939). Does the 'vocabulary' which announces his academic 'membership' also represent a distinctively coloured 'set of spectacles . . . a veritable a priori form of perception and cognition' through which he 'sees' the world? (Mills 1963, pp. 459–60). The reader of this book has confronted some of the 'special language' of sociolinguistics, the dictionary of which contains some esoteric terms (e.g. diglossia, domain) and many more which are old words with new meanings, or nuances of meaning (e.g. competence, code, marker). Does it offer or facilitate new insights, new ways of observing, classifying and relating the phenomena? Or does it seem to be a 'translation' which adds nothing to the commonsense knowledge, a new way of *talking about* language which mystifies but does not enlighten?

Clearly, the line between the 'intellectual' and the 'conventional' is very blurred. This is nicely illustrated in Merton's addition of 'manifest' and 'latent' functions to the special language of sociology. 'Function' replaced 'purpose' because it avoided confusing observable and objective consequences with subjective intentions. 'Manifest' and 'latent' made the further distinction between consequences which were intended and recognized, and those which were neither. Christening the distinction would rightly be regarded by laymen as 'an affront to their intelligence and an offence against common intelligibility' unless it helped sociologists towards more systematic observation and analysis (Merton 1957, p. 61). The terms passed quickly into normal sociological discourse. But they have been attacked as a mere re-labelling, 'devoid of any explanatory or predictive power' (Andreski 1974, p. 58). And in a virtuoso display of slapdash aggression leavened by some sharp epigrams, Andreski makes a general attack on the 'smoke-screen' of social scientific jargon, the 'heavy clouds of opaque verbiage' which conceal platitudes because no one knows what is really being said. If truisms are made to seem obscure, profundity may be inferred. All disciplines have their 'verbal substitutions masquerading as contributions to knowledge', words which do no cognitive work but which create a sense of 'mystery'. Unfortunately, they are not as easily unmasked as Andreski suggests. One man's opaque verbiage is another man's necessary clarification. For example, role theory is notorious for its confusion of terms, a confusion which begins with the misuse of 'theory'. 'Role' itself is certainly no 'magic incantation which opens the sesame of otherwise inaccessible knowledge', but it is *not* replaceable by 'position' or 'place' (Andreski 1974, p. 82) without losing essential distinctions which role-analysis tries to make.

Barnes (1969, p. 43) gives a classroom example of 'hunting the label' which the non-specialist might dismiss as cognitively irrelevant and the specialist defend as a necessary item in the vocabulary of geography. The shape of sand-dunes, which the teacher calls 'an unusual, a specific . . . a special shape', has to be described as a 'crescent'. 'Like waves', 'an arc', and 'humpy up and down' are welcomed only as steps towards a precisely located terminological target. The 'right' word eventually snared is not the idiosyncratic preference of the teacher, but a 'technical' term judged to be necessary for future learning. Elsewhere, Barnes quotes a classroom explanation of why men pray—because 'God *provides*'—which also depends on a 'right' word, but one totally lacking any professional agreement that other words (and reasons) would not do as well (1969, p. 49). These are easy examples. In practice, the distinction between the linguistic-intellectual and conventional is usually hard to make. In principle, it may be critical in analysing problems of linguistic discontinuity between home and school because it attempts to separate the 'necessary' *cognitive* barriers to learning from those which are *socio-cultural* and 'unnecessary'. This separation has been a large part of the argument against 'deficit theory' (pp. 132–40), and will be touched on again in relation to 'classroom register'. If a subject register *is* apparent, are pupils expected to use it, or just understand it; is a receptive or a productive competence required? Do they learn it by imitation, or by coping with subject-specific tasks in which the form is determined by the function? How does the teacher 'mediate' between the language of his pupils, and that which he considers appropriate to his subject? When a teacher says something like this, is it a one-man performance which he does not yet expect his pupils to match, or does he expect an approximation to it, or does he 'translate' pupil contributions into the appropriate form while responding to the content of what they say?

> Put that into the distillation flask and then distil off, and then we get thermometer recording the correct temperature which is boiling point for acetone. Then we collect the acetone which came over as a distillate.
>
> (Barnes 1969, p. 51.)

L.C.C.—6

The questions indicate something of the range and longitudinal nature of the evidence which would be needed to provide the answers. They also indicate the importance of the teacher providing frequent opportunity for his pupils to try out their new vocabulary, and test their meanings against his. Periodic samples of their contributions might show the gradual acquisition of a subject-identity, and their differential knowledge of the 'language' might provide a measure of their absorption in the 'sub-culture' (cf. Lerman 1967). What is most likely is an unpredictable mixture of specialist and non-specialist language, frequent and rapid 'code-switching' being what we would expect from research into 'second-dialect' learning. Indeed, this is likely to be a feature of teachers' speech too, their sudden awareness of a gulf in expression and understanding between themselves and their pupils leading to frequent breaches of the normal stylistic 'rules of co-occurrence'.

The 'linguistic intellectual' refers to forms of expression which make the structure of the subject available to the pupil, and are a necessary part of it. But teachers' preoccupation with terminology goes far beyond this, to particular selections among referential equivalents which carry powerful *social* meanings. These can usefully be seen as situational *markers*. The alternative formulation offered by the teacher may often be a 'substitution masquerading as a contribution to knowledge', but it helps to symbolize and reinforce a different 'reality'. It marks off academic from everyday knowledge, *and* a *particular* academic territory. The pupil learns that he is entering a different world of experience in which his commonsense knowledge is largely irrelevant, and may well be excluded. The use of a subject register, in the sense in which we have used the term here, is inseparable from the authority of the teacher, and is a main means of signalling the appropriate teacher and learner roles. The implications for classroom interaction will be considered later. But by the language he uses, the teacher is effectively saying—'This is the reality which is chemistry, and this is how we talk about it. Other kinds of reality don't matter for the next forty minutes, and you must see things my way.' It is a means of *framing*, as Bernstein describes the separation of knowledge from not-knowledge, the 'degree of control (by the teacher) over the selection, organisation and pacing of the knowledge transmitted and received' (1971, p. 50).

However valid it may seem to the observer, the distinction between the linguistic and the conventional is likely to seem unreal to the pupil. What the teacher regards as cognitively indispensable is still experienced by the pupil as a form of social control, emphasizing his dependence on the teacher's definition of what is acceptable. It is part of the larger process by which the 'worlds' of home and school are separated.

'Classroom register'

In what Rosen has called 'the language of secondary education', a consistent formality of speech is seen as a means of preserving social distance between teacher and pupil, and as a persistent reminder of the special and serious business of learning. Like conventional subject-usage, but in a more general way, it involves linguistic constraints which are social rather than intrinsic to the material being learned. Houston's (1970) term 'classroom register' refers to a *range* of styles. It is a range which includes the language expected of anyone in 'authority', and which excludes much of the everyday language of children. Both approaches represent the predominant use of 'standard' or 'formal' language in schools as an essential part of the transmission of the mainstream culture, with its 'authoritative' definitions of what is normal and proper. Its acquisition marks a social rather than a cognitive change in the learners, and is a test of their acculturation. The main argument has been stated at length, especially in Chapter 4, and will be restated briefly as preliminary to analysing the situation in which classroom language is used.

Non-standard language may be 'intrinsically usable for the full range of language functions' (Cazden 1972, p. 156), but its potential utility is irrelevant beside the strong social barriers to its use. Language is a social denominator in any stratified society, and where one language or variety has an obvious prestige, some facility in its use is likely to be seen as an indicator of suitability for secondary or higher education. Access to it can therefore be a critical influence on the distribution of knowledge, and Bourdieu's broader account of 'cultural inheritance' can be given a strong sociolinguistic flavour. The transmission of culture 'is in direct relation to the distance between the linguistic and cultural competence implicitly demanded by the schools, and the competence inculcated by the home'. Cultural wealth belongs to those with the means of acquiring it, 'who hold the code making it possible to decipher cultural goods' (Bourdieu 1973, pp. 73, 81). One vital question is whether the school provides what it demands—whether the 'code' is made available to those not already equipped with it—or whether the initial inequalities are preserved and 'sanctified'. The same question may be asked even if that 'code' is defined as a more appropriate or prestigious *style* rather than as an especially powerful tool of thought. A further question relates to the sensitivity of the school's response to linguistic difference, and to how sharp and pervasive are the boundaries between what is acceptable and what is not. A 'sensitive' approach does not mean a denial of difference, but an explicit recognition that 'standardness' is appropriate for some occasions and purposes—for example, in written language, where its functional advantages are most obvious. The point is argued by Fishman and Salmon (1972) in an analogy with the co-existence in Swabian classrooms of regional dialect and Standard German. Here, 'getting educated' and using the standard are not considered identical, and teachers themselves use the dialect in class discussion. There is no persistent stylistic gulf between them and their students, with its connotations of intellectual and social distance and its effects on teacher expectations (the prizes going 'to the best mimics'). Intended as an inspirational tale for American urban classrooms, the analogy underestimates the depth of the deficiencies associated with ethnic and social class dialects, and the importance of the *cognitive* superiority ascribed to standard and formal speech. The concreteness and in-explicitness associated with more colloquial usage are contrasted with the necessary abstractions of classroom language, the frequent generalizations at the 'apex of some pyramid of experience' which provide few links with the personal, everyday world (Rosen 1967). As we saw in Chapter 4, this cognitive superiority has been disputed as at least unproven, its assumed existence leading to a frequent disregard of ideas not expressed in the 'proper' form. In what ways *are* standard-ness and explicitness related? When a speaker tries consciously to be explicit, does he shift to more formal usage as well? If he does so, the explanation may be social—the tendency to formality when talking to people and about topics from outside the everyday world. Explicitness may be less *likely* in colloquial or dialect form because of their association with familiar relationships in which explicitness is not normally required. Kochman (1972b) makes a Bernstein-like distinction between 'high contexts', where there is a high degree of familiarity with the situation and the participants, and 'low contexts' where the gap in experience must be bridged in more verbally elaborate ways. There is some evidence that black children are more likely to define classrooms as high contexts, at least where they are the majority, and to use more casual speech than their teachers expect. There have been similar suggestions of social class differences in the way situations are categorized, and of the importance of devising classroom situations which 'demand' more elaborated style.

Register describes the co-relation of linguistic and situational features, and its description requires detailed analysis of content, purpose and participant-relations, as well as of any distinctive features of style. It is part of that situational perspective on language outlined in Chapter 2—and it faces the same problem of identifying the structures that 'serve' the social functions.

2. THE CLASSROOM AS 'SITUATION'

Communicative competence includes knowledge of the 'etiquette' of speech in particular situations. Without this knowledge, the participants risk being disvalued themselves, or having what they say ignored or misunderstood. Observers need some of this knowledge too if they are to follow what is going on, and especially if they are to interpret the fine shades of meaning carried by various linguistic choices. Their interpretation of everyday, personalized, conversation depends largely on a knowledge of basic rules by which an ordered interchange of words is created and sustained—for example, the conventional ways of claiming, keeping and relinquishing 'the floor' (pp. 65–6)—and an awareness of part of that back-cloth of shared meanings to which the speakers implicitly refer. The participants create and sustain a conversation because they know what 'conversation' is, and because they know each other. To follow it successfully, the observer needs knowledge which is both general (to that culture or sub-culture), and specific (to those speakers). His task is much easier when they are not 'free' to wander within the bounds of referential intelligibility, grammatical 'correctness' and general cultural appropriateness—i.e. when there are relatively well-defined constraints on the distribution of talk, the communicative purposes, and the level of formality. As identified by Firth, the main task of 'sociological linguistics' was the identification of *typical* situations, where the communicative roles were partly predefined, and where the appropriate 'lines' and 'episodes' could be recognized with relative ease.

School classrooms offer such a situation. Aspects of the language used *can* be seen as 'both patterned and predictable on the basis of certain features of the local social system' (Blom and Gumperz 1972, p. 409). An overtly recognized division of roles, and manifest communicative functions, constrain what can be said, by whom and how. Because of them, the teacher is normally 'entitled' to speak, first, most and last, and to make most of the initiating moves. He can avoid flaunting his authority by using modes of control which are not 'imperative' in *form* ('Do I hear someone talking?'; 'Would you please open your books'), but which are clearly understood as commands in *that* context. The 'functional limits' on pupils' classroom language may therefore be more relevant to what they say than any 'grammatical constraints' (Sinclair *et al.* 1972, p. 189). In other words, whatever the 'underlying' social class or other persistent limitations on their performance, the immediate social context exerts its own powerful influence. Studying classroom language can be seen as *basic* socio-linguistic research, with very accessible opportunities of relating 'the structure of language to the structure of speaking' (see Stubbs 1975).

The following examples show interaction where order is an on-going achievement, and interaction which is relatively ritualized and formalized. The first is from a small-group discussion of a poem ('Five Ways to Kill a Man'), a method of working familiar to this comprehensive school class (I am grateful to Mr Sidney Wilson for the transcript). The second is from one of my own lessons, taught with no prevision of its present use. The pupils are third-formers in a grammar school, and are being instructed in the danger to peace in 1914 of two opposing European alliances.

Garry	Well, the bows and arrows were the start of all that, wasn't it?
Tim	What?
Glen	Ah, the bow and arrow.
Garry	They could get 'em from long distance.
Tim	Yeah, but ever since—
Glen	Yeah, but that was only killing one. That wasn't killing thousands, was it?
Garry	Yes it was—at the Battle of Agincourt.
Glen	Oh, that's one arrow though, isn't it?
Ian	With one arrow you can only kill one person.
Tim	Yeah.
Ray	Not unless you—
Tim	I know what you mean, yeah.
Glen	But the bomb—just need one bomb to kill a load of them, don't you?
Dean	Right. Arishe . . . Arisimina . . . I mean Arishima.
Garry	Hiroshima.

T	So you've got three countries on one side, three on the other. Why is this a danger to peace?
P	If Germany quarrels with the other side and, say, Austria won't do anything to help.
T	Yes . . . (*pause*) That's not the biggest danger but I suppose . . . yes . . . if one of the side backs out, it's a problem for the others. But what's the biggest danger of these two sides facing each other?
P	Well, if anyone did start a war um . . . um . . . the countries have so many other places in the world each, so it'll be a world war.
T	Yes, that's a good answer. It doesn't follow from my sketch-map, but

it's quite true. Just look at the map though, think of the way the two sides line up. Yes?

P   Well, if war breaks out, Germany and the rest of Germany's allies can cut Britain and France off from Russia.

T   Yes ... you're thinking of the war now ... (*pause*) If it *comes* to a war, that *is* an advantage. But before the war—if you were a German, you wouldn't much like the look of that map. Why not?

P   They're surrounded on all sides.

T   Yes, *right*. They often said they were encircled. . . .

Though entirely task-oriented, the first extract is relatively personalized and the participants are talking *to* each other rather than simply *about* something. It resembles everyday conversation in its inexplicitness, simultaneous bids for the 'floor', and apparently incomplete utterances. The second extract is more orderly, and the 'T-P' labels symbolize the *role* basis of the communication. The teacher asks all the questions, and there is no doubt who should answer. Each answer is evaluated. And while each is acknowledged as 'relevant', only the last fits the predetermined pattern. The teacher reclaims the floor after each contribution, and his 'right' to do so is not challenged. There is no stylistic gulf between teacher and pupils, but while a *formal* analysis might not reveal who was talking, a functional analysis would show the initiative remaining consistently with the teacher. The resulting orderliness is not the precarious accomplishment of the moment. It is 'typical' in Firth's sense of being repeatedly observable because of a 'constellation' of constraints on what is said, and how it is said.

The 'components' of situation examined in Chapter 2 will now be considered in relation to classrooms. In this section, the analysis will be deliberately static and idealized. There will be little reference to the methods used in observing classroom interaction, or to *how* such orderly interaction is achieved. Uniformity will also be exaggerated. Even in well-defined contexts, there are many variants of appropriateness, and too much concern with what is 'typical' may obscure how much of the interaction is governed by rules particular to *that* teacher, with *those* pupils, on *that* occasion (Jackson and Lahaderne 1967: Mishler 1972). It may seem from this preface that the structure is going to be described only for the pleasure of dismantling it. But compared with the *apparent* formlessness of everyday conversation, teacher-pupil relationships and the purposeful nature of their interaction are sufficiently well defined to be apparent in their discourse. Classrooms represent a set of 'congruent' influences on speech. At least, they do so if attention is diverted from their more 'open' and 'progressive' forms. A concentration on traditional structures and

functions—on class-teaching and subject-teaching—will exaggerate
the consistency of the constraints. But these are the classrooms we know
most about, and they are still the most prevalent.

(i) *Setting*

> The basic grid of rows and aisles helps to define the area of attention . . . and
> enables the teacher to supervise the class and, when necessary, to become a
> focus of attention. The desk helps to indicate the sobriety of behaviour
> expected . . . and the formation as a whole represents a 'unit' for class
> teaching . . . many teachers would feel uneasy if they had not these rows to
> deal with—they might consider that the classroom had become slovenly and
> unbusinesslike.   (Mannheim and Stewart 1962, p. 136.)

This traditional setting involves a clearly defined and enclosed 'stage',
a podium for the 'star', and a physically regimented supporting cast
who must frequently double as 'audience' for the star's performance.
Despite progressive pressures to collapse away the sides of the box,
break up the grid of desks and remove the dais, its appearance remains
familiar, and its communicative consequences (or correlatives) are
marked. The teacher is physically the natural focus of attention. He
can direct his questions to any part of the room. The natural flow of
pupil-talk is to him, and to each other through him. Direct communication among the pupils is inhibited (see pp. 71–2). These
physical constraints on interaction are highly visible (Oeser 1955,
pp. 52–5: Gump 1964). And the dramatic analogy is not too far-
fetched. The centre-front of such a room provides the teacher with a
'spiritual and temporal home', the location of a 'footlight parade'
which often lasts for most of the lesson (Adams and Biddle 1970,
pp. 37 and 65). One investigation suggested that pupils attached such
ritualistic importance to this central position that when the teacher
strayed from it, the associated interaction was most unlikely to be
concerned with the central academic business of the lesson. Pupils
situated outside this 'central action zone' were rarely involved in the
'action', either as contributors or as targets (Adams and Biddle 1970:
Adams 1971). It may seem from this that participation is determined by
location. But the relationship may of course be reversed, participants'
awareness of the normal 'flow' of communication leading them to take
up a position outside it. The teacher's awareness of their awareness may
lead *him* to direct his questions 'against the tide'. The desks can be
moved, and the dais can be abandoned. As was argued in Chapter 2,
settings are *cultural* units, arrangements of the environment into
possibly discrete categories with sets of communicative expectations
attached to them. The traditional classroom lay-out both reinforces

and symbolizes a definition of learning as dependent on one teacher with many children, engaged in a highly organized sequence of activities. Whether he is with them all day, or for the period formally assigned to his subject, he is for that time in charge. He is the source of orders, advice, judgments and instruction—above all of instruction, because that traditional arrangement of desks announces and supports the vertical transmission of knowledge.

Before considering this process, some obvious organizational implications must be mentioned. Where large numbers are gathered into a confined space for hours of each day, mundane matters of management are prominent. These pervasive institutional features of classroom life were coded by Jackson and Lahaderne (1967) as the *instructional*, the *managerial* and the *prohibitory*. Though the balance between the three varied widely in the classrooms they studied, organizational problems were prominent. Where order is precarious, they can absorb most of the lesson time. But even in the typical primary school session described by Hilsun and Cane (1971), 'instruction' took up only half of the time. The sheer quantity of interpersonal exchanges with which the teacher must cope means that pupils have to learn to queue, wait, share, and have their immediate needs denied while the teacher allocates scarce resources of equipment, attention and praise (Jackson 1968). This persistent distributive aspect of his work may seem to demand a central position from which to supervise and direct. As long as he occupies it, no pupil is likely to say very much. Of course, classrooms do not always constitute a single interacting group. Some pupils will not be involved at all. Some will form peripheral groups whose activities are unrelated to, or opposed to, the main stream of events. But the existence of these groups is likely to be challenged by the teacher, and to be transitory. In the 32 lessons recorded by Adams and Biddle (1970), a 'central communication system' was evident for 85% of the time, and was the *only* communication system for three-quarters of it. Their categorization of communicative roles into emitter, target and audience showed the last of these as the role most readily available to pupils. The classroom, then, is very much a public arena. Indeed, it is a highly unusual situation in the public nature of the performances given within it, the 'persistent reference for individual behaviour' being an ever-present audience (Adams 1971, p. 117). A major *qualitative* consequence is the 'public' style of speaking likely to result. Hesitant, exploratory talk is more likely in small groups, at least where the members know each other well. There talk can be 'tentative, discursive, inexplicit and uncertain of direction . . . The intimacy of the context allows this to happen without strain. In an atmosphere of tolerance, of hesitant formulation and of co-operative effort, the children can "stretch" their language to accommodate their own second thoughts and the opinions of others' (Bullock 1975, p. 146: see also Barnes and Todd 1975a). Large groups encourage declamation and categoric statements. Where they are also a setting for frequent evaluations of what is said, then the risk of public exposure of error will often make it seem safer to say nothing, or stay close to the obvious. As was suggested earlier in relation to language research, 'concreteness' of expression may then be a *socio*linguistic phenomenon arising in a particular kind of communicative context. It is already clear that the contextual pressures on the quantity and quality of classroom speech arise not only from spatial and demographic factors, but from the role-relationship of teachers and pupils and from the purposes that bring them together.

(ii) *Participants*

All social interaction is constrained by general cultural knowledge of what to expect and what is expected. Interaction of a personalized kind is influenced by the experience each has of the other, and these are *individualized* expectations. Between the two 'levels' of expectation come those which arise from the relative status of the participants, their role-relationship, and the topic and function of their discourse. All these may be linguistically relevant—they may indicate the appropriate stylistic choice.

Classrooms are, or have been, status-marked situations in which personal feelings and personalized responses are largely masked. The overwhelming predominance of task-related talk in those studied by Flanders led him to describe them as an 'affective desert'. Seen in the 'vertical' dimension of power and solidarity, the central relationship is highly asymmetrical, the pupil's responses being far more contingent on the teacher than the teacher's are on his (Hargreaves 1972, p. 139). The unequal use of first-name (or last-name only) is an obvious illustration of this, the reciprocated first-names allowed by some teachers and in some schools being an indicator and marker of 'radical' educational attitudes (cf. Brown and Gilman 1960). Seen in the 'horizontal' dimension of formality and intimacy, it is marked by a considerable social distance. *Why* this is so obviously relates to the functions of schooling, and also to certain characteristics of teachers and pupils.

The teacher is adult in the company of the young. There are still pervasive cultural expectations that the adult will be 'in charge', even when no formal instruction is taking place. When it is, the inevitable subordination of the 'ignorant' to the 'knowledgeable' may be more bearable when age provides a status-basis for the teacher's authority. In Waller's famous account, the teacher's ascendancy is seen as more acceptable when it is made impersonal, when it is filtered through the sieve of formality. It is also easier for the teacher, because only the most charismatic can rely on a *personal* leadership 'which must be recreated every hour' (Waller 1932, repr. 1965, pp. 189–90: 1942, p. 208). Most teachers need strong institutionalized supports, and 'set phrases and conventionalised verbal formulae' are an important means of maintaining the 'necessary' distance (Waller 1932, repr. 1965, pp. 279–89). They 'must keep state in order to control', because their pupils' attendance is involuntary, and may be acutely felt as such. And given the facts of large numbers and physical restriction, the pupil too must learn to 'leave most of his personality outside the classroom door'. Both 'sides' must subordinate their behaviour to the role-relationship.

Waller saw the teacher's authority as a 'perilous despotism' because it was exerted over the most tractable *and* the most unstable members of the community. He saw it as justified by the teacher's responsibilities as a 'paid agent of cultural diffusion', hired to carry the light into dark places and set apart from his pupils by his knowledge and his attachment to less local values. The institutionalization of learning aligns the schools with other public spheres of activity. To an increasing extent with older pupils, the 'high' values of power and formality are likely to be emphasized. Some stylistic consequences were outlined earlier. Briefly, the variety normally used will be that appropriate to a relationship based on roles rather than one in which *persons* interact against a wide background of shared meanings. The roles are there because *new* meanings are being transmitted. And in any relationship involving a transfer of knowledge, the element of power is apparent. The 'teacher' is, at least temporarily, the superior. As long as his expertise is accepted, he is entitled to initiate interaction, elicit responses, and evaluate performance (Geer 1968). The status of an accredited expert is most easily claimed when he commands a 'subject', a body of knowledge marked off from other subjects and from 'everyday knowledge'. He can then define what contributions are appropriate, and how much of his pupils' previous knowledge is relevant for his purposes.

(iii) *Purposes*

Any school child playing teacher will produce most of the behaviour used by most teachers. Typical behaviours are: standing in front of a group of relatively passive onlookers (a position of authority), doing most of the talking (telling), asking questions to which they already know the answers (testing), and evaluating by passing judgements.

(Simon and Boyer 1970, Vol. 2, p. 2.)

Such a role-performance would lie squarely within the mainstream of research into teacher behaviour, which has tended to erect polarized models around the central fact of teacher dominance (e.g. authoritarian-democratic, dominative-integrative, direct-indirect). Without too much over-simplification, this research has shown that teachers expect to take charge, that pupils expect to be taught, and that 'being taught' has meant acquiring information of which the teacher was the source. The central communicative purpose of classrooms has been the vertical transmission of facts, opinions and skills from those who know to those who do not. Where this knowledge is sharply separated from the pupil's out-of-school experience, he is at the mercy of the teacher's definitions, and of his decisions about how much and how fast it is to be made available. Classrooms also provide frequent public displays of success and failure, the teacher regularly judging the correctness and relevance of what the pupil says. The communicative results of this dual process of instruction and evaluation are roughly summarized in Flanders' 'rule of two-thirds', a generalization from many hours of classroom observation. 'About two-thirds of the time spent in a classroom, someone is talking. The chances are two out of three that this person is the teacher. When the teacher talks, two-thirds of the time is spent in many expressions of opinion and fact, giving some directions, and occasionally criticising the pupils' (Flanders 1967b, p. 285).

The supporting evidence comes from a category-system of analysis which, within its considerable limitations, has provided strikingly consistent accounts of teacher dominance. Teachers may talk less, and less 'directively', with younger pupils; if they teach English and Social studies; and if they are regarded as 'superior' by colleagues (Furst and Amidon 1967: Amidon and Giammateo 1967). But the differences seem less significant than the limited range of variation. In Flanders' plain words, 'teachers usually tell pupils what to do, how to do it, when to start, when to stop, and how well they did whatever they did' (1970, p. 14). The same 'facts' can be expressed in more abstract form. Teachers usually initiate and pupils respond (Amidon and Hunter 1967). Teachers make most of the 'moves' in a classroom game in which they act as player, coach and referee; most of the 'soliciting moves' are theirs, and most of the 'responding moves' are their pupils' (Bellack et al. 1966). The teacher is mainly an emitter, often a target, and rarely one of the 'audience': three types of communicative-role allocation dominate classrooms—a teacher emitter, and a student audience; a teacher emitter, a single student target and an audience; a single student emitter, a teacher target and an audience (Adams and Biddle 1970). The most typical interaction sequence is: teacher question—pupil answer—teacher evaluation. The teacher-feedback is so common 'that if it does not occur, we feel confident in saying that the teacher has deliberately withheld it for some strategic purpose' (Sinclair *et al.* 1972, p. 103).

The linguistic relevance of classroom setting, status, role and function makes sense of utterances which would be ambiguous, or misunderstood, or not understood at all, when taken out of context. But the analysis in this section has been too static. The emphasis in the next is on *how* the participants in classroom interaction announce, recognize, maintain or challenge the rules they apply to it, and on how far the observer can recover the underlying assumptions.

3. THE STRUCTURING OF CLASSROOM INTERACTION

An orderly exchange of words depends on the actors' recognition and *implementation* of the norms of appropriate usage relevant to their situation and relationship. Indeed, the linguistically relevant roles are 'realized' *through* what is said. *How* the social structure of the classroom is produced and maintained seems a more interesting research problem than producing generalizations about what its typical structures are. It suggests that the observer must 'immerse himself in the life of the natives', and record the actual words used. Yet it is the distillation of words into categories that has dominated the observation of classrooms.

(i) *Coding classroom language*

It is part of the rationale for a recent study of classroom interaction that such research can contribute to the mainstream of sociolinguistic enquiry because the communicative roles and purposes are relatively well defined (Sinclair *et al.* 1972). A more practical reason also offered in its support is largely irrelevant to this professed sociolinguistic concern—that there has already been extensive research into classroom language on which that study could build. This is true only in the obvious sense that most classroom activity involves talk, and the talk must be recorded somehow. Most methods have involved category systems, more or less ruthless filters through which the rich stream of speech is sieved. The talk itself has rarely received close attention. Some examples of these methods are now given, and the difficulties of coding outlined.

Taba *et al.* (1964) tried to establish causal relationships between methods of teaching and 'levels' of pupil thinking. Lesson transcripts were analysed in terms of who said what, to whom, and for what purpose. Was the speaker a pupil, was he giving or seeking information, did the information refer to class management or to the content of the lesson? Coding the transcripts made it possible to construct a 'cognitive flow-chart' showing how far the teacher had tried to stimulate 'abstract' thinking (the application of known facts and ideas to explain new phenomena or to develop hypotheses), and how far he had been able to do so. Teacher's questions were especially critical in opening out or 'closing' the meanings available to the pupil. So was his willingness to allow pupils to question him and each other, so avoiding the monotony of teacher-pupil-teacher-pupil sequences of the kind illustrated on page 158.

Waimon and Hermanowicz (1965) also concentrated on the functions of teacher talk. How did the teacher gain his pupils' attention, state a learning goal or state a problem (procedural statements)? How did he define terms, state facts, and offer explanations (substantive statements)? How did he accept, correct or disagree with pupil responses (rating statements)? The whole system contained more than a hundred categories, and the detail intensifies the difficulty of assuming that the observer's decision somehow represents the interpretation of the participants. How did the *pupils* recognize when the teacher was restating, rather than rejecting, their response? 'That's one way of putting it' is offered as an example of a *mild positive rating*. But did the participants interpret this as meaning—'That's a good idea which I hadn't thought of'; or as—'That's nonsense, but I'm not going to show you up'; or as 'That's quite irrelevant to the problem as I've defined it': or as 'That's a silly suggestion'. Their decision will depend on intonation, facial expression, the location of the utterance in a sequence of utterances, and a great deal of other information available because of their knowledge of the teacher and the situation. It is interesting that student-teachers exposed to this fine-meshed analysis of lesson transcripts expressed a strong preference for direct classroom observation.

The best-known method of classroom observation offers no opportunity to reinterpret the data. Flanders assumes that an adequate sample of all classroom behaviour can be recorded in ten mutually exclusive categories. These represent instant judgments of what is being 'done' with words. Is the teacher (for example) 'praising or encouraging', 'accepting or using pupil ideas', or 'criticizing or justifying his authority'? The observer makes his decision at three-second intervals, and can produce from his record both a simple quantitative breakdown of the interaction (the % tallies in each category) and a profile of 'interactive sequences' (what followed what). The method is variously described as *only* an observational technique, a means of thinking about teacher behaviour, and a non-evaluative way of feeding back to the teacher information from which he can assess his own performance and make whatever change he wishes (Flanders 1968). Though the approach can be criticized as atomistic, breaking the 'stream' of verbal behaviour into arbitrary units, 'interaction' and 'events' are claimed to be its key concepts. By 'events', Flanders means teacher acts which are significantly correlated with pupil attitudes and achievements. A 'critical teaching behaviour' is a *pattern* of acts 'logically related to certain educational outcomes', and following a certain sequence with 'measurable probability' (Flanders 1967a, p. 361). For example, an especially critical moment of decision for the teacher is what to say—in effect, what to *do*—when a pupil ends his reply to a question. If the teacher resumes his exposition, the 'dialogue' is over. If he remains silent, that pupil may elaborate his answer, or another pupil may take over from him. If he makes use of the pupil's contribution, this may signal an invitation to debate, and his own dominance may be temporarily suspended. Without being merely pedantic about the label, it is hard to see this as *interaction* analysis. We are told what follows what in a bluntly categorical way. As Flanders himself recognizes, 'interaction analysis systems seek to abstract communication by ignoring most of its characteristics. Once the same code symbol is used for different statements, the differences among them are lost for ever' (1970, p. 29).

The small number of categories and the preponderance of those devoted to teacher-talk are not a necessary part of Flanders' approach. His system can be adapted to the particular interests of the observer. One offshoot of it separates teacher-pupil from pupil-pupil talk, 'broad' from 'narrow' questions, and the acceptance or rejection of ideas from acceptance or rejection of feelings and behaviour (Amidon and Hunter 1967). These are refinements in pursuing the same purpose —to provide 'objective' data from which the teacher can make his own decisions, and through which he can free himself from the alternative evils of 'mere tradition' and 'blind experimentation'. They in no way reduce basic objections to the approach. Another modification of the system uses the same categories for teacher- and pupil-talk, on the 'reciprocity principle' that a corresponding student verbal behaviour exists 'for every teacher verbal behaviour that can either be observed in the classroom or theoretically conceived' (Ober *et al.* 1971, p. 38). Again, the emphasis is on systematic observation by an observer who knows what he is looking for, and is confident that he can record what is 'going on'.

'Systems for analysing classroom talk can tell us what actually occurs in classrooms' (Amidon and Hunter 1967). The statement is bold, deceptively straightforward, and quite misleading. At least two large claims are contained in it. The lesser of them is that the systems are reliable. And from Anderson (1939) onwards, their devisers have been able to claim high levels of agreement among coders. They allow 'any trained person who follows stated procedures to observe, record and analyse interactions with the assurance that others viewing the same situation would agree to a great extent with his recorded sequence of behaviours' (Ober *et al.* 1971, p. 16). But they do so for reasons which raise profound social scientific issues. Coders are trained to perceive interaction in ways appropriate to the system they use. They see what they are looking for, and there is an important latent function in the instruction to coders to keep the categories clearly in mind. It is claimed that most systems use low-inference measures—i.e. that observers have to make few inferences (or few problematic inferences) from what they see and hear to some higher-order construct. It is apparently much easier to record a teacher as 'lecturing' or asking questions than to rate him as 'boring' or 'warm', and so the record appears objective. Those inferences which are made are claimed to be 'based on events which can be said to have occurred with a greater degree of certainty than is usually true of classroom observation' (Flanders 1970, pp. 6–7). This 'objectivity' is achieved partly by the sheer holding-capacity of the categories, into which disparate behaviours can be fitted.

The larger claim is that the observational record gives the essence of what 'really' happened. Flanders (1970) describes the 'game of blind matrix analysis', in which part of a lesson is 'reconstructed' from the three-second tallies. No doubt this can be done for such conventional sequences as teacher-directed drill sessions, though even then at a high level of generality. The interesting questions are still how the original coder 'fixed' the meaning of what he heard, and how far his interpretations might have coincided with those of the members. Major difficulties are evaded in conventional references to the precision and 'accuracy' of the observations (Allon 1969: Robinson 1974: Hamilton and Delamont 1974). They are unwittingly revealed in

Ober's analogy between the agreed frame of reference provided by an observation schedule, and the 'rules of sport where a foul is a foul'. One man's foul is another man's competitive tackle. The observer's view is a view from the outside, a 'second reality' partly constructed *in advance* by what he is 'set' to see. It is a bold assumption that the events in it represent, in their due proportion, events in the 'first reality' of the members (Smith and Geoffrey 1968, p. 255). He will lack knowledge of the history of the interaction, during which certain forms of speaking have acquired special meanings which elude him. It is a general problem of coding that it tends to fix meaning prematurely at the expense of messages carried beneath the surface. Yet the interaction analysts' freedom from any assumptions about the actors' intentions is seen as an *advantage*, 'making the data analysis less dependent on the observer's prior understanding of the system' (Adams 1971, p. 105). It is precisely this prior understanding that the sociolinguistically oriented observer would need.

Flanders partly recognizes the problem when he indicates the need to separate 'genuine praise' from 'superficial habits' (e.g. a too frequent and automatic use of 'Good'), and the greater difficulty of distinguishing between the teacher's *use* of a pupil's idea, and a restatement of it so extensive that the pupil would no longer recognize it as his own. The problem is not recognized at all in his recipe for distinguishing student-response from student-initiation: if the contribution is 'predictable' by the observer (as well as by teacher and class), it should be coded as a 'response'. But this is a judgment which may have to wait on events, the predictability of what the pupil says being apparent only in the *teacher*'s response to its 'relevance'. And there is no possibility of retrospective coding in the Flanders' system; the observer's decisions must be instant. The objection is even stronger to the coding of 'narrow' and 'broad' questions (Amidon and Hunter 1967, pp. 10–14). A question is narrow when 'the specific nature of the response can be predicted'. This is sometimes obvious even when the question is taken out of its context—e.g. 'What is the date of the Battle of Hastings?'. It is much more likely to be obvious only in the context of the immediate discourse, and in the wider context of the kind of questions that particular teacher asks. Amidon and Hunter give as an example of a 'broad' question—'What are some of the reasons why Paris became the capital of France?'. But if the teacher has already provided three 'good' reasons why, and now expects them to be repeated, then that question too is 'narrow'. What came before defines what is appropriate now. What is appropriate now is recognizable retrospectively in the teacher's response. It is necessary to wait for what is said later to interpret what was meant before (Garfinkel 1964).

Systems of interaction analysis have made it possible to 'document' the teacher's dominance of the classroom by both counting and categorizing his talk. They tell us who speaks longest and most often, who opens and closes the sequence, who initiates and who responds. But beyond a superficial level, interpreting who 'did' what with words depends on detailed knowledge of the situations as the participants see it. Only then can we show 'how particular grammatical forms are interpreted as moves', and what is the function of a particular utterance 'in a particular social situation and at a particular place in a sequence as a specific contribution to a developing discourse' (Sinclair et al. 1972, p. 43).

A number of other approaches will now be outlined. Some were not at all sociolinguistic in intention but are open to a measure of 'translation'. Indeed, the scarcity of directly relevant research makes such reinterpreting inevitable. The attempt to do so revives the questions asked earlier—whether the translation is merely a re-labelling or a means to fresh insight.

(ii) *Asking questions*

Social categories like status and role have been described as having a function in the *whole* process of communication like that of syntax in the communication of referential meaning (Gumperz and Herasimchuk 1972, p. 101). The analogy suggests a level beneath the surface of the interaction to which the actual items used can be referred and so made meaningful. These categories are 'signalled in the act of speaking'; linguistic choice demonstrates how the speakers categorize the setting, participants and topic, and it 'does the categorising'. This is rarely done unambiguously through the formal properties of speech, but through complex and subtle relationships between the utterances and their social context. Extensive social assumptions underly their interpretation.

Mood has been called 'the grammar of communicative roles', a main means of 'realizing' semantic options (Halliday 1971). Of course, a question may be asked in other ways than through the interrogative mood, and what seems from its surface to be a question may realize quite different functions (e.g. a 'rhetorical' question, which indicates not a dialogue but a continued monologue, or a command when the 'question' draws attention to a rule which has been broken—'Is that someone talking in the back?'). But however they are asked, questions are an essential method by which teachers claim and retain the initiative, and allocate the complementary respondent roles. The type of question asked also has far-reaching communicative consequences, as well as the possible cognitive implications suggested by other investigators (Gallagher and Aschner 1963: Taba *et al.* 1964: Sanders 1966). The proportion of 'factual' to 'reasoning' questions is seen by Barnes (1969) as indicating to pupils whether the content of the lesson is to be received ready-made, whether it can be challenged, and whether their own experience has anything relevant to contribute. This is how they are socialized into the appropriate learner-roles, into an appropriate stance towards the knowledge being transmitted. This is how the teacher defines the *content* of the interaction and controls the 'participant-structures' (Philips 1970: Barnes and Todd 1975b). In Barnes' analysis, teachers' instructional questions were placed in inclusive categories, though with a clear awareness of the need for frequent retrospective identification:

(a) *Factual* ('*what*') *questions*—either naming ('What is this called?') or informative ('What happened when we added the acid to the zinc?').
(b) '*Open*' *questions not calling for reasoning.* The answers may be factual ('Tell me something about Magellan') or observational ('What do you notice in this picture?').
(c) *Reasoning* ('*how*', '*why*') *questions.* These are 'open' when alternative answers are permitted or encouraged. They are 'closed' when they invite the recall of already disclosed sequences of cause-and-effect, or when the 'right' approach is marked out by the teacher. They are 'pseudo-open' when an apparent openness in the form of the question is contradicted by the teacher's rejection of feasible replies. These relate to unstated but well-understood criteria of relevance; pupils learn to ignore the formally expressed openness, and to guess what answer (or kind of answer) the teacher wants. To do this successfully, they must select from the enormous amount of talk that washes over them those utterances which *do* reveal the criteria by which their performance will be judged.

This is a sociolinguistic approach in its emphasis on situated interpretation and its concentration on the creation of roles through verbal interaction. Broadening the discussion beyond the examples and arguments provided by Barnes, I want to consider what communicative consequences might be predicted for certain types of question. A 'closed' question is likely to elicit a teacher-pupil-teacher-pupil interactive sequence until the 'right' answer is achieved and announced. It is probably more realistic to see this as a triadic sequence of teacher-pupil-teacher, in which the teacher evaluates or comments on each response as his pupils proceed through a tightly structured content (see the extract on page 158). The teacher's 'intermediate' contributions may be no more than a look or a pointed finger, but some invitation to continue the replies means that the 'prize' is still to be won. A 'closed' question is also likely to elicit short responses. This is obviously so when a label or other item of information is being sought for, and the appropriate reply can be a word or a phrase. Even when an explanation is demanded, brevity is possible because implicit reference can be made to a backcloth of shared meanings provided by teacher or text-book. 'To ask children to tell each other or the teacher things which they know about already simply invites inadequate accounts because detailed and explicit ones are not necessary, and the children know they are not' (Gahagan and Gahagan 1970, p. 30). And the pupil may 'parrot' the teacher's language like an incantation, giving the outward appearance of understanding. 'Closed' questions may focus attention on the teacher as 'authority', or on a fixed body of facts or opinions of which he is the custodian. Either way, the emphasis is on the product and not on the search—hence the frequency of evaluative feedback to keep contributions 'on track' for relevance and 'correctness'. 'Pseudo-open' questions tend to direct attention to the teacher as the source of approval. They can emphasize the hierarchical relationship even more than 'closed' questions do, for the latter may announce the subordination of pupils *and* teacher to some body of unproblematic knowledge. They are also likely to heighten pupils' sensitivity to the various verbal and non-verbal means by which 'correctness' is signalled by the teacher. Mishler's (1972) microscopic study of three classrooms shows how radically different learning strategies are expressed in the kind of statements the teacher makes, and the kind of pupil-teacher interaction initiated or permitted by them.

Both forms of question relate to meanings which are already determined. Though they may be explicitly stated and 'universalistic', they have some of the characteristics associated with meanings transmitted in a restricted code. To challenge them is to challenge the academic sub-culture. Their basis is not open to question, curiosity is inhibited, and 'creative' ambiguity is rare. From what little evidence is available, teachers usually ask questions to which they already know *the* answers, and their pupils know that they know. When they ask questions to which there is no apparent 'right' answer, quite different 'participant-structures' may be created. Immediate evaluation of responses is no longer appropriate. The teacher does not demand the 'floor' again once a response is given, and a teacher-pupil-pupil-pupil . . . sequence is more likely. Pupils are also encouraged to make lengthier and more verbally explicit contributions. Both these effects are evident in some of the 'creative classroom encounters' described by Massialas and Zevin (1967). In the first example, the teacher's contributions are given in full. The number in brackets after each of them is the number of consecutive responses (by different pupils) which followed. The teacher makes nine contributions to his pupils' fifty-nine. Their function is to ask for clarification or evidence, or to return a question to the group; and they are shorter than almost all the pupil contributions, some of which are quoted in the second example. The class is 'testing an autonomously developed generalisation about secret societies' after working on documentary material (Massialas and Zevin 1967).

(a) T. 'What if I asked you to prove your rule?' (1)
'Well?' (14)
'How would you know that all other governments *were* oppressive?' (3)
'That's assuming they *were* ruled by foreigners. Aren't you taking Lenin's word for that?' (11)
'Ah, that's a very good question.' (1)
'I like your choice of words.' (1)
'What do you think it means?' (10)
'I don't know. Can we tell?' (18)
'Don't look at me, *you're* deciding the question.'

(b) P1. 'I just thought of a new problem. Maybe we're all being too agreeable with our own rule. We didn't consider the Ku Klux Klan. We studied it, and we have their oath, but where do they fit our rule?'
T. 'Ah, that's a very good question.'
P2. 'They thought that the American government in Washington was being oppressive to white people in the South, so they formed their organization to protect their rights.'
T. 'I like your choice of words.'
P2. 'What does that mean?'
T. 'What do you think it means?'
P3. 'Oh, I think I see what you're getting at. Janet said that the Ku Klux Klan *thought* the U.S. government was bad. But was it? For whom? It wasn't bad for the Negroes in the South.'
P4. 'No, it was giving the Negroes their rights for the first time. The KKK was oppressing the Negroes.'
P5. 'The KKK obviously thought that the U.S. government was interfering with their old way of life, and since they couldn't get their old life back legally, they resorted to violence and formed a sort of secret club to frighten Negroes and Northerners who came South.'
P4. '. . .

Massialas and Zevin comment on the relative ambiguity (and insecurity) of such *relatively* 'open' teacher and learner roles. Like the solution to the problem being investigated, the method of working towards it has to be achieved. They describe the teaching role as being transformed from the 'didactic' to the 'dialectical'. But what does the 'dialectical' teacher do to create more varied participant-structures? Their suggestions (pp. 25–6) are summarized below, with a constructed example of each. They highlight the importance of 'open' questions, and of other ways of eliciting frequent and elaborated student talk. And they also emphasize the virtual disappearance of exposition and evaluation, the bases of teacher-dominated verbal interaction.

introduces new material, or a problem, e.g.	'Do you think this account is biased?'
challenges pupils to explore it	'How would we start looking for bias?'
challenges pupils to test alternatives	'That's one possibility. Is there any other way of explaining it?'
insists on evidence	'You might guess that. But what have you got to go on?'
asks for clarification	'I'm not sure what you mean by that.'
asks for information	'Can you think of events anywhere else which might throw light on this?'
redirects question	'Yes, that's a real problem. Does anyone have any ideas on that?'
legitimates creative thought	'Yes, that's not in the book but it's a real possibility. How would the problem look if we saw it that way?'
summarizes and recapitulates	'What we've done so far is . . . That still leaves us the problem . . .'

As was suggested earlier, the teachers' most effective move might be to increase the proportion of 'talking time' spent in smaller, less public groups, in which the possibility of avoiding talk altogether is less while that of exploring and testing meanings is very much greater (Barnes and Todd 1975a).

(iii) Classroom control
The preceding discussion concentrated on the central classroom activity of instruction, and took discipline for granted. In an important sense, the distinction is arbitrary anyway, the teacher's control over the knowledge he transmits being a pervasive form of *social* control. The form of the social relationship is implicit in the frequency with which the teacher asks questions, evaluates the answers, and defines

the parameters of 'relevant' knowledge. But special problems arise from those institutional features of classroom life outlined earlier. Formality of 'style' or formal modes of address are powerful means of maintaining social distance and expressing a role- rather than a personal relationship. If the teacher needs to 'keep state to keep control', then verbal routines and a deliberate impersonality in speech and 'tone' help him to do so. For example, teacher and student may have relaxed in a 'man-to-man' conversation. Then the student complains about another teacher. Professional solidarity is asserted, and social distance re-established, by stylistic and paralinguistic means that both will recognize—'I feel sure that MR So-and-So is quite competent to run his classes.' The tone is dry, uninterested and disapproving (Waller 1965, p. 281). 'Buffer phrases' also help the teacher to correct pupils' behaviour and their academic errors without arousing undue antagonism, personal feelings being 'filtered' through conventionalized forms of expression. Some of the difficulties experienced by student-teachers arise from the lack of this facility to formalize *or* personalize their relationship with their pupils as the situation changes.

In most classrooms most of the time, it is tempting to describe control as *positional* (see pp. 108–9). The main justification for the teacher's commands is inherent in the role-relationship, and the norms regulating it. Pupils are generally expected to do as instructed without much argument or delay; to begin, suspend and end activities on demand; to answer questions whenever asked, or to make it apparent that silence indicates ignorance rather than an improper refusal to reveal appropriate knowledge; to show at least some outward respect in speech and behaviour; and to accept restrictions on their range of discretion in ways that may have little relation to their individual wishes. The rules to which conformity is expected are partly institutional (operational throughout the school), largely specific to particular settings, activities and teachers. Most of them are not stated explicitly. The principles underlying 'correct' behaviour are rarely brought directly to the pupil's attention, and he learns by experience how an item of behaviour comes under a relevant rule. At least in this respect, the 'language of classrooms' seems to represent a restricted code; the speech controlled in this way 'cannot be understood apart from the context, and the context cannot be read by those who do not share the history of the relationship' (Bernstein 1973a, p. 201).

The institutionalization of teacher-control depends on a wide base of taken-for-granted meanings which remove the apparent ambiguities. In the early stages of a teacher's interaction with a new class, he will spell out many of his demands, hoping to create a set of shared perceptions of the rules which will eventually stabilize into group norms of a prescriptive kind. Moving them from an understanding of how things *are* done to an appreciation that this is how they *ought to be* done has been described as 'grooving the children' (Smith and Geoffrey 1968, p. 49). The gradual deepening of the grooves provides an extensive background knowledge from which to interpret what is said. Certainly, the rules governing classroom interaction are so numerous, and the occurrence of at least mild infractions so numerous, that explicit acts of identification by the teacher would make his authority too obtrusive. The outside observer then faces the problem mentioned earlier—that the behaviour governing the immediate interaction may have taken place some time ago, and be referred to implicitly. The relevant rules are so situationally embedded that one recent study of classroom deviance was 'pushed' unwillingly into 'close and careful analysis of the changing contexts of lessons' (Hargreaves *et al.* 1975, pp. 54–5). Pupils seemed to make fine quantitative and qualitative discriminations —for example, in relation to when talking was permissible, and how much, and how loud, and with whom, and about what. How then did teacher and pupils know when a rule had been broken, and how were rules 'attached' to acts when the 'same' action may be variously labelled according to the context, and so interpreted as breaking different rules on different occasions? Studying much younger pupils, Kounin (1970) coded the intensity (or attention-demanding properties), firmness and clarity of what he called 'desist-techniques'. Did the teacher make it clear *who* was deviant, *what* was deviant, and *why*? Such clarity is not evident in most of the categories of 'verbally explicit' deviancy imputations suggested by Hargreaves and his associates (pp. 50–1). I have reduced their eleven categories to nine:

Direct statement of the rule, e.g.	'You must not talk when I am talking.'
Statement of deviant behaviour (rule implied)	'You are talking.'
Attention-drawer	'Jones,' '3B.'
Direct command	'Shut up.' 'Stop talking.'
Command in the form of a question	'Do I have to tell you again.'
Warning (implied serious short-term consequences)	'I'm going to lose my temper with you.'
Warning (long-term consequences)	'You won't pass the exam, acting like that.'
Evaluative labelling of conduct	'That is very silly.'
Evaluative labelling of pupil	'You are very silly.'

In few of these examples is the action which occasioned the imputation overtly identified. Most are highly compressed, and their formal structure conveys very little of their meaning. To take them out of context would destroy their meaning by removing the ways in which the actors fill in the necessary detail from their background knowledge, and from their understanding of the immediate sequence of events. The context is something far more refined and detailed than a 'lesson', which is divided into 'phases' in Hargreaves' analysis. These involve different rules (and participant-structures). For example, even task-related pupil talk may be discouraged during teacher-exposition; it may be demanded, according to a strict etiquette of communication, during discussion; it may be allowed during individual work, with or without control over its relevance to the task. The point of transition from one phase to another is marked by a 'switch-signal', usually verbal and often drawn from a very limited conventional repertoire (e.g. 'Right', 'O.K.', 'Now', 'If you'll just stop work for a moment'). Though developed quite independently of it, this part of the analysis has some similarity to the method outlined in the next section of this chapter (Hargreaves *et al.* 1975, p. 65).

A final point of interest is that teachers were often unable to account for their particular choice of expression in imputing deviance—e.g. why they said 'Jones, if you don't stop talking you'll be in trouble' rather than simply 'Shut up'. But the expectation that they might be able to do so mistakes the nature of the social constraints on linguistic choice. These are rarely determinants of a particular selection, but parameters within which an appropriate choice is made. A teacher's selection from the limited repertoire quoted is a matter of 'free variation', any of the alternatives constituting unmarked usage. But if he said—'Please be quiet because all this noise is making my head ache, and you know how I suffer from nerves', or 'Please give me a chance, because I spent hours on this lesson last night, and now you're spoiling it, and I'm getting very upset'—these would be such person-alized appeals as to constitute *marked* usage, the significance of which would be immediately sought. In such status-marked settings as classrooms, especially in secondary schools, imperative and positional forms of control are likely to predominate. They will be 'realized' verbally in a variety of ways within these impersonal limits.

(iv) *Acts, moves and exchanges*
Although the approaches to classroom interaction outlined so far have implications for sociolinguistic enquiry, they were directed by different concerns. My last examples have a more direct relevance.

Descriptions of teaching behaviour by Flanders and by Amidon and Hunter are centred on the concepts of initiative and response. A similar orientation is found in Bellack's analysis of classroom language, though in more ostentatiously academic form. It is an account of 'the patterned processes of verbal interaction that characterise classrooms in action', guided by Wittgenstein's theory of 'language games' (Bellack *et al.* 1966). The results reinforce those of more mundane studies. Teachers speak most of the lines, make most of the 'moves', and make almost all the 'soliciting moves'. They provide the rules, train the players, and control the game. Part of the analysis concerns the content of social studies lessons, and is relevant here only in showing the predominance of information over discussion even in the teaching of controversial topics. A body of 'solid' facts at the teacher's back clearly reinforces his control of the interaction. The rest of the analysis is an attempt to break the lessons up into 'chunks of socio-linguistic reality' (Coulthard 1974, p. 235). A clear separation is made between what is said, and what is being 'done' with words in the act of speaking. Four 'basic verbal actions' are identified in the form of pedagogical 'moves'—i.e. in terms of functions which have to be recognized by the participants in a variety of verbal forms. 'Structuring moves' set the scene for subsequent behaviour by, for example, terminating one 'piece' of interaction, or announcing a new topic ('What I want to go to now is . . .'). 'Soliciting moves' elicit a verbal response directly—by command, question or request. 'Responding moves' are their obvious complement. 'Reacting moves' are not directly elicited, but are related to some previous move; they include a teacher's evaluation of a pupil's response, but not his answer to a pupil's question. Such moves are an important means of maintaining coherence across a number of teacher and pupil contributions, so building up an 'exchange'. The definitions imply what the ensuing account makes explicit—that the moves occur in regular 'cycles'. A common example is a teacher stating a problem (structuring), asking a question, eliciting a reply, and commenting on it (reacting). His pupils have to recognize, in whatever form of words is used, that a new stage has begun, that a question has been asked, that someone must reply, and that the evaluation must be identified. This concern with 'the functions that language actually serves in verbal interplay' brings the approach close to a sociolinguistic account of how participants announce and respond to the moves governing their interaction. It has an obvious influence on the most detailed investigation so far of the 'organisation of spoken discourse' in a classroom setting (Sinclair *et al.* 1972).

The report of that investigation is preceded by a lightning sketch of symbolic interactionist and ethnomethodological approaches. As is admitted, however, the methods of language description owe most to the immediate problems of coping with the data, and were derived from it rather than imposed on it from a precisely prepared theoretical position. From the vantage point of 'systematic' observation of classrooms, this might look like a 'look-and-see exercise with a catch-what-you-can outcome' (Ober *et al.* 1971, p. 16). In fact, the broad intentions are clear enough. There is a rejection of any fragmenting of the discourse in ways that destroy its coherence, and of any attempt to assign labels to decontextualized segments of behaviour. The analysis used a rank-scale of units—i.e. all but the 'highest' being subsumed in the one above. The 'lowest' unit was the 'act' (e.g. an elicitation, directive or cue), expressed verbally in ways that could only be interpreted in their social context and in their place in a sequence of acts. 'Acts' build up into 'moves', and 'moves' into 'exchanges'. The 'exchange' is the central concept, its primary structure being described in terms of initiation, response and feedback. These in turn build up into 'transactions', like giving information or question-and-answer sessions, and 'transactions' into lessons. The research showed how orderly discourse was created and sustained, and this could not have been made apparent by either an analysis of the *content* of the interaction or of the purely linguistic devices for coding communicative function. The description of the meaning of grammatical forms *as moves* involved a description of 'what normally competent interaction is in the classroom situation'.

That situation is one with strongly defined communicative roles and purposes, which is its attraction for sociolinguistic research. Everyday conversation is inexplicit, full of ambiguities and apparently incomplete utterances, lacking any overall theme or stylistic consistency and likely to give an impression of disjointedness (Crystal and Davy 1969, pp. 95–116). The orderly nature of the classroom texts was the outcome of strong central direction (Sinclair *et al.* 1972, pp. 182–3). Everyday conversation also raises 'problems' of turn-taking and topic-switching which would be baffling if we were to approach them with conscious deliberation (see p. 66). In classrooms, some of these are 'solved' by the teacher's 'right' to decide. This is apparent in Sinclair's analysis. For example, the teacher marks off the stages in the discourse. 'Focusing' moves announce what is to happen next, or what the next topic is to be, so directing attention to the appropriate contributions and activities. 'Framing' moves indicate boundaries, showing that a phase has been completed. The teacher usually indicates the next speaker, his 'nomination' often being preceded by a 'cue' that the moment for a verbal response by some pupils is approaching, or by the evoking of a pupil 'bid'. Of course, the pupil may make his own unprompted 'bid', but he must normally wait until authorized to speak. Regaining the floor is rarely a problem for the teacher, however difficult for his pupils, because of his 'right' to speak (and interrupt) when he likes. He can reclaim the initiative with a question, an evaluation, or even an 'acceptance' of a pupil contribution which incorporates it into the developing exposition.

These brief examples make the orderliness of the discourse seem too easily achieved. But they illustrate the starting-point of the research, that *how* such order is created and sustained is more easily seen in a 'typical' situation where it is possible to 'recover the social assumptions which underlie the verbal communicative process' and so relate the linguistic forms used to the ways in which they are interpreted in *that* situation. The results of the research suggested that formal education may be characterized by *too* limited a range of communicative acts and moves, and by tight 'functional limits' on communicative skills. Grammatical differences between teachers and pupils seemed less significant than variations in the semantic options available to individuals in these roles (Sinclair *et al.* 1972, p. 59). Whatever the underlying social class or other persistent limitations on linguistic performance, the immediate communicative context brought its own stringent constraints.

In their 'traditional' form, classrooms are places contrived for the controlled transmission of knowledge. This is what gives them their peculiar identity as settings for talk. Most of the time, there *is* talk; most of the talk is by the teacher; and most of his talk is 'telling'—the giving out of information and instructions. Since it is systematic inter-action analysis which has provided most of the 'facts' about classrooms like these, it could be said that they have had the research methods they 'deserved'. The more fragmentary, allusive and personalized talk likely to occur in 'informal' classrooms would be largely inaccessible to any category system. It would also raise acute problems for socio-linguistic analysis, as Sinclair recognized. His attempt to relate the structure of classroom discourse to the 'pedagogical' structure of the interaction depends on predefined communicative roles and purposes. These provide the participants with a means of interpreting much of what is said. An outside observer can also make sense of it, in so far as it conforms to 'type', because he knows what competent classes inter-action is like. In 'informal' learning groups, the participants have to do more communicative work to 'create and maintain the social situation' (Gumperz and Herasimchuk 1972). Relationships are more fluid, and there are fewer 'ready-made' clues to meaning.

Barnes' recent work has focused on these potentially creative uncertainties (Barnes 1976: Barnes and Todd 1975). What he defines as 'exploratory' talk occurs when pupils 'talk their way into' a problem, while simultaneously negotiating how they are to relate to each other in arriving at some solution. The possibility of such talk depends on pupils being 'placed in a social context which supports it'—one in which the boundary between 'everyday' and 'school' knowledge is lowered. Where that boundary is high, most pupil-talk is likely to be 'talk as performance', a series of 'final-draft versions' in which uncertainties are concealed so as to reveal the speaker as a 'good' pupil who knows the appropriate answers. Where it is low, at least for the moment, pupils may collaborate in shaping new meanings, rather than reflecting back those which they have passively received. Whether or not they do so will depend on social relationships within the group— for example, on their sense of security with each other and their willingness to tolerate disagreement. But at least the possibility is there. Barnes takes a highly situational view of 'exploratory' talk. Its occurrence is seen to depend not on the linguistic abilities of the pupils, but on 'the degree of control over knowledge which they feel themselves to have' (Barnes 1976, p. 18). His position can be restated in 'Bernsteinian' form. Where the 'framing' of classroom knowledge is relatively weak, meanings have to be negotiated and achieved, rules of procedure have to be constructed, and difficulties cannot be resolved by an appeal to 'authority'. The conditions seem to exist for the use of an elaborated code.

I feel no temptation to end this book prescriptively. The present state of knowledge cannot support a platform from which to offer 'solutions' to educational problems, and as Hymes has remarked of linguistics, the prestige of any social science should not be abused by 'pretending to tell more than it knows'. The sociology of language is too new an enterprise to expect much in the way of 'results'. It *can* offer useful perspectives on some of the problems and practices of education. 'Speaking is the first and primary mode for communicating competency in all of the areas of skill and knowledge which schools purport to teach' (Philips 1970, p. 79). It is the main means by which children daily demonstrate their ability to meet the behavioural and academic demands of the classroom, and to cope with the 'realities' of speaking 'requires a theory in which socio-cultural factors have an explicit and constitutive role' (Hymes 1972a, p. 271). Sociological analysis first concentrated on those socio-cultural influences which arise from the distribution of power and opportunities in society at large. These may be reflected in the 'interference' between some children's understanding of communicative roles and stylistic appropriateness in other contexts, and the demands which confront them in schools. But they may also be reinforced, or insufficiently challenged, by the kind of 'critical contexts' for language use which classrooms commonly provide. The 'may' must be emphasized, because while formal education is founded on talk, we still know very little about the kind of talk which goes on. Studying classroom language can be seen as basic sociolinguistic research, with special opportunities of relating 'the structure of the language to the structure of speaking'. It offers the rare possibility in the sociology of education for contributing directly to the mainstream of social scientific enquiry, rather than waiting for work in the 'core' discipline which is then applied, more or less aptly, to educational concerns.

Bibliographical Index

The page numbers in square brackets refer to main references in the present book.

Abrahams, R. (1970), 'Rapping and Capping: Black Talk as Art', in J. Szwed (ed.), *Black America*, Basic Books. [48]

Abrahams, R. (1972a), 'Joking: the Training of the Man of Words in Talking Broad', in T. Kochman (ed.), *Rappin' and Stylin' Out*, op. cit. [33]

Abrahams, R. (1972b), 'The Training of the Man of Words in Talking Sweet', *Language in Society*, **1**.1, pp. 15–30. [48, 78]

Adams, R. (1971), 'A Sociological Approach to Classroom Research', in I. Westbury and A. Bellack (eds.), *Research into Classroom Processes*, Teachers' College Press. [160–1, 169]

Adams, R. and Biddle, B. (1970), *Realities of Teaching: Explorations with Videotape*, Holt, Rinehart and Winston. [160–1, 165]

Alatis, J. (ed.) (1969), *Linguistics and the Teaching of Standard English to Speakers of Other Languages or Dialects*, Georgetown University Monograph Series on Language and Linguistics, Number 22, Georgetown University Press. [139]

Allen, V. (1969), 'A Second Dialect is not a Second Language', in J. Alatis, op. cit., pp. 189–202. [139]

Allon, N. (1969), 'Systems of Classroom Interaction', *Journal of Experimental Education*, **38**, pp. 1–4. [168]

Allport, G. and Cantril, H. (1934), 'Judging Personality from Voice', *Journal of Social Psychology*, pp. 5, 37–55. [30]

Amidon, E. and Giammateo, M. (1967), 'The Verbal Behaviour of Superior Elementary Teachers', in E. Amidon and J. Hough (eds.), *Interaction Analysis: Theory, Research and Application*, Addison-Wesley. [164]

Amidon, E. and Hunter, E. (1967), *Improving Teaching: the Analysis of Classroom Interaction*, Holt, Rinehart and Winston. [164, 167–9]

Anderson, H. (1939), 'The Measurement of Dominative and Socially Integrative Behaviour in Teachers' Contacts with Children', *Child Development*, **10**, pp. 73–89. [168]

Andreski, S. (1974), *Social Science as Sorcery*, Penguin. [152–3]

Anisfeld, E. and Lambert, W. (1964), 'Evaluational Reactions of Bilingual and Monolingual Children to Spoken Languages', *Journal of Abnormal & Social Psychology*, **69**, pp. 89–97. [29]

Anisfeld, M., Bogo, N., and Lambert, W. (1962), 'Evaluational Reactions to

Accented English Speech', *Journal of Abnormal & Social Psychology*, **65**, pp. 223–31. [29]

Argyle, M. (1972a), *The Psychology of Inter-personal Behaviour*, Penguin. [67]

Argyle, M. (1972b), 'Non-Verbal Communication in Human Social Interaction', in R. Hinde (ed.), *Non-Verbal Communication*, Cambridge University Press. [67]

Argyle, M., Slater, V., Nicholson, H., Williams, M., and Burgess, P. 'The Communication of Inferior and Superior Attitudes by Verbal and Non-Verbal Signals', *British Journal of Social and Clinical Psychology*, **9**, pp. 222–31. [67]

Austin, J. (1962), *How To Do Things With Words*, Oxford University Press. [78]

Bailey, B. (1965), 'Toward a New Perspective in Negro English Dialectology', *American Speech*, **40**, pp. 171–7. [48, 50]

Bailey, B. (1966), *Jamaican Creole Syntax*, Cambridge University Press. [9, 43, 116]

Bales, R. (1950), *Interaction Process Analysis*, Addison-Wesley. [78]

Baratz, J. (1969a), 'Linguistic and Cultural Factors in Teaching Reading to Ghetto Children', *Elementary English*, **46**, pp. 199–203. [134]

Baratz, J. (1969b), 'A Bi-Dialectal Task for Determining Language Proficiency in Economically Disadvantaged Negro Children', *Child Development*, **40**, pp. 889–901. [121, 134]

Baratz, J. (1971), 'Teaching Reading in an Urban School System', in F. Williams (ed.), op. cit. [121, 134]

Baratz, S. (1970), 'Social Science's Conceptualization of the Afro-American', in J. Szwed (ed.), *Black America*, Basic Books. [131, 133]

Baratz, S. and Baratz, J. (1969), 'Negro Ghetto Children and Urban Education: a Cultural Solution', *Social Education*, **33**, pp. 401–4. [123]

Baratz, S. and Baratz, J. (1970), 'Early Childhood Intervention: The Social Science Base of Institutional Racism', *Harvard Educational Review*, **40**, pp. 29–50. [131, 135]

Barber, B. (1957), *Social Stratification*, Harcourt Brace. [84]

Barber, C. (1962), 'Some Measurable Characteristics of Modern Scientific Prose', in F. Behre (ed.), *Contributions to English Syntax and Philology*, Gothenburg University Press. [151]

Barker, R. (ed.) (1963), *The Stream of Behaviour*, Appleton-Century-Crofts. [116]

Barker, R. (1968), *Ecological Psychology*, Stanford University Press. [71].

Barnes, D. (1969), 'Language in the Secondary School Classroom', in D. Barnes, J. Britton and H. Rosen, *Language, the Learner and the School*, Penguin. [149, 153, 171]

Barnes, D. (1976), *From Communication to Curriculum*, Penguin. [180–1]

Barnes, D. and Todd, F. (1975a), *Communication and Learning in Small Groups*, S.S.R.C. Report, Leeds University Institute of Education. [162, 174]

Barnes, D. and Todd, F. (1975b), *Frames: How To Understand Conversation*, S.S.R.C. Report, Leeds University Institute of Education. [78, 171]

Basso, K. (1972), 'To Give Up On Words: Silence in Western Apache Culture', in P. Giglioli (ed.), *Language and Social Context*, Penguin. [74]

Becker, H. (1963), *The Outsider: Studies in the Sociology of Deviance*, Free Press. [25]

Bellack, A., Kliebard, H., Hyman, R. and Smith, F. (1966), *The Language of the Classroom*, Teachers' College Press. [165, 178]

Bereiter, C. (1965), 'Academic Instruction and Pre-School Children', in R. Shuy (ed.), *Language Programs for the Disadvantaged*, National Council for the Teaching of English. [139]

Bereiter, C. and Engelmann, S. (1966), *Teaching Disadvantaged Children in the Pre-School*, Prentice-Hall. [112, 127-8]

Bernstein, B. (1958), 'Some Sociological Determinants of Perception', *British Journal of Sociology*, **9**, pp. 159-74. [89, 106, 143]

Bernstein, B. (1959), 'A Public Language: Some Sociological Implications of a Linguistic Form', *British Journal of Sociology*, **10**, pp. 311-26. [143]

Bernstein, B. (1961a), 'Social Class and Linguistic Development', in A. Halsey, J. Floud and C. Anderson (eds.), *Education, Economy and Society*, Free Press. [88, 143]

Bernstein, B. (1961b), 'Social Structure, Language and Learning', *Educational Research*, **3**, pp. 163-76. [88-9, 106, 143]

Bernstein, B. (1962a), 'Linguistic Codes, Hesitation Phenomena and Intelligence', *Language & Speech*, **5**, pp. 31-46. [89-90, 96, 106]

Bernstein, B. (1962b), 'Social Class, Linguistic Codes and Grammatical Elements', *Language & Speech*, **5**, pp. 221-40. [89, 96]

Bernstein, B. (1965), 'A Socio-linguistic Approach to Social Learning', in J. Gould (ed.), *Penguin Survey of Social Sciences*, Penguin. [35, 90-2, 94]

Bernstein, B. (1967), 'Open Schools, Open Society', *New Society*, **14**, pp. 351-3. [146]

Bernstein, B. (1970a), 'A Critique of Compensatory Education', in D. Rubinstein and C. Stoneman (eds.), *Education for Democracy*, Penguin. [94, 146]

Bernstein, B. (1970b), 'Education Cannot Compensate for Society', *New Society*, **15** (387), pp. 344-47. [94, 100]

Bernstein, B. (1971), 'On the Classification and Framing of Educational Knowledge', in M. Young (ed.), *Knowledge and Control: New Directions in the Sociology of Education*, Collier-Macmillan. [146, 154]

Bernstein, B. (1973a), *Class, Codes and Control: Vol. 1—Theoretical Studies Towards a Sociology of Language*, Paladin Books; first published Routledge and Kegan Paul 1971. [88, 90-102, 105-8, 145-6, 175]

Bernstein, B. (ed.) (1973b), *Class, Codes and Control: Vol. 2—Applied Studies Towards a Sociology of Language*, Routledge and Kegan Paul. [102]

Bernstein, B. and Young, D. (1967), 'Social Class Differences in the Conception of the Use of Toys', *Sociology*, **1**, pp. 131-40. [109]

Bernstein, B. and Henderson, D. (1969), 'Social Class Differences in the Relevance of Language to Socialisation', *Sociology*, **3**, pp. 1-20. [110]

Bernstein, B. and Brandis, W. (1970), 'Social Class Differences in Communication and Control', in W. Brandis and D. Henderson, *Social Class, Language and Communication*, Routledge & Kegan Paul. [111]

Bickerton, D. (1971), 'Inherent Variability and Variable Rules', *Foundations of Language*, **7**, pp. 457-92. [9]

Bickerton, D. (1972), 'The Structure of Polylectal Grammars', in R. Shuy (ed.), *Sociolinguistics*, op. cit. [9]

L.C.C.—7

Blank, M. and Soloman, F. (1968), 'A Tutorial Language Program to Develop Abstract Thinking in Socially Disadvantaged Pre-School Children', *Child Development*, **39**, pp. 379–90. [127]

Blank, M. and Soloman, F. (1969), 'How Shall the Disadvantaged Child be Taught?', *Child Development*, **40**, pp. 47–61. [127]

Blom, J-P. and Gumperz, J. (1972), 'Social Meaning in Linguistic Structures', in J. Gumperz and D. Hymes (eds.), *Directions in Sociolinguistics*, op. cit. [30, 32, 52, 60, 70, 77]

Bloomfield, L. (1926), 'A Set of Postulates for the Science of Language', *Language*, **2**, pp. 153–6. [1]

Bloomfield, L. (1927), 'Literate and Illiterate Speech', *American Speech*, **2**, pp. 432–9. [45, 81]

Bloomfield, L. (1933), *Language*, Holt, Rinehart and Winston. [45]

Boas, F. (1964), 'Linguistics and Ethnology', in D. Hymes (ed.), *Language in Culture and Society*, op. cit. [103]

Bossard, J. (1945), 'Family Modes of Expression', in J. Bossard and E. Boll, *The Sociology of Child Development* (4th Edition), Harper International 1966. [87]

Bourdieu, P. (1973), 'Cultural Reproduction and Social Reproduction', in R. Brown (ed.), *Knowledge, Education and Cultural Change*, Tavistock. [155]

Brandis, W. and Henderson, D. (1970), *Social Class, Language and Communication*, Routledge & Kegan Paul. [91]

Brent, S. and Katz, E. (1967), *A Study of Language Deviations and Cognitive Processes*, Psychology Department, Wayne State University, Detroit. [120]

Bright, W. (ed.) (1966), *Sociolinguistics*, Mouton. [8, 10]

Brottman, M. (ed.) (1968), 'Language Remediation for the Disadvantaged Pre-School Child', *Monographs of the Society for Research in Child Development*, **33**.8. [127]

Brown, R. and Gilman, A. (1960), 'The Pronouns of Power and Solidarity', in T. Sebeok (ed.), *Style in Language*, M.I.T. Press. [75]

Brown, R. and Ford, M. (1961), 'Address in American English', *Journal of Abnormal Psychology*, **62**, pp. 375–85. [75]

Bullock, A. (chairman) (1975), *A Language for Life* (The Bullock Report), Department of Education and Science, H.M.S.O. [149, 162]

Burling, R. (1969), 'Linguistics and Ethnographic Description', *American Anthropology*, **71**, pp. 817–27. [69]

Burling, R. (1970), *Man's Many Voices: Language in its Cultural Context*, Holt, Rinehart and Winston. [8, 67]

Burling, R. (1973), *English in Black and White*, Holt, Rinehart and Winston. [48]

Byers, P. and Byers, H. (1972), 'Non-Verbal Communication and the Education of Children', in C. Cazden et al., op. cit. [140]

Byrne, D. and Williamson, B. (1972), 'The Myth of the Restricted Code', *Working Paper in Sociology No. 1*, Durham University Department of Sociology and Social Administration. [106, 124]

Carroll, J. (1953), *The Study of Language*, Harvard University Press. [7]

Cassidy, F. (1961), *Jamaica Talk: Three Hundred Years of the English Language in Jamaica*, Macmillan. [43–4]

Cassidy, F. (1969), 'Teaching Standard English to Speakers of Creole in Jamaica', in J. Alatis (ed.), op. cit. [42–4, 124]

Cazden, C. (1966), 'Sub-Cultural Differences in Child Language', *Merrill-Palmer Quarterly*, **12**, pp. 185–220. [82, 102, 133]

Cazden, C. (1970), 'The Neglected Situation in Child Language Research and Education', *Journal of Social Issues*, **25**, pp. 35–60. [117, 147]

Cazden, C. (1971), 'Approaches to Social Dialects in Early Childhood', in *Sociolinguistics: A Cross-Disciplinary Perspective*, Centre for Applied Linguistics.

Cazden, C. (1972), *Child Language and Education*, Holt, Rinehart and Winston. [122, 128, 130, 155]

Cazden, C., John, V., and Hymes, D. (eds.), *The Functions of Language in the Classroom*, Teachers' College Press. [140]

Cheyne, W. (1970), 'Stereotyped Reactions to Speakers with Scottish and English Regional Accents', *British Journal of Social and Clinical Psychology*, **9**, pp. 77–9. [51]

Chinoy, E. (1961), *Society: An Introduction to Sociology*, Random House. [84]

Chomsky, N. (1965), *Aspects of the Theory of Syntax*, M.I.T. Press. [2, 37]

Chomsky, N. (1972), *Language and Mind* (2nd Edition), Harcourt, Brace & World. [2, 4]

Cicourel, A. (1973), *Cognitive Sociology*, Penguin. [69]

Cohen, R. (1968), 'The Relation Between Socio-Conceptual Styles and Orientation to School Requirements', *Sociology of Education*, **41**, pp. 201–20. [128]

Cohen, R. (1969), 'Conceptual Styles, Culture Conflict and Non-Verbal Tests of Intelligence', *American Anthropology*, **71**, 828–56. [130]

Cole, M., Gay, J., Glick, J., Sharp, D. et al. (1971), *The Cultural Context of Learning and Thinking*, Methuen. [118, 129–30]

Cook-Gumperz, J. (1973), *Social Control and Socialisation: A Study of Class Differences in the Language of Maternal Control*, Routledge & Kegan Paul. [98, 107–9]

Coulthard, M. (1969), 'A Discussion of Restricted and Elaborated Codes', *Educational Review*, **22**, pp. 38–50. [93, 99, 102]

Coulthard, M. (1974), 'Approaches to the Analysis of Classroom Interaction', *Educational Review*, **26**, pp. 229–40. [178]

Coulthard, R. and Robinson, W. (1968), 'The Structure of the Nominal Group and Elaboratedness of Code', *Language & Speech*, **11**, pp. 234–50. [98]

Cowan, P., Weber, J., Hoddinott, B., and Klein, J. (1967), 'Mean Length of Spoken Response as a Function of Stimulus, Experimenter and Subject', *Child Development*, **38**, pp. 199–203. [120]

Creber, J. (1972), *Lost For Words: Language and Educational Failure*, Penguin. [149]

Crystal, D. (1971), 'Prosodic and Paralinguistic Correlates of Social Categories', in E. Ardener (ed.), *Social Anthropology and Language*, Tavistock. [28, 67]

Crystal, D. and Davy, D. (1969), *Investigating English Style*, Longmans. [150–1, 179]

Davies, A. (1968), 'Some Problems in the Use of Language Varieties in Teaching', *Educational Review*, **20**, pp. 107–22. [150]

Davies, A. (1969), 'The Notion of Register', *Educational Review*, **22**, pp. 64–77. [150–1]

Davis A. (1948), *Social Class Influences Upon Learning*, Harvard University Press. [84–5]

De Camp, D. (1969), 'Is a Sociolinguistic Theory Possible?', in J. Alatis (ed.), op. cit. [3, 8–9, 15, 92]

Denison, N. (1968), 'Sauris: A Trilingual Community in Diatypic Perspective', *Man* (New Series), **3**, pp. 578–92. [56–7, 72, 77]

Denison, N. (1971), 'Some Observations on Language Variety and Plurilingualism', in E. Ardener (ed.), *Social Anthropology and Language*, Tavistock. [56–7, 72]

Deutsch, C. (1967), 'Learning in the Disadvantaged', in M. Deutsch (ed.), op. cit. [113]

Deutsch, M. (1965), 'The Role of Social Class in Language Development and Cognition', *American Journal of Orthopsychiatry*, **35**, pp. 78–88. [112, 120, 123–5, 128]

Deutsch, M. (ed.) (1967), *The Disadvantaged Child*, Basic Books. [130–1]

Deutsch, M., Maliver, A., Brown, B. and Cherry, E. (1967), 'The Communication of Information in the Elementary School Classroom', in M. Deutsch (ed.), op. cit. [114, 120, 129–31]

Dillard, J. (1972), *Black English: Its History and Usage in the United States*, Random House. [48, 50]

Douglas, J. (ed.) (1971), *Understanding Everyday Life*, Routledge & Kegan Paul. [118]

Dreitzel, P. (ed.) (1970), *Patterns of Communicative Behaviour*, Recent Sociology No. 2, Collier-Macmillan. [8]

Drucker, E. (1971), 'Cognitive Styles and Class Stereotypes', in E. Leacock (ed.), *The Culture of Poverty: A Critique*, Simon & Schuster. [133]

Dumont, R. (1972), 'Learning English and How to be Silent: Studies in Sioux and Cherokee Classrooms', in C. Cazden et al. (eds.), op. cit. [128]

Dumont, R. and Wax, M. (1969), 'Cherokee School Society and the Inter-Cultural Classroom', *Human Organisation*, **28**, pp. 217–26. [128]

Dundes, A. (1972), 'The Strategy of Turkish Boys' Duelling Rhymes', in J. Gumperz and D. Hymes (eds.), op. cit. [32]

Edwards, A. (1974), 'Social Class and Linguistic Inference', *Research in Education*, **12**, pp. 71–80. [90]

Edwards, A. (1976a), 'Social Class and Linguistic Choice', *Sociology*, **10**, pp. 101–10. [101]

Edwards, A. (1976b), 'Speech Codes and Speech Variants: Social Class and Task Differences in Children's Speech', *Journal of Child Language*, **3.2**. [15, 101, 120]

Edwards, A. and Hargreaves, D. (1976), 'The Social Science Base of Academic Radicalism', *Educational Review*, **28**, pp. 83–93. [132–3]

Entwisle, D. (1966), 'Developmental Sociolinguistics: A Comparative Study in Four Sub-Cultural Settings', *Sociometry*, **29**, pp. 67–84. [113]

Entwisle, D. (1968a), 'Developmental Sociolinguistics: Inner-City Children', *American Journal of Sociology*, **74**, pp. 37–49. [113]

Entwisle, D. (1968b), 'Sub-Cultural Differences in Children's Language Development', *International Journal of Psychology*, **3**, pp. 13–22. [113]

Ervin-Tripp, S. (1964), 'An Analysis of the Interaction of Language, Topic and Listener', *American Anthropology*, **66.6** (part 2), pp. 86–102. [70]

Ervin-Tripp, S. (1971a), 'Sociolinguistics', in J. Fishman (ed.), *Advances in the Sociology of Language*, Mouton. [10, 70, 75]

Ervin-Tripp, S. (1971b), 'Social Dialects in Developmental Sociolinguistics', in *Sociolinguistics: A Cross-Disciplinary Perspective*, Centre for Applied Linguistics. [121–2, 134, 136]

Fasold, R. (1969), 'Distinctive Linguistic Characteristics of Black English', in J. Alatis (ed.), op. cit. [50]

Fasold, R. (1970), 'Two Models of Socially Significant Language Variation', *Language*, **46**, pp. 551–63. [50]

Ferguson, C. (1959), 'Diglossia', *Word*, **15**, pp. 325–40. [58–9]

Ferguson, C. (1962), 'The Language Factor in National Development', *Anthropological Linguistics*, **4**, pp. 23–7. [18]

Ferguson, C. (1964), 'Baby Talk in Six Languages', *American Anthropology*, **66.6** (Part 2), pp. 103–14. [73]

Ferguson, C. (1966a), 'Sociolinguistically Oriented Language Surveys', *Linguistic Reporter*, **8**, pp. 1–3. [11]

Ferguson, C. (1966b), 'National Sociolinguistic Profile Formulas', in W. Bright (ed.), op. cit. [11]

Ferguson, C. and Gumperz, J. (1960), 'Linguistic Diversity in South Asia', *International Journal of American Linguistics*, **26**, pp. 1–8. [37]

Fillmore, C. (1972), 'A Grammarian Looks To Sociolinguistics', in R. Shuy (ed.), op. cit. [4–5, 9]

Firth, J. (1935), 'On Sociological Linguistics', in D. Hymes (ed.), *Language in Culture and Society*, Harper & Row 1964. [7, 15, 64, 157]

Firth, J. (1957), *Papers in Linguistics 1934–1951*, Oxford University Press. [63–4]

Fischer, J. (1958), 'Social Influences on the Choice of a Linguistic Variant', *Word*, **14**, pp. 47–61. [13, 61, 68]

Fischer, J. (1964), 'Words For Self and Others in Some Japanese Families', *American Anthropology*, **66.6** (Part 2), pp. 115–26. [74]

Fishman, J. (ed.) (1968), *Readings in the Sociology of Language*, Mouton. [8]

Fishman, J. (ed.) (1971), *Advances in the Sociology of Language*, Mouton. [8–9, 61]

Fishman, J. (1972a), 'The Sociology of Language', in P. Giglioli (ed.), op. cit. [10, 17–18, 70]

Fishman, J. (1972b), 'Domains and the Relationship Between Micro- and Macro-Sociolinguistics', in J. Gumperz and D. Hymes (eds.), op. cit. [16, 59–60, 68–9]

Fishman, J. and Salmon, E. (1972), 'What Has the Sociology of Language to Say to the Teacher?', in C. Cazden et al. (eds.), op. cit. [57–8, 156]

Flanders, N. (1967a), 'Interaction Models of Critical Teaching Behaviour', in E. Amidon and J. Hough (eds.), *Interaction Analysis*, Addison-Wesley. [167]

Flanders, N. (1967b), 'Intent, Action and Feedback', in E. Amidon and J. Hough (eds.), op. cit. [168]

Flanders, N. (1968), 'Interaction Analysis and In-Service Training', *Journal of Experimental Education*, **37**, pp. 126–32. [167]

Flanders, N. (1970), *Analysing Teacher Behaviour*, Addison-Wesley. [164–9]

Foster, G. (1964), 'Speech Forms and Perception of Social Distance in a

Spanish-Speaking American Village', *South-West Journal of Anthropology*, **20**, pp. 107–22. [68]

Foster, H. (1974), *Ribbin', Jivin' and Playin' the Dozens: The Unrecognised Dilemma of Inner-City Schools*, Bollinger. [32–3, 67, 141]

Frake, C. (1964), 'How To Ask for a Drink in Subanun', *American Anthropology*, **66.6** (Part 2), pp. 127–32. [65, 78]

Freeburg, N. and Payne, D. (1965), 'Parental Influence on Cognitive Development in Early Childhood', *Child Development*, **38**, pp. 65–87. [127]

Frender, R. and Lambert, W. (1972), 'Speech Style and Scholastic Success', in R. Shuy (ed.), op. cit. [138]

Frey, J. (1945), 'Amish Triple Talk', *American Speech*, **20**, pp. 85–98. [18, 59–60, 72]

Friedrich, P. (1966), 'The Linguistic Reflex of Social Change', in S. Lieberson (ed.), op. cit. [12]

Friedrich, P. (1972), 'Social Context and Semantic Feature: The Russian Pronominal Usage', in J. Gumperz and D. Hymes (eds.), op. cit. [12]

Fries, C. (1940), *American English Grammar*, Appleton-Century. [82–3]

Furst, N. and Amidon, E. (1967), 'Teacher-Pupil Interaction Patterns in the Elementary School', in E. Amidon and J. Hough, *Interaction Analysis*, Addison-Wesley. [164]

Gahagan, D. and Gahagan, G. (1970), *Talk Reform: Explorations in Language for Infant School Children*, Routledge & Kegan Paul. [144–5, 172]

Gallagher, J. and Aschner, M. (1963), 'A Preliminary Report on Analyses of Classroom Interaction', *Merrill-Palmer Quarterly*, **9**, pp. 183–94. [171]

Garfinkel, H. (1964), 'Studies in the Routine Grounds of Everyday Activities', *Social Problems*, **11**, pp. 225–50. [169–70]

Garfinkel, H. (1972), 'Remarks on Ethnomethodology', in J. Gumperz and D. Hymes (eds.) op. cit. [65]

Geer, B. (1968), 'Teaching', in D. Sills (ed.), *International Encyclopaedia of Social Science*, Vol. 15, pp. 560–65, Collier-Macmillan. [163]

Geertz, C. (1960), *The Religion of Java*, Free Press. [35–6, 73, 77]

Gerber, S. and Hertel, C. (1969), 'Language Deficiency of Disadvantaged Children', *Journal of Speech & Hearing Research*, **12**, pp. 270–80. [114]

Giglioli, P. (ed.), *Language and Social Context*, Penguin. [8]

Giles, H. (1970), 'Evaluative Reactions to Accents', *Educational Review*, **22**, pp. 211–27. [12, 30, 51]

Giles, H. (1971), 'Patterns of Evaluation to RP, South Welsh and Somerset-Accented Speech', *British Journal of Social and Clinical Psychology*, **10**, pp. 280–1. [30, 51]

Goffman, E. (1964), 'The Neglected Situation', *American Anthropology*, **66.6** (Part 2), pp. 133–6. [63]

Goffman, E. (1971), *The Presentation of Self in Everyday Life*, Penguin. [28]

Golden, M. and Birns, B. (1968), 'Social Class and Cognitive Development in Infancy', *Merrill-Palmer Quarterly*, **14**, pp. 139–49. [114]

Goldfarb, W. (1943), 'The Effects of Early Institutional Care on Adolescent Personality', *Journal of Experimental Education*, **12**. [85]

Goldfarb, W. (1945), 'Effects of Psychological Deprivation During Infancy and Subsequent Stimulation', *American Journal of Psychology*, **102**, pp. 18–33. [85]

Greenberg, J. (1948), 'Linguistics and Ethnology', *South-West Journal of Anthropology*, **4**, pp. 140–7. [3]

Greenberg, J. (1971), *Language, Culture and Communication*, Stanford University Press. [3, 11]

Greenberg, J. and Berry, J. (1966), 'Sociolinguistic Research in Africa', *African Studies Bulletin*, **9.2**, pp. 1–9. [11]

Gump, P. (1964), 'Environmental Guidance of the Classroom Behavioural System', in B. Biddle and W. Ellena (eds.), *Contemporary Research on Teacher Effectiveness*, Holt, Rinehart & Winston. [160]

Gumperz, J. (1962), 'Types of Linguistic Communities', *Anthropological Linguistics*, **4**, pp. 28–40. [37–8]

Gumperz, J. (1964), 'Linguistic and Social Interaction in Two Communities', *American Anthropology*, **66.6** (Part 2), pp. 137–53. [12, 16, 38, 52, 70]

Gumperz, J. (1968), 'The Speech Community', in D. Sills (ed.), *International Encyclopaedia of the Social Sciences*, **9**, pp. 381–6. [38–9, 54–5]

Gumperz, J. (1971), *Language in Social Groups*, Stanford University Press. [42, 55–6]

Gumperz, J. and Herasimchuk, E. (1972), 'The Conversational Analysis of Social Meaning: A Study of Classroom Interaction', in R. Shuy (ed.), op. cit. [170, 180–1]

Gumperz, J. and Hymes, D. (1972), *Directions in Sociolinguistics: The Ethnography of Communication*, Holt, Rinehart and Winston. [8, 69, 90, 95]

Haas, M. (1944), 'Men and Women's Speech in Koasati', *Language*, **20**, pp. 142–9. [73]

Hall, E. (1963), 'A System for the Notation of Proxemic Behaviour', *American Anthropology*, **65**, pp. 1003–26. [67]

Hall, R. (1972), 'Pidgins and Creoles as Standard Languages', in J. Pride and J. Holmes (eds.), *Sociolinguistics*, Penguin. [42]

Halliday, M. (1964), 'The Users and Uses of Language', in M. Halliday, A. McIntosh and P. Strevens, *The Linguistic Sciences and Language Teaching*, Longmans. [31, 47, 150]

Halliday, M. (1969), 'Relevant Models of Language', *Educational Review*, **22**, pp. 26–37. [107]

Halliday, M. (1971), 'Language in a Social Perspective', *Educational Review*, **23**, pp. 165–88. [79, 170]

Halliday, M. (1973), *Explorations in the Functions of Language*, Arnold. [79]

Halliday, M. (1975), 'Talking One's Way In: A Sociolinguistic Perspective on Language and Learning', in A. Davies (ed.), *Problems of Language and Learning*, Heinemann Educational Books. [9]

Hamilton, D. and Delamont, S. (1974), 'Classroom Research: A Cautionary Tale', *Research in Education*, **11**, pp. 1–16. [168]

Hargreaves, D. (1972), *Interpersonal Relations and Education*, Routledge & Kegan Paul. [162]

Hargreaves, D., Hestor, S. and Mellor, F. (1975), *Deviance in Classrooms*, Routledge & Kegan Paul. [176–7]

Hasan, R. (1968), 'Grammatical Cohesion in Spoken and Written English', Longman's *Programme in Linguistics and English Teaching*, Paper 7. [31, 65, 99]

Hasan, R. (1973), 'Code, Register and Social Dialect', in B. Bernstein (ed.), op. cit. [99, 101]

Haugen, E. (1966), 'Dialect, Language and Nation', *American Anthropology*, **68**, pp. 922–35. [39–41, 44, 46, 58]

Hawkins, P. (1969), 'Social Class, the Nominal Group and Reference', *Language & Speech*, **12**, pp. 125–35. [99]

Hawkins, P. (1973), 'The Influence of Sex, Social Class and Pause Location in the Hesitation of Seven Year Old Children', in B. Bernstein (ed.), op. cit. [100]

Heider, E., Cazden, C. and Brown, R. (1968), 'Social Class Differences in the Effectiveness and Style of Children's Coding Ability', *Project Literacy Reports No. 9*, Cornell University. [115, 118]

Henderson, D. (1970a), 'Social Class Differences in Form-Class Usage among Five Year Old Children', in *W. Brandis and D. Henderson*, op. cit. [99, 118, 120]

Henderson, D. (1970b), 'Contextual Specificity, Discretion and Cognitive Specialisation', *Sociology*, **4**, pp. 311–38. [108]

Herman, S. (1961), 'Explorations in the Social Psychology of Language Choice', *Human Relations*, **14**, pp. 149–64. [12, 30]

Herriott, P. (1970), *An Introduction to the Psychology of Language*, Methuen. [102]

Hertzler, J. (1953), 'Towards a Sociology of Language', *Social Forces*, **32**, pp. 109–19. [8, 84]

Hertzler, J. (1965), *A Sociology of Language*, Random House. [8, 125]

Hess, R. and Shipman, V. (1965), 'Early Experience and the Socialization of Cognitive Modes in Children', *Child Development*, **36**, pp. 869–86. [109–10, 127–9]

Hess, R. and Shipman, V. (1968), 'Maternal Influences Upon Early Learning', in R. Hess and R. Beer, *Early Education*, Aldine. [109–10, 127, 130]

Hilsun, S. and Cane, B. (1971), *The Teacher's Day*, National Foundation for Educational Research. [161]

Hoggart, R. (1957), *The Uses of Literacy*, Chatto & Windus. [88, 105]

Horner, V. and Gussow, J. (1972), 'John and Mary: A Pilot Study in Linguistic Ecology', in C. Cazden et al. (eds.), op. cit. [132, 142]

Houston, S. (1969), 'A Sociolinguistic Consideration of the Black English of Children in Northern Florida', *Language*, **45**, pp. 599–607. [49–50, 119]

Houston, S. (1970), 'A Re-Examination of Some Assumptions about the Language of Disadvantaged Children', *Child Development*, **41**, pp. 947–63 [119, 132, 155]

Humphreys, L. (1970), *The Tea-Room Trade*, Duckworth. [76]

Hymes, D. (1964), 'Towards Ethographies of Communications', *American Anthropology*, **66.6** (Part 2), pp. 12–25. [3, 64]

Hymes, D. (ed.) (1964b), *Language in Culture and Society*, Harper & Row. [8]

Hymes, D. (1967a), 'Models of the Interaction of Language and Social Setting', *Journal of Social Issues*, **22**, pp. 8–28. [54, 70]

Hymes, D. (1967b), 'Why Linguistics Needs the Sociologist', *Social Research*, **34**, pp. 632–47. [14]

Hymes, D. (1971), 'Sociolinguistics and the Ethnography of Speaking', in E. Ardener (ed.), *Social Anthropology and Language*, Tavistock. [3, 5, 61, 64]

Hymes, D. (1972a), 'On Communicative Competence', in J. Pride and J. Holmes (eds.), *Sociolinguistics*, Penguin. [3–4, 7, 141, 180]

Hymes, D. (1972b), 'The Scope of Sociolinguistics', in R. Shuy (ed.), op. cit. [4, 16, 58, 79]

Hymes, D. (1972c), 'Editorial Introduction', *Language in Society*, 1, pp. 1–14. [35]

Inkeles, A. (1966), 'Social Structure and the Socialization of Competence', *Harvard Educational Review*, 36, pp. 265–83. [104]

Jackson, L. (1974), 'The Myth of Elaborated and Restricted Codes', *Higher Educational Review*, 6, pp. 65–81. [102]

Jackson, P. (1968), *Life in Classrooms*, Holt, Rinehart and Winston. [161]

Jackson, P. and Lahaderne, H. (1967), 'Inequalities of Teacher-Pupil Contacts', *Psychology in the Schools*, 4, pp. 204–11. [159, 161]

Jencks, C. et al. (1973), *Inequality: A Re-Assessment of the Effects of Family and Schooling in America*, Allen Lane: The Penguin Press. [124]

Jensen, A. (1967), 'The Culturally Disadvantaged: Psychological and Educational Aspects', *Educational Research*, 10, pp. 4–20. [127, 129]

Jensen, A. (1968), 'Social Class and Verbal Learning', in J. De Cecco (ed.), *The Psychology of Language, Thought and Instruction*, Holt, Rinehart and Winston. [102, 114, 129]

John, V. (1963), 'The Intellectual Development of Slum Children', *American Journal of Orthopsychiatry*, 33, pp. 813–22. [114]

John, V. (1971), 'Language and Educability', in E. Leacock (ed.), op. cit. [132]

John, V. and Goldstein, L. (1964), 'The Social Context of Language Acquisition', *Merrill-Palmer Quarterly*, 10, pp. 265–75. [112, 114]

John, V. and Moskovitz, S. (1970), 'Language Acquisition and Development in Early Childhood', in *National Society for the Study of Education Year-Book*, 69 (Part 2). [85, 115]

Jones, J. (1966), 'Social Class and the Under-Fives', *New Society*, No. 221, pp. 935–6. [109]

Joos, M. (1952), 'The Medieval Sibilants', *Language*, 28, pp. 222–31. [13]

Joos, M. (1962), '*The Five Clocks*', *International Journal of American Linguistics*, 28.2 (Part 5). [79, 148–9]

Jordan, C. and Robinson, W. (1972), 'The Grammar of Working-Class and Middle-Class Children Using Elicited Imitations', *Language & Speech*, 15, pp. 122–40. [121]

Kendon, A. (1967), 'Some Functions of Gaze Direction in Social Interaction', *Acta Psychologica*, 28, pp. 1–47. [71]

Kessler, J. (1965), 'Environmental Components of Measured Intelligence', *School Review*, 73, pp. 339–58. [112]

Klein, J. (1965), *Samples From English Cultures, Vol. 2—Child-Bearing Practices*, Routledge & Kegan Paul. [105]

Kloss, H. (1967), 'Bilingualism and Nationalism', *Journal of Social Issues*, 23, pp. 23–47. [40]

Kochman, T. (1972a), *Rappin' and Stylin' Out: Communication in Urban Black America*, University of Illinois Press. [33, 61]

Kochman, T. (1972b), 'Black Speech Events and a Language Programme for the Classroom', in C. Cazden et al. (eds.), op. cit. [33, 130, 135, 141–2, 156]

L.C.C.—7*

Kohn, M. (1959), 'Social Class and the Exercise of Parental Authority', *American Sociological Review*, **24**, pp. 352–66. [105, 109]

Kohn, M. (1963), 'Social Class and Parent-Child Relationships: an Interpretation', *American Journal of Sociology*, **68**, pp. 471–80. [105]

Kohn, M. and Schooler, C. (1969), 'Class, Occupation and Orientation', *American Sociological Review*, **34**, pp. 659–78. [105]

Kounin, J. (1970), *Discipline and Group Management in Classrooms*, Holt, Rinehart and Winston. [176]

Krauss, R. and Rotter, G. (1968), 'Communicative Abilities of Children as a Function of Status and Age', *Merrill-Palmer Quarterly*, **14**, pp. 161–73. [115, 128]

Labov, W. (1964), 'Phonological Correlates of Social Stratification', *American Anthropology*, **66.6** (Part 2), pp. 164–76. [12]

Labov, W. (1966a), *The Social Stratification of English in New York City*, Centre for Applied Linguistics. [6, 12–13, 19–21, 52]

Labov, W. (1966b), 'Hyper-Correction by the Lower Middle-Class as a Factor in Linguistic Change', in W. Bright (ed.), op. cit. [21]

Labov, W. (1966c), 'The Effect of Social Mobility on Linguistic Behaviour', in S. Lieberson (ed.), op. cit. [20]

Labov, W. (1968), 'The Reflection of Social Processes in Linguistic Structures', in J. Fishman (ed.), op. cit. [12, 19]

Labov, W. (1969a), 'Contraction, Deletion and Inherent Variability', *Language*, **45**, pp. 715–62. [22, 49–50, 117]

Labov, W. (1969b), 'The Logic of Non-Standard English', in J. Alatis (ed.), op. cit. (also in P. Giglioli, op. cit.). [92, 119, 133, 137, 142]

Labov, W. (1971), 'The Study of Language in its Social Context', in J. Fishman (ed.), op. cit. [27, 117]

Labov, W. (1972), 'Rules for Ritual Insults', in D. Sudnow (ed.), *Studies in Social Interaction*, Free Press. [32–3]

LaCivita, A., et al. (1966), 'The Socio-Economic Status of Children and the Acquisition of Grammar', *Journal of Educational Research*, **60**, pp. 61–4. [113]

Lambert, W., Hodgson, R., Gardener, R. and Fillenbaum, S. (1960), 'Evaluational Reactions to Spoken Languages', *Journal of Abnormal Social Psychology*, **60**, pp. 44–51. [29]

Lambert, W., Anisfeld, M. and Yeni-Kamshian, G. (1965), 'Evaluational Reactions of Jewish and Arab Adolescents to Dialect and Language Variations', *Journal of Personal and Social Psychology*, **2**, pp. 84–90. [29–30]

Lambert, W. (1967), 'A Social Psychology of Bilingualism', *Journal of Social Issues*, **23**, pp. 91–109. [12, 29–30]

Landar, H. (1964), *Language and Culture*, Oxford University Press. [8]

Langendoen, D. (1968), *The London School of Linguistics*, M.I.T. Press. [63–4]

Laver, J. (1968), 'Voice Quality and Indexical Information', *British Journal of Disorders of Communications*, **3**, pp. 43–54. [28, 67]

Lawton, D. (1968), *Social Class, Language and Education*, Routledge & Kegan Paul. [85, 89, 97, 118]

Leach, E. (1972), 'The Influence of Cultural Context on Non-Verbal Communication in Man', in R. Hinde (ed.), *Non-Verbal Communication*, Cambridge University Press. [67]

Leacock, E. (ed.) (1971), *The Culture of Poverty: a Critique*, Simon & Schuster. [131-2]

Lennard, H. and Bernstein, A. (1968), 'The Inter-dependence of Therapist and Patient Verbal Behaviour', in J. Fishman (ed.), op. cit. [12]

Le Page, R. (1968), 'Problems to be Faced in the Use of English as the Medium of Education in Four West-Indian Territories', in J. Fishman et al. (eds.), *Language Problems of Developing Nations*, Wiley. [44]

Lerman, P. (1967), 'Argot, Symbolic Deviance and SubCultural Delinquency', *American Sociological Review*, **32**, pp. 209-24. [11, 24-5]

Lesser, G., Fifer, G. and Clark, D (1965), 'Mental Abilities of Children from Different Social Class and Cultural Groups', *Monographs Society Research in Child Development*, **102**, Vol. 30, No. 4. [119]

Levine, L. and Crockett, H. (1966), 'Speech Variation in a Piedmont Community: Post-Vocalic r', in S. Lieberson (ed.), op. cit. [15, 73]

Lewis, M. (1947), *Language and Society*, Nelson. [23, 151]

Lieberson, S. (ed.) (1966), *Explorations in Sociolinguistics*, International Journal of American Linguistics, **33.4** (Special Issue). [8]

Loban, W. (1963), *The Language of Elementary School Children*, National Council for the Teaching of English, Research Report No. 1. [100, 111-12]

Loban, W. (1965), 'Language Proficiency and School Learning', in J. Krumboltz (ed.), *Learning and the Educational Process*, Rand McNally. [111]

McCandless, B. (1969), 'Childhood Socialisation', in D. Goslin (ed.), *Handbook of Socialisation Theory and Research*, Rand McNally. [143]

McCarthy, D. (1954), 'Language Development in Children', in L. Carmichael (ed.), *Manual of Child Psychology*, Wiley. [85-6, 117]

McDavid, R. (1946), 'Dialect Geography and Social Science Problems', *Social Forces*, **25**, pp. 168-72. [3, 11, 84]

McDavid, R. (1966), 'Dialect Differences and Social Differences in an Urban Society', in W. Bright (ed.), op. cit. [3, 138-9]

McDavid, R. (1968), 'Variations in Standard American-English', *Elementary English*, **45**, pp. 561-4 and 608. [39]

McDavid, R. (1969a), 'Dialects: British and American Standard and Non-Standard', in A. Hill (ed.), *Linguistics*, Voice of America Forum Lectures. [138, 140]

McDavid, R. (1969b), 'A Theory of Dialect', in J. Alatis (ed.), op. cit. [41]

McDavid, R. and McDavid, V. (1951), 'The Relationship of the Speech of American Negroes to the Speech of Whites', *American Speech*, **26**, pp. 3-17. [48]

Mackay, D., Thompson, B. and Schaub, P. (1970), *Breakthrough to Literacy: Teachers' Manual*, Longmans. [135]

Malinowski, B. (1923), 'The Problem of Meaning in Primitive Languages', Supplement to C. Ogden and I. Richards, *The Meaning of Meaning*, Kegan Paul. [62-3]

Malinowski, B. (1935), *Coral Gardens and Their Magic*, republished by Indiana University Press 1965. [62-3]

Malinowski, B. (1937), 'The Dilemma of Contemporary Linguistics', *Nature*, **140**, pp. 172-3. [7]

Mannheim, K. and Stewart, W. (1962), *Introduction to the Sociology of Education*, Routledge & Kegan Paul. [160]

Massialas, B. and Zevin, J. (1967), *Creative Encounters in the Classroom*, Wiley. [172–4]

Maurer, D. (1939), 'Prostitutes and Criminal Argots', *American Journal of Sociology*, **44,** pp. 544–50. [24]

Maurer, D. (1940), *The Big Con*, Bobbs-Merrill. [24]

Maurer, D. (1950), 'The Argot of the Dice Gambler', *Annals of American Academy of Political and Social Science*, **269,** pp. 114–33. [24]

Mehrobian, A. and Diamond, S. (1971), 'Seating Arrangements and Conversation', *Sociometry*, **34,** pp. 281–89. [71]

Merton, R. (1957), *Social Theory and Social Structure*, Free Press. [152]

Miller, D. and Swanson, G. (1960), *Inner Conflict and Defence*, Holt. [128]

Mills, C. W. (1939), 'Language, Logic and Culture', *American Sociological Review*, **4,** pp. 670–80. [13–14, 152]

Mills, C. W. (1940), 'Situated Actions and Vocabularies of Motive', *American Sociological Review*, **5,** pp. 439–52. [13–14]

Mills, C. W. (1963), *Power, Politics and People*, Oxford University Press. [1, 152]

Milner, E. (1951), 'A Study of the Relationship of Reading-Readiness and Patterns of Parent-Child Interaction', *Child Development*, **22,** pp. 95–112. [86]

Mishler, E. (1972), 'Implications of Teacher Strategies for Language and Cognition', in C. Cazden et al. (eds.), op. cit. [159, 172]

Mitchell-Kernan, C. (1972a), 'Signifying and Marking: Two Afro-American Speech Acts', in J. Gumperz and D. Hymes (eds.), op. cit. [33]

Mitchell-Kernan, C. (1972b), 'On the Status of Black English for Native Speakers', in C. Cazden et al. (eds.). [50]

Moerman, M. (1972), 'Analysis of Lue Conversation', in D. Sudnow (ed.), *Studies in Social Interaction*, Free Press. [69]

Moffett, J. (1968), *Teaching the Universe of Discourse*, Houghton-Mifflin.

Moscovici, S. (1967), 'Communication Processes and the Properties of Language', *Advances in Experimental Psychology*, **3,** pp. 225–70. [71]

Moscovici, S. (ed.) (1972), *The Psychosociology of Language*, Markham. [8]

Nash, W. (1971), *Our Experience of Language*, Batsford. [33]

Newson, J. and Newson, E. (1970), *Four Years Old in an Urban Community*, Penguin. [109]

Nisbet, J. (1953), 'Family Environment and Intelligence', *Eugenics Review*, **45,** pp. 31–40. [85]

Ober, R., Bentley, E. and Miller, E. (1971), *Systematic Observation of Teaching*, Prentice-Hall. [168–9, 179]

Oeser, O. (ed.) (1955), *Teacher, Pupil and Task*, Tavistock. [160]

Olim, E. (1971), 'Maternal Language Styles and the Cognitive Development of Children', in F. Williams (ed.), op. cit. [127]

Olim, E., Hess, R. and Shipman, V. (1967), 'The Role of Mothers' Language Styles in Mediating Their Pre-School Children's Cognitive Development', *School Review*, **75,** pp. 414–24. [111, 127]

Opie, I. and Opie, P. (1959), *The Lore and Language of Schoolchildren*, Oxford University Press. [25–6]

Osser, H., Wang, D. and Zaid, F. (1969), 'The Young Child's Ability to

Imitate and Comprehend Speech: a Comparison of Two Sub-Cultural Groups', *Child Development*, **40**, pp. 1063–75. [121]

Peisach, E. (1965), 'Children's Comprehension of Teacher and Peer Speech', *Child Development*, **36**, pp. 467–80. [115]

Philips, S. (1970), 'Acquisition of Rules for Appropriate Speech Usage', in J. Alatis (ed.), *Monograph Series on Language and Linguistics*, No. 23, Georgetown University Press. [128, 142, 171, 180]

Philips, S. (1972), 'Participant Structures and Communicative Competence: Warm Springs Children in Community and Classroom', in C. Cazden et al. (eds.), op. cit. [128, 142]

Pickford, G. (1956), 'American Linguistic Geography: a Sociological Appraisal', *Word*, **12**, pp. 211–33. [3, 11, 84]

Pieris, R. (1951), 'Speech and Society: A Sociological Approach to Language', *American Sociological Review*, **16**, pp. 499–505. [84]

Plumer, D. (1971), 'A Summary of Environmentalist Views and Some Educational Implications', in F. Williams (ed.), op. cit. [117, 124, 140]

Pride, J. (1971), *The Social Meaning of Language*, Oxford University Press. [8]

Pringle, M. and Tanner, M. (1958), 'The Effects of Early Deprivation on Speech Development', *Language & Speech*, **1**, pp. 269–87. [85]

Putnam, G. and O'Hern, E. (1955), 'The Status Significance of an Isolated Urban Dialect', *Language*, **31**, No. 4 (Part 2); *Language Dissertations*, No. 53. [84]

Quay, L. (1971), 'Language Dialect, Reinforcement and the Intelligence-Test Performance of Negro Children', *Child Development*, **42**, pp. 5–15. [134]

Quirk, R. (1968), *The Use of English*, Longmans. [46]

Rackstraw, S. and Robinson, W. (1967), 'Social and Psychological Factors Related to Variability of Answering Behaviour in Five-Year Old Children', *Language & Speech*, **10**, pp. 88–106. [98]

Raph, J. (1965), 'Language Development in Socially Disadvantaged Children', *Review of Educational Research*, **35**, pp. 389–400. [112]

Raph, J. (1967), 'Language and Speech Defects in Culturally Disadvantaged Children', *Journal of Speech & Hearing Disorders*, **32**, pp. 203–14. [113]

Riessman, F. (1962), *The Culturally Deprived Child*, Harper. [128]

Robins, R. (1971), 'Malinowski, Firth and the Context of Situation', in E. Ardener (ed.), *Social Anthropology and Language*, Tavistock. [63]

Robinson, P. (1974), 'An Ethnography of Classrooms', in J. Eggleston (ed.), *Contemporary Research in the Sociology of Education*, Methuen. [168]

Robinson, W. (1965a), 'Cloze Procedure as a Technique for the Investigation of Social Class Differences in Language Usage', *Language & Speech*, **8**, pp. 42–55. [97]

Robinson, W. (1965b), 'The Elaborated Code in Working-Class Language', *Language & Speech*, **8**, pp. 243–52. [97, 120]

Robinson, W. (1971), 'Restricted Codes in Socio-Linguistics and the Sociology of Education', in W. Whiteley (ed.), op. cit. [107, 124]

Robinson, W. (1972), *Language and Social Behaviour*, Penguin. [8, 107]

Robinson, W. and Creed, C. (1968), 'Perceptual and Verbal Discriminations of Elaborated and Restricted Code Users', *Language & Speech*, **11**, pp. 182–93. [98, 144]

Robinson, W. and Rackstraw, S. (1967), 'Variations in Mothers' Answers to Children's Questions as a Function of Social Class, Verbal Intelligence Scores, and Sex', *Sociology*, **1**, pp. 259–79. [110]

Robinson, W. and Rackstraw, S. (1972), *A Question of Answers* (2 Vols.), Routledge & Kegan Paul. [102, 110]

Rosen, H. (1967), 'The Language of Text-Books', in J. Britton (ed.), *Talking and Writing*, Methuen. [151, 155]

Rosen, H. (1972), *Language and Class: A Critical Look at the Theories of Basil Bernstein*, Falling Wall Press. [102, 106]

Rubin, J. (1962), 'Bilingualism in Paraguay', *Anthropological Linguistics*, **4**, pp. 52–68. [18, 74]

Rushton, J. and Young, G. (1974), 'Elements of Elaboration in Working-Class Writing', *Educational Research*, **16**, pp. 181–8. [101]

Sacks, H. (forthcoming), *Social Aspects of Language: The Organisation of Sequencing in Conversation*, Prentice-Hall. [66]

Sanders, N. (1966), *Classroom Questions: What Kinds?*, Harper & Row. [171]

Sankoff, G. (1972), 'Language Use in Multilingual Societies', in J. Pride and J. Holmes (eds.), *Sociolinguistics*, Penguin. [70]

Sapir, E. (1949), *Selected Writings of Edward Sapir in Language, Culture and Personality*, (ed.), D. Mandelbaum, University of California Press. [11, 13, 23, 37, 112]

Schatzman, L. and Strauss, A. (1955), 'Social Class and Modes of Communication', *American Journal of Sociology*, **60**, pp. 329–38. [83, 87-8, 104]

Seabrook, J. (1967), *The Unprivileged*, Longmans. [105]

Seligman, C., Tucker, G. and Lambert, W. (1972), 'The Effects of Speech Style and Other Attributes on Teachers' Attitudes Towards Pupils', *Language in Society*, **1**, pp. 131–42. [138]

Shriner, T. and Miner, L. (1968), 'Morphological Structures in the Language of Disadvantaged and Advantaged Children', *Journal of Speech & Hearing Research*, **11**, pp. 605–10. [113]

Shuy, R. (1969), 'Subjective Judgments in Sociolinguistic Analysis', in J. Alatis (ed.), op. cit. [49, 52-3]

Shuy, R. (1971), 'The Sociolinguists and Urban Language Problems', in F. Williams (ed.), op. cit. [52-3]

Shuy, R. (ed.) (1972), *Sociolinguistics: Current Trends and Prospects*, Georgetown University Monograph Series on Language and Linguistics, No. 25. Georgetown University Press.

Simon, A. and Boyer, G. (eds.) (1970), *Mirrors for Behaviour: An Anthology of Classroom Observation Instruments*, Research for Better Schools Inc. [163–4]

Sinclair, J., Forsyth, I. and Coulthard, R. (1972), *The English Used by Teachers and Pupils*, S.S.R.C. Report—Birmingham University Department of English (also reported in Sinclair, J. and Coulthard, R., *Towards an Analysis of Discourse*, Oxford University Press 1974). [157, 165, 170, 178–80]

Sledd, J. (1969), 'Bi-Dialectalism: The Linguistics of White Supremacy', *English Journal*, **58**, pp. 1307–15. [139]

Slobin, D. (1963), 'Some Aspects of the Use of Pronouns of Address in Yiddish', *Word*, **19**, pp. 193–202. [75]

Slobin, D. Miller, S. and Porter, L. (1968), 'Forms of Address and Social

Relations in a Business Organisation', *Journal of Personal & Social Psychology*, **8**, pp. 289–93. [12, 75–6]

Smith, L. and Geoffrey, W. (1968), *The Complexities of an Urban Classroom*, Holt, Rinehart and Winston. [169, 176]

Sommer, R. (1965), 'Further Studies of Small-Group Ecology', *Sociometry*, **28**, pp. 337–48. [71]

Soskin, W. and John, V. (1963), 'The Study of Spontaneous Talk', in R. Barker (ed.), op. cit. [72, 78]

Speier, M. (1973), *How To Observe Face-To-Face Communication: A Sociological Introduction*, Goodyear. [65]

Stewart, W. (1969), 'Historical and Structural Bases for the Recognition of Negro Dialect', in J. Alatis (ed.), op. cit. [48]

Stewart, W. (1970), 'Understanding Black Language', in J. Szwed (ed.), *Black America*, Basic Books. [48, 135]

Stewart, W. (1971), 'Towards a History of American Dialect', in F. Williams (ed.), op. cit. [48]

Strauss, A. and Schatzman, L. (1955), 'Cross-Class Interviewing', *Human Organisation*, **14**, pp. 28–31. [117]

Strodtbeck, F. and Hook, L. (1961), 'The Social Dimensions of a Twelve-Man Jury Table', *Sociometry*, **24**, pp. 397–415. [71]

Strongman, K. and Woosley, J. (1967), 'Stereotyped Reactions to Regional Accents', *British Journal of Social and Clinical Psychology*, **6**, pp. 164–7. [29]

Stubbs, M. (1975), 'Teaching and Talking: A Sociolinguistic Approach to Classroom Interaction', in G. Chanan and S. Delamont, *Frontiers of Classroom Research*, National Foundation for Educational Research. [158]

Taba, H. Levine, S. and Elzey, F. (1964), *Thinking in Elementary School Children*, San Francisco State College, Co-operative Research Project, p. 1574. [166]

Tanner, N. (1967), 'Speech and Society among the Indonesian Elite', *Anthropological Linguistics*, **9**, pp. 15–39. [58, 74, 77]

Templin, M. (1957), 'Certain Language Skills in Children', *Institute of Child Welfare Monographs*, no. 26. [86, 112]

Templin, M. (1958), 'The Relation of Speech and Language to Intelligence and Socio-Economic Status', *Volta Review*, **60**, pp. 331–34. [86, 119–20]

Thorne, J. (1970), 'Generative Grammar and Stylistic Analysis', in J. Lyons (ed.), *New Horizons in Linguistics*, Penguin. [150]

Tough, J. (1970), *Some Differences in the Use of Language in Groups of Three-Year Old Children*, Leeds University Institute of Education. [100]

Troike, R. (1969), 'Receptive Competence, Productive Competence and Performance', in J. Alatis (ed.), op. cit. [9, 121, 136]

Trudgill, P. (1974a), *The Social Differentiation of English in Norwich*, Cambridge University Press. [11, 21–2, 53, 73]

Trudgill, P. (1974b), *Sociolinguistics: An Introduction*, Penguin.

Tucker, G. and Lambert, W. (1969), 'White and Negro Listeners' Reactions to Various American-English Dialects', *Social Forces*, **47**, pp. 463–68. [29]

Turner, G. (1973), 'Social Class and Children's Language of Control', in B. Bernstein (ed.), op. cit. [93, 109]

Turner, G. and Mohan, B. (1970), *A Linguistic Description and Computer Programme for Children's Speech*, Routledge & Kegan Paul. [96]

Turner, G. and Pickvance, R. (1971), 'Social Class Differences in the Expression of Uncertainty in Five-Year Old Children', *Language & Speech*, **14**, pp. 303–25. [98]

Turner, R. (1972), 'Some Formal Properties of Therapy Talk', in D. Sudnow (ed.), *Studies in Social Interaction*, Free Press. [72]

Waimon, M. and Hermanowicz, H. (1965), 'A Conceptual System for Prospective Teachers to Study Teaching Behaviour', *Paper to the American Educational Research Association*, Chicago. [166]

Waller, W. (1932), *The Sociology of Teaching*, republished by Wiley 1965. [163, 175]

Waller, W. (1942), 'The Teacher's Roles', in J. Rouck (ed.), *Sociological Foundations of Education*, Thomas Crowell. [163]

Weener, P. (1969), 'Some Dialect Differences in the Recall of Verbal Messages', *Journal of Educational Psychology*, **60**, pp. 194–9. [81, 121]

Wells, J. (1973), *Jamaican Pronunciation in London*, Blackwell. [116]

Whiteley, W. (1966), 'Social Anthropology, Meaning and Linguistics', *Man* (New Series), **1**, pp. 139–57. [3]

Whiteley, W. (ed.) (1971), *Language Use and Social Change*, Oxford University Press. [11]

Whiteley, W. (1972), 'Socio-linguistic Surveys at the National Level', in R. Shuy (ed.), op. cit. [11, 40, 42]

Whiteman, M. and Deutsch, M. (1968), 'Social Disadvantage as Related to Intellective and Language Development', in M. Deutsch et al. (eds.), *Social Class, Race and Psychological Development*, Holt, Rinehart and Winston [131]

Whorf, B. (1956), *Language, Thought and Reality: Selected Writings of Benjamin Lee Whorf*, (ed.), J. Carroll, M.I.T. Press & Wiley. [13, 39]

Wight, J. (1971), 'Dialect in School', *Educational Review*, **24**, pp. 47–58. [134]

Wight, J. and Norris, R. (1970), *Teaching English to West Indian Children*, Schools' Council Working Paper, **29**, Evans & Methuen. [122, 134]

Wilkinson, A. (1965), 'Spoken English', *Educational Review*, **17**, Supplement. [51]

Williams, A. Powell (1972), 'Dynamics of a Black Audience', in T. Kochman (ed.), op. cit. [141–2]

Williams, F. (1970), 'Psychological Correlates of Speech Characteristics: On Sounding Disadvantaged', *Journal of Speech & Hearing Research*, **13**, pp. 472–488. [137]

Williams, F. (ed.) (1971a), *Language and Poverty*, Markham. [30, 124]

Williams, F. (1971b), 'Social Dialects and the Field of Speech', in *Sociolinguistics: Cross-Disciplinary Perspectives*, Centre for Applied Linguistics. [122]

Williams, F. and Naremore, R. (1969), 'Social Class Differences in Children's Syntactic Performance', *Journal of Speech & Hearing Research*, **12**, pp. 778–93. [118–9]

Williams, F. and Wood, B. (1970), 'Negro Children's Speech: Some Social Class Differences in Word Predictability', *Language & Speech*, **13**, pp. 141–50. [115]

Wilson, T. (1970), 'Conceptions of Interaction and Forms of Sociological Explanation', *American Sociological Review*, **35**, pp. 697–710. [68]

Wolfram, W. (1969), *A Sociolinguistic Description of Detroit Negro Speech*, Centre for Applied Linguistics. [11, 22]

Wright, R. (1975), 'Black English', *Language in Society*, **4**, pp. 185–98. [45]

Wyld, (1920). *A History of Modern Colloquial English*, Blackwell. [44, 47]

Subject Index